A Childhood Adrift

THE AZRIELI SERIES OF HOLOCAUST SURVIVOR MEMOIRS: PUBLISHED TITLES

ENGLISH TITLES

A Childhood Adrift

René Goldman

THE AZRIELI FOUNDATION
www.azrielifoundation.org

Cover and book design by Mark Goldstein
Endpaper maps by Martin Gilbert
Map on page xxv by François Blanc

LIBRARY AND ARCHIVES CANADA CATALOGUING IN PUBLICATION

Goldman, René, 1934– , author
    A Childhood Adrift / René Goldman.

(Azrieli series of Holocaust survivor memoirs. Series IX)
Includes index.
ISBN 978-1-988065-17-5 (softcover)

1. Goldman, René, 1934–. 2. Goldman, René, 1934– — Childhood and youth. 3. Hidden children (Holocaust) — France — Biography. 4. Jewish children in the Holocaust — France — Biography. 5. Holocaust, Jewish (1939–1945) — France — Personal narratives. 6. Holocaust survivors — Canada — Biography. I. Azrieli Foundation, issuing body II. Title. III. Series: Azrieli series of Holocaust survivor memoirs. Series IX

D804.48.G64 2017   940.53'18083   C2017-904414-1

PRINTED IN CANADA

The Azrieli Series of Holocaust Survivor Memoirs

Naomi Azrieli, Publisher

Jody Spiegel, Program Director
Arielle Berger, Managing Editor
Farla Klaiman, Editor
Matt Carrington, Editor
Elizabeth Lasserre, Senior Editor, French-Language Editions
Elin Beaumont, Senior Education Outreach and Program Facilitator
Catherine Person, Educational Outreach and Events Coordinator,
    Quebec and French Canada
Stephanie Corazza, Education and Curriculum Associate
Marc-Olivier Cloutier, Educational Outreach and Events Assistant,
    Quebec and French Canada
Tim MacKay, Digital Platform Manager
Elizabeth Banks, Digital Asset Curator and Archivist
Susan Roitman, Office Manager (Toronto)
Mary Mellas, Executive Assistant and Human Resources (Montreal)

Mark Goldstein, Art Director
François Blanc, Cartographer
Bruno Paradis, Layout, French-Language Editions

Contents

Series Preface:
In their own words...

In telling these stories, the writers have liberated themselves. For so many years we did not speak about it, even when we became free people living in a free society. Now, when at last we are writing about what happened to us in this dark period of history, knowing that our stories will be read and live on, it is possible for us to feel truly free. These unique historical documents put a face on what was lost, and allow readers to grasp the enormity of what happened to six million Jews — one story at a time.

David J. Azrieli, C.M., C.Q., M.Arch
Holocaust survivor and founder, The Azrieli Foundation

Since the end of World War II, over 30,000 Jewish Holocaust survivors have immigrated to Canada. Who they are, where they came from, what they experienced and how they built new lives for themselves and their families are important parts of our Canadian heritage. The Azrieli Foundation's Holocaust Survivor Memoirs Program was established to preserve and share the memoirs written by those who survived the twentieth-century Nazi genocide of the Jews of Europe and later made their way to Canada. The program is guided by the conviction that each survivor of the Holocaust has a remarkable story to tell, and that such stories play an important role in education about tolerance and diversity.

Millions of individual stories are lost to us forever. By preserving the stories written by survivors and making them widely available to a broad audience, the Azrieli Foundation's Holocaust Survivor Memoirs Program seeks to sustain the memory of all those who perished at the hands of hatred, abetted by indifference and apathy. The personal accounts of those who survived against all odds are as different as the people who wrote them, but all demonstrate the courage, strength, wit and luck that it took to prevail and survive in such terrible adversity. The memoirs are also moving tributes to people — strangers and friends — who risked their lives to help others, and who, through acts of kindness and decency in the darkest of moments, frequently helped the persecuted maintain faith in humanity and courage to endure. These accounts offer inspiration to all, as does the survivors' desire to share their experiences so that new generations can learn from them.

The Holocaust Survivor Memoirs Program collects, archives and publishes these distinctive records, and the print editions are available free of charge to educational institutions and Holocaust-education programs across Canada. They are also available for sale to the general public at bookstores. All revenues to the Azrieli Foundation from the sales of the Azrieli Series of Holocaust Survivor Memoirs go toward the publishing and educational work of the memoirs program.

~

The Azrieli Foundation would like to express appreciation to the following people for their invaluable efforts in producing this book: Doris Bergen, Sherry Dodson (Maracle Inc), Dianne Hildebrand, Barbara Kamieński, Nina Krieger, Therese Parent, and Margie Wolfe & Emma Rodgers of Second Story Press.

About the Glossary

The following memoir contains a number of terms, concepts and historical references that may be unfamiliar to the reader. For information on major organizations; significant historical events and people; geographical locations; religious and cultural terms; and foreign-language words and expressions that will help give context and background to the events described in the text, please see the glossary beginning on page 249.

Introduction

In the foreword to this highly unusual memoir, René Goldman writes, "The panorama of my past has been marked by a succession of moves from place to place, moves prompted by the necessity to survive during the war and by more benign reasons in the years and decades that followed."

This is an understatement. Every survivor of the Shoah (Holocaust) has his or her unique life story, but I have never read or heard of one that was more interrupted and disrupted, or so full of unexpected twists. Beginning in 1934 with a more or less ordinary childhood in the small Jewish community of Luxembourg, René Goldman narrates an astonishing tale of two years with his parents in Belgium, eight years of placement with strangers and in children's homes in France, three years of high school in postwar Poland, eight years of college in China, a few years of doctoral studies in New York, and, ultimately, a career in Asian Studies at the University of British Columbia.

This extraordinary trajectory is described in detail by a narrator who has spent his academic life steeped in a culture not implicated in the Shoah. Unlike his fellow child survivors Elie Wiesel or Saul Friedländer, he has not studied the events of World War II and takes pains to verify what he remembers with documents and visits to the many sites of his past. He is careful to situate his personal history within the relevant political, cultural and sociological contexts. In so doing, Goldman draws on many other survivor memoirs and books of historians, archivists and scholars. He also is careful to interview as many of his wartime protectors and surviving members of their families as possible.

A Childhood Adrift is unusual, too, because of Goldman's dispassionate adult perspective on the relatives and strangers he knew and depended on as a child, and his adult understanding of the Jewish, Catholic and communist institutions and ideologies that inspired and sheltered him. He is also aware of some of the psychological coping mechanisms he developed along the way. For example, early on in René's travels, to distract him from the trauma of dislocation, an adult gave him paper and pencil and suggested that he draw a map. Map-making and writing became his refuge within a refuge. They've also proved to be good skills for a memoirist.

Goldman often compares his own situation to that of fellow children in hiding and makes clear that it is a very heterogeneous group: children who were murdered; children who survived in hiding with their families; children who were sent away, alone, to foreign countries; children who were orphaned at home.

He points out that:

…the place and country in which we survived and the circumstances of our survival differ, as do our individual personalities and outlooks on history. How we lived the events and how deeply we were marked by them, the intensity of the pain and suffering, are also to no small degree a function of the age we were at the time. Some children were too young to be aware that they faced death should their whereabouts be discovered, while adolescents understood enough to be fearful every waking moment. My age fell somewhere between these two poles of childhood.

I consider myself relatively fortunate to have been too young to comprehend the political and military events that influenced my destiny and, consequently, my suffering was perhaps less intense than that of children, such as Anne Frank, who were several years older than I was.

Unlike Anne, René was an only child whose parents, Mira Shaindl Arenstein and Wolf Goldman, were among the thousands of Polish Jews who emigrated west in the 1920s. They met in France but in 1931 moved to Luxembourg, where Goldman estimates that the pre-war Jewish community numbered about 4,000. Wolf Goldman was a tailor and a communist who found work in the shop of a landsman. René was born in March of 1934 and, for his first six years, lived in a multilingual environment, speaking Lëtzebuergesch and hearing German and Yiddish.

After the German invasion of Luxembourg in May of 1940, the Goldmans moved to Brussels where René attended two years of Flemish elementary school. In one of his many speculations about what his parents might have been thinking, he notes that Flemish is related to the Germanic languages he already knew; perhaps they thought it would be easier for him to pick up than French? Or maybe cheap housing was the decisive factor for school district? There is much about his parents that he will never know.

In one of his many editorial asides, René writes admiringly of Belgium's conduct toward its Jews, comparing it favourably to France and Holland. Anti-Jewish legislation was slow to be enacted, he writes, due to the strong opposition of the Belgian legal profession to the Occupation. René recalls walking to music lessons and frequenting parks, theatre and the movies until May 1942, when Jews were forced to wear the yellow star. That summer, his parents told him that they were leaving for Montevideo. In the summer of 1942, the family was smuggled hundreds of miles out of Belgium and across occupied France by a series of *passeurs*. They were caught a few kilometres away from Switzerland, arrested, and then interned in France.

René's parents told him that in the fall he would be attending school in Lons-le-Saunier, the city to which the French police had assigned them to live. But two weeks after their arrest, there was a *rafle*: Wolf Goldman escaped, Mira Goldman was deported; and in a truly miraculous fashion René was rescued by his maternal aunt Fella.

Aunt Fella and Uncle David are two of René's relatives who managed to survive the war unscathed in the unoccupied part of France, often at odds or out of sorts. His depiction of them reminds the reader that surviving the Shoah depended as much on temperament and interpersonal relationships as on food and lodging. One day René wakes up with an unannounced stranger sleeping beside him. She works for one of a network of organizations charged with the protection of Jewish children in France and takes him to the château du Masgelier, administered by the Œuvre de secours aux enfants (OSE), originally founded in Russia in 1912 to help victims of the pogroms and now funded by the American Jewish Joint Distribution Committee.

The eight-year-old only child does not adjust well to institutional life with two hundred hidden children, twelve to a room, and sends letters of complaint to Aunt Fella, which are unanswered. A few weeks later, without explanation, he is abruptly moved to the first in a series of private homes in the countryside.

School becomes the only constant thread in René's life. In France, he repeats in French the two grades he had completed in Flemish, learning French curriculum — grammar, composition, geography and civics — so well that he soon requires a translator to decipher his father's (German) letters.

Soon, another stranger appears and relocates René to a Catholic convent school for boys. At Pensionnat des Besses, the nine-year-old is given a new name — René Garnier — and a Catholic education: strict religious discipline, allegiance to Marshal Pétain, poor food, and a Dickensian atmosphere of gloom.

In his memoir, Goldman does not dwell on the psychological effects of these multiple dislocations or lack of explanations; in hiding, as in the concentration camps of which René as yet knows nothing, no answers are given to the question "why?" He leaves it to the reader to feel disbelief and an erosion of trust in his caretakers, noting only, "From the rambunctious little boy prone to mischief that I had once been, I now grew into a timorous child, anxious not to displease any-one: not the teacher at school, not my classmates and least of all, not the kind people who sheltered me."

In the spring of 1944, when he has turned ten, another stranger turns up at his school and takes him to Lyon to see his father. Wolf now lives in a one-room flat with several other members of Main-d'œuvre immigrée (MOI), a Jewish section of an organization created by the Communist Party that was part of the French Resistance. On June 6 (D-Day) he heard about the Allied invasion over the illegal radio. As the Gestapo intensified its anti-Resistance activity in Lyon, Wolf Goldman was able to board René with a peasant family, where he witnessed American troops entering the village on their way to liberate Lyon on September 2, 1944.

Since his father was still fighting the Nazis and his mother's where-abouts were unknown, René once again returned to his relatives in Lyon, where he resumed school. But in the spring, they sent him to a group home in the foothills of the Alps near Grenoble. Operated by the Œuvre de protection des enfants juifs (OPEJ), this home was a transit point where children waited for their parents to return home while attending the community school and receiving a rigorous Zion-ist education in the event that they might immigrate to Palestine.

It was there, in May 1945, shortly after turning eleven, that René had his first encounter with the Shoah. The OPEJ group was invited to the office of Grenoble's Jewish community to view an exhibit of photographs from the concentration camps. "Is that what happened to Mama?" Goldman does not write any more about that day but quotes a French Jewish journalist who later wrote, "Liberation was not for us a day of joy: it was the day of truth." Goldman adds, "While the French nation rejoiced without reservation, our minds were filled with anguished questions about those who were absent."

Children were waiting for their parents; parents were searching for their children. Some would never know the fate of their parents. It would not be until two years later, when he was thirteen, that René was told that his father had been arrested one month before the liberation of Lyon, and it would be many more years before he learned the fate of both of his parents.

In the fall of 1945, the eleven-year-old was placed by his aunt with the Commission centrale de l'enfance (CCE), the Jewish communist organization now charged with caring for Jewish war orphans. René was sent to the first Maison d'enfants de déportés et fusillés in a suburb of Paris, then to a beautiful castle, the manoir de Denouval, in Andrésy. The children of the deported attended the community school, but at what they called "the enchanted manor" sang revolutionary communist songs led by communist counsellors.

Goldman is one of the only child survivors I've read who writes about his attachment to communism as a teenager. This may be because refugees applying to the United States for citizenship were required to expunge any trace of communism in their resumés — or because René was part of a small minority.

He describes the three CCE homes in which he lived from 1945 to 1948 as the first places in which he felt truly at home. The ethos of these homes encouraged looking to the future rather than to the past and to political rather than psychological problems. "Rather than allow our thoughts to dwell on the fate of our murdered parents," he writes, the children and teenagers were taught to draw inspiration from heroes of the French communist resistance and Soviet heroes. "We were excessively politicized for our ages and some of us were more susceptible to this indoctrination than others. I was, unfortunately, one of these."

When René's paternal uncle invited him to immigrate to Canada with his family, the fourteen-year-old refused because of his hostility to North American capitalism. Instead, after a trip to Poland the following summer, he made the extraordinary decision to live in Poland — the country his parents had fled in the 1920s. Many of the people he admired were communists. His father had been a communist. He persuaded himself that had his parents survived, they would have returned to the country of their births.

The CCE supported his decision. On August 19, 1950, sixteen years old and knowing no Polish, he began attending high school outside bombed-out Warsaw. He lived with CCE-affiliated guardians, met other child survivors, and befriended a sinology student at Warsaw University who introduced him to the field. Meanwhile he struggled to master Polish, missed France, and viewed 1951 as one of the unhappiest years of his young life, until he finished high school and was accepted into a Polish-Chinese exchange program. Then he made his most extraordinary move of all — to Beijing, where he studied Chinese language, literature and history from 1953 to 1958, the year of Mao's Great Leap Forward.

Goldman continues to describe his trajectory from place to place, giving the reader only short glimpses of his complicated relationship to Poland and to Soviet-style communism. He is disturbed by dorm mates informing to the Party and by news reports of the antisemitic Slánský trial in Czechoslovakia and the antisemitic "doctors' trial" in the Soviet Union, but does not analyze his options. Instead, he keeps moving. He describes the excitement of his trip via the Soviet Union to Beijing University at the age of nineteen, happy to immerse himself in a culture and country that had no tradition of antisemitism. He planned to graduate with an M.A. in 1960.

Instead, he left Beijing University in October of 1958 and returned to Poland. "My disenchantment with Mao's China and communism in general was profound," Goldman writes. "Luckily in 1958 I succeeded in renewing contact with my family in France and in Canada.... I became anxious to return to Poland as soon as possible, fearful lest the exceptionally liberal political climate of the country of which I was a citizen might deteriorate."

At the age of twenty-five, after living for nine years under communism, Goldman defected from Poland. For over a year he lived in Paris, keeping his distance from the communist organization that had helped shelter him during the war, translating and studying Chinese. He does not say how he won a scholarship to pursue graduate study at Columbia University, just that he fell in love with New York

City and lived there from 1960 to 1963, after which he found a teaching position at the University of British Columbia.

I had many questions for René Goldman when I finished his memoir. Starting from the end of his memoir, how is it that though he loved NYC he wound up in Canada? Did his embrace of communism as a younger man make him unacceptable to American immigration authorities? Or did he simply find a good post-doc at UBC? Does he think that his study of Chinese literature and history gives him perspective on twentieth-century Europe? Does Chinese philosophy help him cope with the after-effects of the Shoah in his life? Who did he eventually marry and why? Does he have children? How does a childhood and adolescence without parents affect parenting?

René Goldman's is such an unusual odyssey that it will provoke many more thoughts and questions. Read it and marvel at the miracle of human resilience.

Helen Epstein
2017

Helen Epstein (helenepstein.com) is the author of *Children of the Holocaust* and nine other books of non-fiction. She is also co-founder of Plunkett Lake Press (plunkettlakepress.com), which publishes out-of-print books of Jewish interest as ebooks.

SUGGESTIONS FOR FURTHER READING

Friedländer, Saul. *When Memory Comes*. Madison: University of Wisconsin Press, 2003.

Heller, Fanya Gottesfeld. *Strange and Unexpected Love: A Teenage Girl's Holocaust Memoir*. Jersey City: Ktav Publishing House, Inc., 1996.

Kestenberg, Judith, and Ira Brenner. *Last Witness: The Child Survivor of the Holocaust*. Arlington: American Psychiatric Publishing, 1996.

Kovaly, Heda Margolius. *Under a Cruel Star: A Life in Prague 1941–1968*. New York: Holmes and Meier, 1997.

Krell, Robert. *Memories: Sounds from Silence*. Vancouver, B.C., 2016.

Richman, Sophia. *A Wolf in the Attic: The Legacy of a Hidden Child of the Holocaust*. New York: Routledge, 2002.

Vegh, Claudine. *I Didn't Say Goodbye: Interviews with Children of the Holocaust*. New York: E.P. Dutton, 1985.

UNITED
KINGDOM

*North
Sea*

English Channel

GERMANY

Antwerp

BRUSSELS

BELGIUM

LUXEMBOURG

Esch-sur-Alzette

Compiègne

Andrésy • Drancy
PARIS

Nancy

Strasbourg

OCCUPIED
ZONE

FRANCE

Atlantic

Pellevoisin

Vendœuvres

Lons-le-Saunier

SWITZERLAND

Le Grand-Bourg

Lyon

Chozeau

Ocean

Limoges

Grenoble

ITALY

UNOCCUPIED
ZONE

Montpellier • Avignon

Rivesaltes

SPAIN

Mediterranean

Sea

LEGEND

Borders 1921-1938

Borders 1939-1944

0   100   200km

N

© 2017 - The Azrieli Foundation

Acknowledgements

I wish to thank the many persons who urged me to put my memories down in writing. Above all, I want to thank my wife, Terry, who was born "on the other side" and, as a virtual orphan, endured many torments during and after the war when she grew up in devastated Berlin. I want to thank her for her lively interest in my project, her observations and suggestions after reading my manuscript, her patience with my frequent monopolizing of our computer and her loving companionship.

I wish also to convey my appreciation to Dianne Hildebrand, my editor, who gave me invaluable assistance by polishing my manuscript and preparing it for publication. Previous to that my manuscript was read at various stages by Dr. Marvin Weintraub, his daughter Lisa, Nancy Ennis and writer Peter Háy; their critical observations were duly considered.

Among the other persons whom I wish to thank with all my heart for their kind and helpful interest in me, I must single out the veteran American journalist Mark R. Arnold: he was the "prime mover" who set in motion the train of events that made it possible for me to leave behind an uncertain future in Europe and embrace a new life in North America, beginning as a scholarship student at Columbia University in New York. For that fortunate outcome I wish to thank also my mentor of the time, the late Professor C. Martin Wilbur, director of the Institute of East Asian Studies of Columbia University, as well as Professor Orlan Lee and the late professor Arthur F. Wright of Yale University. Last, but certainly not least, I must here express my undying gratitude to the late Professor William L. Holland, founder of the Department of Asian Studies at the University of British Columbia in Vancouver, who recruited me for his team and enabled me to find a home, happiness and security in Canada.

Foreword

Memory is everything. It is a passion no less profound or pervasive than love. It is the ability to live in more than one world, to prevent the past from fading, and to call upon the future to illuminate it. — Elie Wiesel

I have nothing in the world but the hour in which I am: it pauses for a moment, and then, like a cloud, moves on. — Samuel HaNagid

Late in the evening of my life I have taken up the challenge of narrating the story of my childhood during the fearful years of the Shoah, the years preceding it and my trajectory afterwards. My first and most weighty motive in so doing is to bring my modest contribution to the mission of ensuring that the greatest tragedy in the long and tormented history of the Jewish people not be forgotten and negated by those bent on further evil. At the same time I wish to unburden myself of personal memories, many of them painful and some, curiously perhaps, tainted with a touch of nostalgia. Peering deep into my soul I appear to myself as somewhat mercurial: in my better moments I feel still young at heart, while in my more moody moments I feel like three thousand years of Jewish history is bearing down on my shoulders. There is no escaping the long shadow cast over my entire existence by the man-made catastrophe in which so many millions of my brethren, among them my parents and almost my entire family, were murdered. The panorama of my past has been marked by a succession of moves from place to place, moves prompted by the necessity to survive during the war and by more benign reasons in the years and decades that followed. It is that particular aspect of my destiny that inspires the title of this book.

From the long path of my life and those memories that still stand out, I wish that I could recapture and convey the intensity of what I felt not only during the sad and tragic moments of my childhood, but also in the midst of its happy moments. The reliving of painful moments has many times inspired in me a sense of communion with orphans I have known or whose stories I have heard or read. Stories of orphaned children always stir my emotions, even when they are heroes of fiction, such as Charles Dickens's David Copperfield or Charlotte Brontë's Jane Eyre.

I belong to the generation of those who, since the 1980s, identify themselves as "child survivors" and "hidden children" of the Shoah. Had we not been hidden among sympathetic gentiles, we would likely not have survived. Our fate during the Shoah and our experience of surviving the genocide of our people gives us a perspective on what happened that is starkly different from that of adult generations. As orphans brought up after the war, we were compelled to silence the trauma that we endured and were prompted to look to the future. In the course of the past thirty-odd years, as our generation advanced into an age that inclines one to look backward more than forward, we emerged from our shells to bear our own testimonies. Coincidentally, an increasingly abundant documentation about World War II has been made available by the opening of archives, and researchers have unearthed facts that were hitherto relegated to obscurity.

My endeavour is therefore not unique: in the past several decades many survivors of the Shoah, including child survivors, have written and published their memoirs. I hope that no publisher or researcher will ever assume that there is a surfeit of such resource material, for each volume of survivor memoirs is original in the sense that our individual experiences, the place and country in which we survived and the circumstances of our survival differ, as do our individual personalities and outlooks on history. How we lived the events and how deeply we were marked by them, the intensity of the pain and suffering, are also to no small degree a function of the age we were at the time. Some children were too young to be aware that they faced death should their whereabouts be discovered, while adolescents understood enough to be fearful every waking moment. My age fell somewhere between these two poles of childhood.

I consider myself relatively fortunate to have been too young to comprehend the political and military events that influenced my destiny and, consequently, my suffering was perhaps less intense than that of children, such as Anne Frank, who were several years older than I was. Anne's profound sensibility and precocious awareness of what perils lurked behind the partition of the closet-sized room in which she was hidden with her sister, Margot, her parents, and several other persons, without ever going out, immensely added to the pain and anguish that were her constant companions. In the end she perished at Bergen-Belsen. As the reader will realize, the conditions in which I survived my brushes with death in France were less dramatic than they might have been, had I been forced into hiding in Holland or Belgium, two very small, densely populated countries with no wilderness regions such as exist in France. Still, even in France, where conditions allowed better chances to survive than was the case in Poland or Lithuania, or even in the Benelux countries, many thousands of Jewish children perished. Those of us who survived owe it mostly to our having been hidden in religious institutions and among a population traditionally less hostile than that of Eastern Europe. Also, the Southern Zone of France was not occupied until the end of 1942 and was liberated by the fall of 1944.

I was immensely fortunate to have escaped the fate met by the majority of the Jews of Europe, including most of my family. The historian Saul Friedländer, who survived in circumstances strikingly similar to the ones in which I did and for a time in the same region of France as I, wrote that we lived "in the margin of the catastrophe." He further observed that we were little more than spectators wandering between several worlds, feeling we belonged to none. Like Friedländer, I have expended much effort to relate to what our parents and others who were swallowed up by the Nazi death camps endured, to imagine the indescribable terrors that they suffered every minute, day and night, before they perished, asphyxiated and burnt to ashes.

Like everyone who puts pen to paper, I write for the generations that succeed our own with a plea that my contemporaries and I not be forgotten and, naturally, in the fervent hope that such tragedy should never happen again: not to the Jews, not to any people. Twenty-two centuries ago China's famed great historian Sima Qian, who suffered torture and humiliation at the hands of one of his country's most murderous tyrants, Emperor Wu of the Han dynasty, reflected on the significance of a human life when he wrote that it could be as weighty as Mount Tài, the highest mountain known to the Chinese of antiquity, or lighter than a feather. Though I would never presume to measure myself up against this giant of the mind, I hope that my life will not have been insignificant either. Will the future illuminate our past, as Elie Wiesel prays? Wiesel was one of the few adolescents who survived the massacre of Hungarian Jewry and the hell of Buchenwald. Brought to France after the war, he grew to become a writer of stature and a spiritual teacher. Gabriel Péri, a hero of the French Resistance, called for "les lendemains qui chantent," the morrows that will sing, as he fell under the bullets of a German execution squad. Alas, the morrows did not sing and the world descends yet again into an age of darkness. At a time such as the present one, we can only hope against hope that Elie Wiesel's prayer is not a voice crying out in the wilderness.

So many decades after the war, the terrors of the past seem to return. Antisemitism, that worm in the apple of Western civilization, is not dead. The cancer was only in remission and reappears now most often in the disguise of anti-Zionism; the true nature of the thing behind the disguise is, however, obvious to anyone who is not wilfully deluded by appearances. Extremists of the left and of the right once fought one another, but nowadays they have in effect merged into a single current of hatred against the state of Israel.

Writing my memoir in a time such as this, I am unavoidably pre-occupied with the renewed threats that hang over the Jewish people. At the same time I seek to extract meaning from our collective past and from the personal one that I endeavour to reconstruct. The psy-chotherapist Victor Frankl, who owed his survival of the Nazi death camps to his spiritual strength, observes in his book *Man's Search for Meaning* that "if there is any meaning in life at all, then there must be meaning in suffering."

In 1979, the psychiatrist Claudine Vegh conducted interviews with fellow child survivors in France, the purpose of which was to in-vestigate the manner in which we live our past and what our feelings are when we think about our lost parents. The result of her research was a book entitled *Je ne lui ai pas dit au revoir* (available in English as *I Didn't Say Goodbye*), in which she notes that the subject is one that we are reluctant to touch upon out of fear of reopening a wound that has never fully healed. In a postscript to Vegh's book, the Austrian-born American psychologist Bruno Bettelheim reflects on the differ-ence between us and children (or adults) who lost relatives in a war or in a natural disaster. The latter are aware of the finality of their loss, he argues, but benefit from the support of society and find in the rites of mourning and other factors an outlet for their grief. The Jewish tradition of shiva is in this regard particularly soothing: mourners remain at home and receive visitors who listen sympathetically, com-fort them and bring them food. For us who never bade adieu to our parents and other relatives, there has not been closure: we have not witnessed their death, don't know the dates on which they died, have no graves where we can go to pay homage and cry. Denied the cer-tainty of finality, many of us even nourished for years varying degrees of vain hopes that our parents might yet return.

In the children's homes in which I was brought up after the war, we were urged not to look back but to look forward. We feared that to dwell on our story of loss and deprivation would invite little sympathy from adults. Our suffering as children torn from their parents, forced to live in hiding and to deny our identity, seemed indeed, even in our own eyes, like nothing compared to the suffering of those who endured the atrocious ordeal of daily life in the death camps, those for whom the slightest misstep could lead to the gas chambers and the crematoria. Theirs was a universe of electrified barbed wire enclosing grey barracks over which hung the smell of burning flesh, while ours was that of the gentle scenery of the French countryside, of old farmhouses set amid gardens and golden wheat fields.

Yet, we had to suppress our grief when we lived in hiding and had to adapt to unfamiliar milieus, some more welcoming than others. We didn't, for the most part, comprehend our loss. In her book *Children of the Holocaust*, Helen Epstein speaks of an "invisible iron box" in which we locked up our emotions and of an "emotional constriction" to the point of "psychic closing off." I recognized myself in her depiction of child survivors and also of their children: vulnerability, a sense of insecurity never entirely shaken off and aversion to opening up emotionally. I do not recognize myself, however, in some of those child survivors studied by Vegh who expressed resentment at their parents for having let themselves be captured and, by so doing, stand accused of having "abandoned" them. I have no recollection of having ever felt anything other than unconditional love for my parents. Though I almost never dream of them any longer, I daily yearn to bring them to life in the meditations of my heart.

My heart blesses the memory of my parents, all the members of my family who perished in the tragic times of my childhood and all those of their generation who joined the ranks of Jewish combat groups everywhere in Europe to defeat the Nazis. Whether they believed in God or not; were communists, Bundists or Zionists; fought in the forests of Belarus, the streets of the ghettos or the Resistance underground in Paris or Lyon — all looked beyond their desperate struggle of the moment to a distant time in which the ideals of justice, righteousness, solidarity and even love, enshrined in our Torah, would be realized. I call them "the Great Generation" of my people. For many of them the end of the most terrible war did not bring the end of grief and disappointments. Those among them who were communists had yet to muster formidable courage to confront the debacle of their idealism and the frightening truth that the cause to which they had given everything of themselves was a cruel hoax.

May the readers of my story find it informative and interesting enough to reflect on those tragic events long past. It is my hope that some will draw lessons from these events that will inspire them in the endeavour of *tikkun olam*, of repairing our badly torn world and making it a better place for all creatures to live.

Luxembourg

Au soir de la vie le passé devient le présent. (In the evening of life the past becomes the present.) — Louis Aragon

The Grand Duchy of Luxembourg is the country of my birth. I lived in its capital, which bears the name of the country, until the age of six. Thereafter, except for a two-week vacation at age thirteen, for nearly thirty years I did not set foot in Luxembourg until a visit in 1976, which lasted, unfortunately, not even a full day.

When, on that memorable day in July 1976, an early train brought me in mid-morning from Brussels to the capital of the Grand Duchy, I wondered, with some trepidation, whether I would recognize any of the surroundings in which the early years of my childhood were cradled, particularly the successive places that had briefly been home to my parents and me. Coming out of the railway station I crossed the raised footbridge that straddles the tracks and separates the central and historical parts of the capital from its modest working-class quarters to the east. These quarters were of single-storey white or grey houses, small, plain, yet rather dainty, nestled along short and narrow streets. I was surprised to discover that many of the current inhabitants of these streets were Turkish immigrant workers.

The first home that I could remember was situated in one of these streets. I probably never knew its name; still, like a homing pigeon guided by some magnetic current, I headed unerringly along a succession of identical lanes until I came upon an intersection where a signpost read "Rue des Trévires." I stood for a moment in amazement: yes, I recognized it; that was indeed "my" street, the first street that I could recall having lived on at the dawn of my life, before I learned to read and write! I turned left and strolled up that gently rising street until my steps led me to a decidedly familiar-looking stretch before the next corner where, alas, I found myself incapable of telling for certain which one among three or four contiguous houses was the one that so long ago had been my home. My birth certificate states, however, that I came into the world in a suburb called Pfaffenthal, where my parents dwelled on Rue Vauban. But that was before the germination of memory in me.

From the Rue des Trévires I turned back across the railway tracks to reconnoitre the city proper, the sites of which I readily identified without the help of a tourist guide. I even walked along a street where I recognized a small apartment house in which we had lived: our third or fourth residence before I reached the age of six. I wonder whether my parents' frequent moves were caused by unaffordable rents or the precariousness of their lives as immigrants. And yet, Luxembourg must have been a hospitable country, considering that it gave asylum to more than a thousand Jews from Germany and Eastern Europe, which is more than was the case of immense Canada, whose prime minister at the time was the heartless William Lyon Mackenzie King.

My mother, Mira Shaindl Arenstein, immigrated to France in 1929 to live with her sister Fella, who was a generation older. Aunt Fella lived with her husband, David Domb, and their son, Simon, and daughter, Ginette (Gitla), in Nancy. Prior to her move, my mother was a native of Kalisz in western Poland, a beautiful thousand-year-old city that boasts of being one of the oldest in Poland. Kalisz was ruled in the thirteenth century by a prince known as Bolesław the Pious, who in 1264 enacted the first edict of religious toleration in Europe, granting Jews various rights and privileges. This happened in the century before Poland's enlightened Renaissance-era king

Casimir the Great widely opened the gates of the country to Jewish immigration. The Jews, who constituted nearly one-third of Kalisz's pre-war population of about 85,000, almost all perished in the Shoah, except for a few who had emigrated before the onset of the cataclysm or had survived the concentration camps. Even the Jews' ancient cemetery was eradicated by the Nazis: they used its tombstones to pave streets. Kalisz author Arkadiusz Pacholski writes in a booklet published in 2001 that before the Shoah, his city, without Jews, was as unimaginable as winter without snow. Thinking of those inhabitants who live in the apartments that once belonged to Jews, he shares the pain and embarrassment he feels at the failure of some Poles to express shame at the crimes perpetrated by their parents and grandparents against their Jewish compatriots. He concludes that unless Poles confront their burden of guilt, their conscience will not be at rest and Poland will remain a haunted country.

My maternal great-grandfather, Rabbi Shimshon Arenstein, was a prominent spiritual leader of the Jewish community of Kalisz at the turn of the nineteenth and twentieth centuries. In the *Sefer Yizkor*, Memorial Book, of Kalisz, published in Israel, I read that in an age when Jewish book peddlers hawked in the marketplaces of the shtetls "scholarly books for men, illustrated books for women," Rabbi Arenstein, who was clearly far ahead of his time, professed that girls ought to be given the same education as boys.

My father, Wolf, was born in Wieruszów, a small town situated, like Kalisz, on the Prosna at a point where that river marked the border between Poland and Germany until 1939. He was afforded not more than a few years of schooling in the local rabbinical cheder, where boys learned to read Hebrew, while the daily languages in the community were Yiddish, Polish and German. Having lost his father at the age of nine, Wolf was forced into apprenticeship as a tailor to help support a family with many children. My father grew to become a self-made man with such a thirst for learning that he taught himself to read and write in German. His yearning for travel to distant countries was likely fed by his passion for the novels of Karl May, a now nearly forgotten German author of fantastic novels about the Indians of America's Far West (which May had never visited).

Unlike the Jewish community of Kalisz, that of Wieruszów was not ancient: according to a local historian its pioneers, who traded in wool, cattle and skins, had migrated there from Silesia in the mid-nineteenth century. Among the Jews who in the year 1856 acquired houses in the town appear the names of Jacob, Alexander and Moses Goldman. Alexander is said to have particularly impressed the city magistrate because he read and wrote Polish and did not look Jewish!

Young Jews of Western Poland who emigrated in search of work usually settled in nearby Germany; comparatively few immigrated to France or North America. Two of my father's uncles, Issar and Pinchas Goldman, lived in Berlin and served in the Imperial German Army in World War I. A series of photos of the two brothers appears in the Memorial Book of Wieruszów: one is dated 1916 and shows them leaning against a tank on the Western front; a second photograph is of Issar in German uniform seated behind the wheel of a car a year earlier. Next come two photos of Pinchas, who was one of the earliest airplane pilots: one is of him seated in his airplane, the other of him standing beside his airplane in Cambrai, in northern France. My mother's elder brother Paul (Kiva) Arenstein likewise immigrated to Germany. He settled in Berlin around 1920 and his daughter, Ginette, and elder son, Freddy (Manfred), were born there. Uncle Paul, his wife, Zilly, and their children fled to France after the advent of the Nazi regime. They found a new home in Lyon, where their younger son, Jacques (Yehuda), was born in the same year as I was. My father had come to Lyon a few years before them to live with his Wieruszów compatriots Moshe and Gitla Schwartz, who were hatters by profession.

France in the 1930s was no longer as receptive to immigrants as it had been in the 1920s. Unable to find work and thus to obtain a *carte de travail*, work permit, without which a foreigner was not allowed to reside in France, my father wandered into Belgium, where he worked for several months as a coal miner in Liège. At the time there were many Jewish workers employed in the coal mines and metallurgical industries of Belgium and Luxembourg. Luckily, a better opportunity beckoned him to Luxembourg, where another landsman from Wieruszów operated a small tailoring workshop and hired him.

As it happened, my mother's brother-in-law David Domb also hailed from Wieruszów; Wolf visited the Dombs in Nancy and there met Mira. On a recent visit to Lyon I was told by the older Schwartz daughter, Lea, that my maternal grandmother, who operated a mikveh, ritual bath, in Kalisz, insisted that Mira should marry Wolf. Lea Schwartz also told me that, according to her mother, my paternal grandparents were reputed to be the most dignified family in Wieruszów, in spite of their poverty. In any event, my parents met in Nancy and then made their home in Luxembourg, where they were married on October 24, 1931, Wolf being only twenty years old and Mira twenty-four. Surprisingly perhaps, I was not born until three years later.

My mother was a woman of very small stature and delicate features; she was soft spoken and rather shy, the very personification of gentleness. I don't remember her ever punishing me when I misbehaved: all she needed to do to bring me back to order was to threaten to report what I did wrong to Papa when he returned from work. I inherited some of her traits, including her flaming red hair, but after the age of eleven my hair grew darker and I grew to resemble my father more. Father was likewise gentle and loving, but he could occasionally be strict, particularly when I became unruly and he deemed it necessary to apply a few whacks of his measuring ruler on my behind! In truth, my parents both spoiled me — I was their only child and my father pinned on me some of the aspirations that life did not enable him to fulfill.

I came into the world on March 25, 1934, which was a Year of the Dog on the Chinese zodiac; that perhaps accounts for my inordinate love of dogs! The first time that I attempted to write the story of my life was at the tender age of eleven, and I still have that school notebook in which I inscribed a single page in elementary school French, a text that ends on an incomplete sentence and contains three spelling mistakes. That childish attempt at an autobiography was inspired by my reading of Charles Dickens's novel *David Copperfield*. I read the novel in an abbreviated French translation at the time and was so entranced with the story of that mistreated orphan boy that I identified with him to the point of not believing that he was a mere creature of fiction. I reread *David Copperfield* several times over my prepubescent years and also saw a film of the novel. I even dreamt of David Copperfield in my sleep.

That earliest "autobiography" of mine contains information that was probably conveyed to me at the time by my Aunt Zilly — such facts as that my parents had lived in Luxembourg since 1933 (which was erroneous) and that my father had considered naming me Abraham but instead followed the suggestion of *une demoiselle*, a young lady, who gave him the idea of calling me René. My paternal uncle Léon, of blessed memory, who lived in Toronto, told me that, in keeping with tradition, I was also given the Hebrew name Yitzhak (Isaac), which was my grandfather's name. However, I dislike the name Yitzhak, which means "laugh": the Bible tells us that Abraham's spouse Sarah laughed incredulously when God informed her that she would bear a child at age ninety-nine, and so her son was named Yitzhak. After a prolonged stay in Israel in 1980, during which I began to learn Hebrew, I gave myself the name Eiran, which means, roughly, "aware." My genial colleague at the University of British Columbia, the late professor Leon Hurvitz, who was a peerless linguist, expressed amazement that my parents should have given me so Christian a name as René/Renatus, which means "reborn," apparently an allusion to the rebirth of Christ. Soon after he made that observation, the Jewish community of France elected as its new *grand-rabbin*, chief rabbi, a man named René-Samuel Sirat!

I grew up in a multilingual environment. I spoke Lëtzebuergesch, the Low German dialect of Luxembourg akin to Alsatian, in kindergarten, and sometimes with Papa; High German when with both my parents; and either Yiddish or German with our family friends. My parents never taught me Polish. The official language of Luxembourg is French, of which I must have picked up some notion at the time. Most Luxembourgeois speak all three languages — French, German and Lëtzebuergesch. French eventually became my preferred language even though I did not actually speak it before the age of eight.

The year of my birth, 1934, was a decidedly eventful one in the descent of the world into the valley of the shadow of wholesale death. Hitler had been in power for more than a year, and the month before I came into the world political tensions in Paris exploded into a riot near the French National Assembly, which some believed was an attempted *coup d'état*, illegal seizure of power. From January 26 to February 10, the Soviet Communist Party held its seventeenth Party Congress at which the cult of Joseph Stalin was officially consecrated, yet in a secret ballot, Sergey Kirov, the Bolshevik boss of Leningrad, won more votes than did Stalin. As a result, Kirov was mysteriously assassinated in December, an event that set the stage for the massive purges of the decade in which millions perished, including most of the delegates to the seventeenth Congress, Lenin's old Bolshevik companions and the entire command of the Soviet army.

I can only imagine the cares that weighed down my parents as they rocked me in my cradle. How their fears must have mounted year by year as they scrutinized the ever-darkening clouds gathering over a future to which, as a young couple with their first child, they ought to have looked forward. My father had tasted poverty in his young years and dreamed of a better life not only for himself and his family, but also for the destitute Jewish masses of the shtetls of Poland and for working people in general.

Unfortunately, wishing to emancipate themselves from the bonds of religion and tradition, many young idealists fell into the trap of an atheistic quasi-religion, which, in the name of the ideals of freedom, equality and brotherhood first proclaimed by the great French Revolution, gave birth to cruel totalitarian regimes. That quasi-religion of communism had its prophets — Marx, Engels and Lenin — who held that the "proletariat" was the agent of humankind's salvation or emancipation from all historical systems of "exploitation of man by man." They called on the workers of the world to unite and break their chains. How uplifting this appeal must have sounded to idealistic Jews, at a time when no one had yet read Marx's "Essay on the Jewish Question" and other testimonies to his scurrilous Judeophobia. Struggling to make a living in often difficult material conditions and faced with the mounting threat of Nazism, the communists of my parents' generation fervently believed in the Soviet Union as the beacon that lit the way to a radiant future, in which there would be no poverty, no "exploitation of man by man" and, just as importantly, no antisemitism or racism. Ill-informed about the horrific reality of the Soviet Union in the 1930s, they allowed no doubt about "the fatherland of the proletariat," and, should any cross their mind, they readily suppressed it, for in their eyes the Soviet Union alone stood to check the deadly and almost palpable threat of the moment: Hitler.

This dream of a just and more humane society in the future drew my father in his adolescence to the youth organization of the Labour Zionist movement Poalei Zion, and then to communism. He became a member of the Communist Party of Luxembourg. I don't know what my mother's political views were and can only surmise that she followed my father's. Perhaps in deference to her family in Poland, she held some reservations.

There is so much about my parents that I shall likely never know. I was circumcised in keeping with tradition, and my parents' friends and acquaintances included some Orthodox Jews, such as the old lady who occasionally invited us over on Friday evening, reverently kissed the prayer book and wished us in Yiddish "a gute Shabbes."

Also, I remember an old skullcapped scholar who spent his days poring over holy books. Whenever my parents visited with his family in their shop, I would creep into his study. Kindly tolerant of my unexpected appearance, he would sit me next to him and cut me a slice from a loaf of delicious dark bread that he always seemed to keep on his desk and then, smiling gently at me, let me watch him in fascination. Such was the taste of that bread that I relished eating it without butter or any other addition.

My parents had a seemingly close circle of friends and acquaintances, chief among them the Lewin family. Max Lewin and his wife owned a small chocolate factory and had five adult children — four sons, named Oscar, Joseph, Bubi and Adi, and a daughter, Rosa. They were true and supportive friends whom we saw often. Among the other members of the circle who come to mind was one man who was so tall that he had to stoop to pass through a door frame. I was thrilled every time he came to our home, for he gushed with vitality and good humour; I would then run into his waiting arms to be lifted over his head and tossed up high in the air, shrieking with delight. I also remember with especial fondness a lovely young couple called Tania and Eugene, whose surname I have unfortunately forgotten, if ever I knew it. They lived in a cottage with a garden and sometimes invited me to spend a few days at their home. They had a dachshund named Amie, who strutted into my room every morning and, having verified that I was awake, would bring her puppies one by one in her mouth to drop them on my bed, after which she jumped on it herself and nestled against my chest. And then there was a cobbler: I have a photo of myself at age three perhaps, wearing a jumper suit, sitting on the doorstep of his workshop. I sometimes wonder what happened to all these kind people in the years of terror, if any of them survived....

On Sunday afternoons in summer my parents would meet up with a band of friends, some married with or without children, some single. Together we strolled along a small country road by the side of a creek, past cottages with gardens. The destination of the walk was

Gantenbeinsmühle, a resort with an immense swimming pool, a large terraced café to one side of it and expanses of lawns on which clusters of people rested and enjoyed themselves, some in their Sunday attire, some in swimwear. My maternal cousins Simon Domb and his sister Ginette (Gitla) often visited from Nancy and joined us at Gantenbeinsmühle. How blessed these precious hours of relaxation and happiness must have been for people who worked six days a week.... Among the old photos that I treasure is one of Ginette standing in the swimming pool holding me in her arms, and another of Simon bending down to hold me against his knees.

Louis Simon (Leyb Shimshon) Domb, who was twenty years older than me, was an exceptionally studious boy. In the late 1930s he was one of the few Jews admitted to the École polytechnique in Paris, an elite school founded by Napoleon I to train engineers and high-ranking government administrators. Simon graduated from Polytechnique just as the war broke out. Holding an engineering diploma and the rank of lieutenant, he was placed in command of a regiment that was entrusted in 1940 with the defence of the city of Vichy.

I reckon that my reminiscences of the first six years of my life are fragmented, disconnected. How far does memory of early childhood reach in any event? How accurate is the retelling? A child's perception of things is conditioned by his small size: he tends to magnify the places he sees and even to adorn them as he stores them away in the treasure chest of the mind. Some landmarks of my childhood years seemed smaller and not as beautiful when I saw them again long after.

Years after the war, when I lived successively in France, Poland, China, the United States and finally Canada, which became my cherished homeland, I almost let go of recollections of my early life, particularly of the wartime years of terror and loss. Thoughts of the moment and of the future became my driving preoccupation. Unfortunately, as a result, I failed to put questions to my uncles and aunts and their contemporaries, which would have substantially enriched my research into the history of my family in the years of the war and before. Eventually, age has brought the past back into the limelight of memory, along with numerous occasions to tell and retell to new generations the story of my life in the dark years of the Shoah.

In 1938, a mere few months before Kristallnacht, my mother took me on a journey to Poland, which lasted weeks, or perhaps even months. There we visited our family on both sides, not only in Wieruszów and Kalisz, but also in Warsaw and Lodz. Ours was a large family, made up of many uncles, aunts and cousins. Alas, I remember few names and no faces, which grieves me all the more since that entire family of mine in Poland, with the single exception of one brother of my father, perished in the Shoah. I was then four years old and of that journey I can retrieve from my memory nothing more significant than a few vignettes or glimpses, such as Mama and I seated on a bench in a railway station; of the two of us seated with a man in an outdoor café, perhaps in Warsaw, watching a streetcar surge from around a street corner ahead and travelling past us; of me lying in bed peering out a window into a large courtyard where a man carried two buckets at the ends of a pole and dipped them in a well; and then of a cousin nicknamed Shlomutek — "Sweet Solly" — home from school, standing by my bed.

But my recollections of Luxembourg are naturally more vivid. Images of the simple happiness of childhood project something like a magic aura over them. Though the size of the country is small, the Grand Duchy of Luxembourg is not in a league with Monaco, Liechtenstein, San Marino or Andorra, as many people tend to assume. Luxembourg, along with Singapore or Hong Kong, belongs among the modern equivalents of the Italian city-states of the Renaissance and the ancient Greek and Phoenician city-states. Like these, it is composed of a capital city of the same name and a stretch of countryside dotted with a number of small towns and villages. Moreover, the hilly terrain of Luxembourg, which measures roughly eighty kilometres from north to south, and fifty-seven from east to west, makes it appear more extensive than it actually is. Though largely rural in appearance, thanks in part to the bucolic scenery of the Ardennes hills in the north, Luxembourg is also an industrialized country, with coal mines and a steel-mill complex at Rodange in the south. The Grand Duchy counts roughly 575,000 inhabitants; Hong-Kong, which occupies an area half its size, counts more than seven million! The city of Luxembourg is today one of the capitals of the European Union and a world financial centre.

Luxembourg is divided into two parts by a most amazing topographical feature: a deep and wide chasm, the Pétrusse Valley, beneath whose wooded slopes a gently flowing little river called Alzette courses amid toy-like villages. To the west of the valley lies the old town surrounded by remnants of its medieval walls. At the heart of it is the Place d'Armes fronted by the Palais Municipal, a community event hall and, a short distance away, Place Guillaume and the Grand Ducal Palace. To the east of the valley rises the modern post-eighteenth-century city, with its avenues and the railway station. The two parts of the city are spanned by two high viaducts. Much as memory may adorn and embellish sights beheld so long ago, I do not think that I am imagining the splendour of the Pétrusse Valley in spring: its slopes were then ablaze with a profusion of lilacs, blooming in all colours, whose fragrance was carried up and around by the breeze.

Among my fondest memories of childhood are the Sunday strolls around the city with my parents, dressed in our formal clothes, as social conventions called for in those times, when people in Europe worked six days a week and Sunday was so special that it called for wearing one's best clothes. Besides the Sunday afternoons with friends at the Gantenbeinsmühle swimming pool, we sometimes travelled to a resort town near the French border called Mondorf-les-Bains, where Papa rowed us in a boat. A sister of Mama, Dora Arenstein, worked there for several months in the Hôtel Hemmendinger. I have a signed certificate — dated March 30, 1939 — in which the owner of that hotel expresses full satisfaction with her work but certifies that, in conformity with Luxembourg's immigration law, he was compelled to terminate her employment. My aunt Dora, whom I do not remember, unfortunately, thus had to return home to Poland; she perished in the hell that would soon engulf the Jewish people there.

I found many years ago, in a torn old handbag of my mother's, sepia and black-and-white photos, some of which bear on the back a dedication in Polish or Yiddish. Alas, I cannot identify these persons and their connection to Mama. One photo, dated November 1938, is of a woman much older than Mama and bears the inscription in Polish "to my sister, Mala." Was she another sister of my mother's, I wonder? I have all my life envied people who, besides growing up with parents, also enjoyed, even in their adult years, the presence of grandparents and even great-grandparents.

I remember with particular fondness the annual celebrations of the birthday of Grand Duchess Charlotte. The city was gaily festooned and burst with illuminations late into the night. Joyful crowds followed the procession of floats up the Avenue de la Liberté, while residents of that thoroughfare, including us, as we lived there for a time, cheered from the windows, tossing confetti and flowers. Then, following the floats, came the little blue train that Papa rode on weekdays to work in the city of Esch-sur-Alzette: for the occasion it was rerouted, magnificently adorned, away from the railway onto the streetcar tracks of the city centre and renamed "la Petite Charlotte" in affectionate tribute to the sovereign.

In retrospect, Luxembourg before the war seemed like a carefree, happy small country, and my parents must have enjoyed living there. Alas, from a mere few kilometres to the east they would have heard echoes of sounds altogether different from the cheering festive noises of our city — sounds of hate-filled barks of a murderous lunatic and of blood-curdling roars of "Sieg heil" and "Death to the Jews" emanating from millions of throats in response. Before the war, roughly 4,000 Jews lived in Luxembourg, about 1,000 of whom were refugees from Germany.

My early childhood ended with the coming of the German occupation. Although the war began with the German invasion of Poland on September 1, 1939, and Britain and France's immediate declaration of war, Western Europe enjoyed an eight-month-long period of armed peace known as *la drôle de guerre*, the phony war. Then, on May 10, 1940, the Germans launched a massive invasion of Holland and Belgium and attacked France. In the process, they violated their promise of respecting the neutrality of Luxembourg.

One Sunday morning Papa and I happened to be walking past the railway station when out of its gates marched columns of German soldiers. Luxembourg now fell under military occupation, but nothing untoward had yet happened. German army bands, trumpets blaring and drums rolling, paraded here and there, followed by amused little boys trying to march in step with them. The German soldiers must have at first surprised and impressed the population by their disciplined and courteous conduct, while the propaganda films shown in the cinemas likely imprinted on many minds the notion that the Germans were an invincible "master race." But it only took two or three months for the velvet gloves to come off and for their *Schrecklichkeit*, terror, to manifest itself. In spite of the presence of a sizable ethnic German population in the country, the occupiers failed to persuade Luxembourg's people of the desirability of annexation to the German Reich. Efforts in that direction, including the enlistment of young men into the Wehrmacht, met with determined resistance in the form of protests, strikes and sabotage. The Germans responded with terror, arrests and executions.

In September 1940, the Nuremberg Laws were enforced in Luxembourg. The Germans seized Jewish property, bank accounts and even personal belongings. Rabbi Robert Serebrenik, spiritual leader of the Jewish community, was summoned to Berlin, where Eichmann personally informed him that Luxembourg must be rendered *judenrein*, free of Jews, within weeks, and that whoever had not left the country by the deadline would be deported to the east. Thanks to what must truly have been untiring efforts on the part of the rabbi, who travelled to Lisbon, several hundred Jews obtained transit visas to Portugal, from where they sailed to the Americas. Those were the fortunate few. Others promptly moved to France or Belgium in a vain hope of escaping deportation to the east. Still, only about half of the Jewish population of Luxembourg succeeded in leaving the country: some with visas, some without. Rabbi Serebrenik left with what must have been the last group to depart, in May 1941. In 1943, the Germans destroyed the synagogue; it was rebuilt after the war with assistance from the Luxembourg government, but the reconstituted Jewish community numbered then only about 1,500 persons. Interestingly enough, it was in the city of Luxembourg that West Germany's chancellor Konrad Adenauer and Israel's foreign minister Moshe Sharett signed, on September 10, 1952, the agreement on German reparations to Israel and Jewish victims of Nazi barbarity.

Soon after I began my graduate studies at Columbia University in New York in October 1960, I made the acquaintance of a Jewish family from Luxembourg named Steinberg, who had known my parents. I became a frequent guest in their home in New Jersey and learned from them that the Jews who left Luxembourg with Rabbi Serebrenik were barred from entering Canada and the United States but found refuge in the Dominican Republic, whose dictator Leonidas Trujillo encouraged European Jews to settle in his country. It is such a tragedy that more Jews were not able to avail themselves of Trujillo's invitation, but the few hundred who did made significant contributions to the development of agriculture and public health in the Dominican Republic. Many of the Luxembourg Jewish refugees in the Dominican Republic obtained American visas in 1947 and settled in New York City and nearby New Jersey. They formed the nucleus of the membership of Congregation Ramath Orah ("Hill of Light," i.e., "Luxembourg" in Hebrew), which in the 1960s still had Rabbi

Serebrenik as its spiritual leader. When I went to meet the rabbi I was astonished to discover that the synagogue was located on West 110th Street, between Broadway and Amsterdam Avenue, a mere five blocks from the campus of Columbia University.

I have often wondered why my parents and I were not among those who managed to reach the Dominican Republic. Was it because my father was a communist and therefore not a member of the synagogue congregation, or perhaps because he could not afford the costs of that distant travel or could not obtain the necessary transit visas? I believe that either of the latter two reasons was the cause of us not escaping from Europe in 1940. Be that as it may, the two years that we next lived in Brussels ended up costing my parents their lives.

Belgium

One sunny morning in the summer of 1940, a month or two after the Germans occupied Luxembourg, my parents and I left the country in the company of Max Lewin, his wife, their daughter, Rosa, and their sons Oscar and Joseph. There was joy when, upon the train's arrival in the Belgian capital, we were met at the station by the other two Lewin sons, cherubic Adi and tall, lanky Bubi. They had travelled ahead to search for accommodation for both our families and had found it in an old building on Boulevard Poincaré in Anderlecht, one of the several boroughs into which Brussels is divided. The Lewins settled in a large upstairs apartment that overlooked the boulevard, and we in a dark, dingy ground-level flat in a wing at the back of the building. The flat, which one entered from a tiny paved courtyard, was L-shaped: its front room was to serve as Papa's tailoring workshop, while the two or three rooms on the side became our living quarters.

As we were moving in with our belongings, one of the Lewin brothers came down to invite me to share their family's noon-hour meal, while my parents sat down to eat soup out of plates placed atop the lid of a wicker trunk. Being neighbours, as well as friends of many years, we and the Lewins saw each other daily. Although the brothers were adults, the two older ones being roughly my parents' age, I often sought their company and frequently went upstairs to listen to records, which they played on a gramophone that was a veritable piece of furniture. I was in this way introduced to the great Italian

tenors Enrico Caruso and Beniamino Gigli; the mellifluous, effemi-
nate voice of Corsican crooner Tino Rossi (who would be briefly imprisoned after the liberation of France for his collaboration with the
Germans); and sundry fashionable songs of the time, such as "Tango
Marina," my first tango, and "Je suis seul(e) ce soir avec mes rêves" (I
am alone tonight with my dreams).

The great event in the lives of our neighbours was the wedding of
Joseph, eldest of the Lewin brothers, in 1941. My parents prepared me
for this happy occasion long in advance by making me learn by heart
the tender and whimsical Yiddish love song "Reyzele." This song,
which I hum to myself to this day, was written by Mordecai Gebirtig,
one of the fathers of modern Yiddish folklore: it is about a shy young
man named Dovidl, who courts a pretty girl named Reyzel. At the
wedding dinner in the Lewins' apartment, I stood on a chair to sing
"Reyzele" to the warm applause of all assembled.

I was awed by the size of Brussels, which was so much larger a city than Luxembourg. I was impressed by its long, tree-lined
boulevards, such as the one on which we lived, and its many imposing buildings. And there were vast parks, such as the woods of la
Cambre and Woluwe, which became the choice places of our Sunday
afternoon outings in summer. When I revisited Brussels in my adult
years, however, the Belgian capital appeared to me as little else than a
very large but unremarkable metropolis, except for the magnificently
ornate Grand Place with its sumptuous Flemish Renaissance architecture and quaint and picturesque restaurant-lined lanes surrounding it. Brussels' most amusing tourist destination is to be found in
one of those quaint lanes: it is a small statue of a cherubic little naked
boy holding his penis, out of which water streams into the fountain,
hence the statue's endearing Flemish nickname of "Manneken Pis."

After living for a short time on Boulevard Poincaré, we moved
into a sunny apartment on Place Alphonse Lemmens in the neighbouring borough of Molenbeek. A few steps around the corner, on
Rue Odon, was an elementary school, which I attended for two years.

There I began my primary education in the Flemish language. Like Canada, Belgium is officially bilingual, but its bilingualism applies only to Brussels, the national capital; in Wallonia public life is conducted in French, while in Flanders it is conducted in Flemish, which is a dialect of Dutch. Most Belgian Jews are Francophones. Had my parents been able to foresee that we might soon find ourselves compelled to leave Belgium, they would probably have sent me to French school. I surmise that they registered me in Flemish school because Flemish is related to the three languages I spoke, all three of which are Germanic: German, Lëtzebuergesch and Yiddish. They reasoned that this would make schooling easier for me at this stage. Eventually, realizing perhaps that they had made a mistake, my parents had Rosa Lewin tutor me in French. That happened when I was in Grade 2, by which time I might have already gleaned some rudiments of that language in the streets, if not at school. In any case, by the time we arrived in France I had some knowledge of French.

After living for some time in two different apartments, we moved back to the slum on Boulevard Poincaré, possibly because we could not afford the higher rents. Papa worked on orders at home and business must have been sluggish, unless one's client was the Wehrmacht, as was the case with a fellow Jewish tailor of our acquaintance, who bore the funny name of Kittenkorn. It seems that the only luxuries that we allowed ourselves were a bottle of beer and one of lemonade, in addition to cake, on Sundays, unless on that one day of leisure we took the streetcar for an afternoon outing in the woods of la Cambre or Woluwe, on which occasions we sat down to a bottle of delicious Spa lemonade on the terrace of a café.

School occupied me six days a week. Some afternoons, after regular school hours, I walked by myself a fairly long distance across town to a music school, where I sat in a class of *solfège* with students ranging in age from my own to young adulthood. The class was taught by a teacher of musical theory, who lectured as he wrote on the blackboard in both French and Flemish. My parents must have

believed that I had musical ability and for a time Mama even travelled with me by streetcar to a piano teacher. Whether I would have
been able to pursue a career in music if the relative placidity of our
life in Brussels had not been terminated by subsequent events, I cannot tell. I remember, however, that I already nourished a profound
love for classical music. My parents certainly exerted themselves to
shelter me from the mounting dread by spinning a cocoon of security
around me.

When the phony war episode ended on May 10, 1940, the Germans
violated the neutrality of Belgium, as they had in 1914, by crossing it
to invade France. The Belgian army fought for nearly three weeks but
was encircled by German troops, causing King Léopold III to surrender rather than emulate the heroic stance of his father Albert I,
who during the First World War personally led the Belgian army to
fight alongside the Allies at Yser. In 1940 the Belgian government fled
to London and the country fell under the rule of a *Gauleiter*, military
governor, Alexander von Falkenhausen. Falkenhausen was said to be
anti-Nazi, a fact which, in practice, was of little consequence, since
the Gestapo and the SS took charge of important matters, such as the
persecution of the Jews. The Germans engaged in that task with the
help of willing native collaborators, notably Flemish nationalists and
Léon Degrelle's far-right political party, Rex.

Unlike what happened in Poland, however, in Belgium, as in Luxembourg, the occupation in its initial stage was not noticeably brutal.
The population suffered material hardships such as rationing of necessities, but life flowed on with a semblance of normality. In Eastern
Europe hell descended suddenly and the Jews were forced out of their
homes and crammed into ghettos as the first stage in the process of
degradation, which culminated in the gas chambers and crematoria
of Treblinka, Majdanek, Chełmno and Auschwitz. However, in Western Europe, the Germans at first concealed the iron fist in a velvet
glove. No ghettos were set up and discrimination and persecution
followed, but one step at a time. When in October 1940, as happened

in the Occupied Zone of France, the German occupation authorities ordered the registration of all Jews and the stamping of the letter "J" on their identity papers, the legal profession protested against this violation of the Belgian constitution; in this they showed considerably more courage than their French colleagues, who that same month voted in favour of the Vichy regime's antisemitic legislation.

Throughout 1941 edicts restricting Jewish property and movement were enacted. On August 29 of that year an order restricted the Jews to residence in four major cities of the country: Brussels, Antwerp, Liège and Charleroi. Malines (Mechelen), which was midway between Brussels and Antwerp, eventually became the site of a camp that, like Drancy outside Paris, served as a gathering centre from where the cattle cars left for the death camps in the east. Yet, as there was no precedent in the history of any nation for the calamity that was to descend on European Jewry, and the Germans, notwithstanding the Nazi regime, were still believed to be a highly cultured nation, our people could not imagine what lay ahead and proceeded with their lives as best they could in circumstances of scarcity and food rationing. In the West we were not aware of the mass murders perpetrated by the Einsatzgruppen since the German invasion of the Soviet Union, nor did we hear of the Wannsee Conference, held five months later in January 1942, where the wholesale massacre of the Jewish people was planned. At the beginning of the occupation, in 1940, there had even been fanciful rumours circulating to the effect that the Germans intended to relocate the Jews of Europe to the French colony of Madagascar in the Indian Ocean. That project is said to have been postponed after the Germans lost the Battle of Britain and abandoned entirely after the Wannsee Conference. In any case, it is doubtful that the French government, otherwise so cooperative, would have agreed to that scheme.

By the time I was six or seven years old, Papa had already bequeathed me his lively interest in the geography of the world. I learned from him the names of the capitals of many countries and also about

Madagascar, where he seemed to believe we might possibly live in the future. I even learned to draw from memory the contours of that magical island, with the straight line of its east coast and the bulge in the middle of the west coast.

Papa did his tailoring, usually at home; Mama kept house and I walked to school and music school. Sometimes I played alongside, rather than with, neighbourhood boys on the boulevard, particularly on Sunday afternoons, when rival teams of men engaged in a sport that I cannot identify and seemed to consist of tossing back and forth little white balls. Whenever players missed their aim and the little balls rolled out of the marked court, we vied with each other in running to catch and hoard them as treasures. But the boys, who probably suspected that I was Jewish, kept me away from their circle and sometimes even roughed me up. Occasionally, my parents sent me on errands to carry something to or back from Mina, a lovely lady who had been a close friend of Mama's since Luxembourg and often stayed with us. My parents had a circle of friends and acquaintances, most of whom were Jews. I remember a couple that had a girl of about my age, whose company I enjoyed greatly; her name was Fela Szeps, but I never learned whether she survived the war. For a time I was also invited almost every weekend for dinner and an overnight stay with a delightful family that had two teenage or adult daughters, cheerful girls who spoiled me like a little brother.

From time to time we travelled by electric train to Antwerp or Malines to visit people we knew. In Brussels we went on outings to parks, cinemas and theatres. As a child of seven, I was fascinated by the theatre stage even more than by the cinema screen. I had a fertile imagination and loved play-acting, dressing up, pretending to be someone else. My parents even allowed me sometimes to go out by myself to the Ancienne Belgique, a small variety theatre that offered light-hearted entertainment and music. I was very proud of the fact that the conductor of that theatre's orchestra, Ludo Langlois, wore a mauve suit tailored for him by Papa. On two occasions my parents took me to Brussels' opera house, the Théâtre Royal de la Monnaie, which to the pint-sized thespian that I had become appeared much larger than it is in reality. The first opera that we watched there was Bizet's *Carmen*. I was so fascinated by the ornately decorated royal lodge to the left of the stage that I half expected the king and queen to appear in it at any moment! Once, when riding a streetcar past a church I fancied it to be a theatre on the stage of which God descended from the tower and produced himself; my parents refrained from contradicting me on that point!

Alas, as time passed I gleaned from the conversations of the adults facts that were disturbing, particularly news of the arrest of one or another family that we knew. I heard the word *déportation*, which in French bears the sinister meaning of "resettlement in the East," the euphemism by which the Germans mendaciously covered up the removal of our people from all over Europe to the death camps. At first only foreign Jews were rounded up, beginning with the men who were sent on work projects before being dispatched to the East. In September 1942, however, Jews who were Belgian citizens were deported as well. Though they knew that nothing good was to be expected of the Germans, as late as the middle of 1942 Jews in Western Europe were not aware of the true meaning of "resettlement" or "deportation." Few realized that the "Final Solution" had come to Belgium. The leaders of the Allied powers knew by then that genocide was in progress, but the intended victims were kept in the dark. *Boches*, the derogatory French epithet pinned on the Germans, was also one that I grasped from overheard adult conversations; yet, strangely enough, I understood it to mean fat men with huge protruding bellies! One day when I was walking along a major street between my parents, who held me by the hands, I distended my belly and rhythmically chanted, "Boche! Boche! Boche!" Petrified, my parents vigorously shook me.

In May 1942, Jews were ordered to sew on their outer garments a yellow star bearing the letter "J" or even the word "Juif" or "Jood" fully spelled out, inside it. The Belgian administration having refused to promulgate such an infamous regulation, the Germans were forced to do it themselves, but they imposed the thankless task of implementing it on the official Association des Juifs de Belgique, which was forced to function like a ghetto Judenrat of Eastern Europe. Signs went up identifying Jewish businesses, many of which were taken over by Germans, and the personal property of those who were deported was confiscated.

One afternoon Mama took me to a cinema, where a special film showing for children was programmed. When I reached my seat and unbuttoned my overcoat the yellow star appeared in full view, whereupon I found myself caught in a crossfire of boos and catcalls of "Juif! Juif! Juif!" Upset beyond words, I burst into tears and ran out of the cinema without waiting for Mama to come for me. I arrived at home breathless and so angry that I shouted to my astonished parents to remove that star, that I did not want to wear it. My parents tried to reason with me, to explain the danger to which I might expose myself if I were caught in the street without the star, but to no avail. Amazingly enough, my resolve swayed my parents; we all three prepared to assume the risk of not wearing the yellow Magen David. This meant that we had to carefully watch where our steps led us. How dangerous the situation became was evident by the appearance on the streets of uniformed Germans, who randomly ordered passersby to produce their identity papers: any Jewish person caught not wearing that yellow star was subject to roundup and deportation.

One time, as we walked along the Boulevard Poincaré a few hundred metres from home, Mama suddenly spotted such a checkpoint. Squeezing my hand, she ordered me to cross to the other side of the boulevard and proceed in the direction of a certain street corner without looking back, until she could meet up with me. Luckily, she was not stopped. We lived not far from the Gare du Midi, Brussels' largest railway station. When I revisited Brussels in my adult years, arriving in that grotty station always revived in my memory the vision of Jews lined up under guard outside.

One beautiful spring day Mama decided to take me on an outing to a park situated at the end of a long streetcar line. As the streetcar reached the entrance to that park, we were preparing to alight, when we noticed a column of Jews who were being herded away. Unnoticed, we rushed back inside the streetcar and rode home.

On another occasion — I don't remember whether it was before or after that incident — Mama and I were returning home by streetcar, after dark, from my last music lesson. When the streetcar reached Place Rouppe, about a fifteen-minute walk from where we lived, I stepped out too fast and was hit by a passing car. Mama, who tried to hold me back, fell on top of me and the contents of her purse scattered over the pavement. Who had been driving that car but three German soldiers! They helped us stand up and gather our things and then drove us home. Luckily, Mama was unhurt and I suffered only minor wounds on my forehead. One of the soldiers bandaged my head and promised to return the next morning to verify that the wounds were healing. They then saluted, apologized and left without asking questions. I can only imagine what kind of a night my parents must have spent waiting for the morrow. Surely enough, the next morning the soldier who had bandaged me returned alone; he undid the bandage and, satisfied that the wounds were healing, apologized again and left!

As dangers mounted and fear became omnipresent in 1942, my parents and some of their friends decided to flee Belgium for France in the hope of reaching the unoccupied southern zone and, once there, book passage on a boat leaving Europe. What we were preparing to do was illegal, for in January of that year Jews had been forbidden to leave the country. How apprehensive my parents must have been as they prepared to abandon home and possessions and face untold dangers to escape into the unknown. Would they succeed in finding a peaceful country far away from the misery and persecution of Europe? Nothing could have been less certain.

Seeking to prepare me for this adventure, my parents explained to me that we were going to travel to Marseille and from there sail to Montevideo. Why the capital of Uruguay, I later wondered: had rumours reached my parents' ears that visas could be obtained to travel there? My parents set out to condition me for long treks on foot. Even though I always walked to and from school, I sometimes complained of fatigue when ambling over greater distances. Mama even chided me for not being able to walk one kilometre without complaining of feeling tired and gently admonished me that we might soon have to go on marches as long as a hundred kilometres. Long walks were not the only major preparation that I had to submit to; Rosa Lewin's French lessons were another.

Papa had established some sort of connection with a very distinguished and well-to-do Belgian gentleman named Monsieur Honoré. That gentleman and his wife lived in a spacious and elegant apartment in a high-class building near the fountain of the Manneken Pis. Papa and I visited that couple several times and they always received us cordially. A short time before our departure from Belgium, my parents and I were riding the streetcar back home one night when suddenly Papa asked me how I would like to live with a rich family: he explained that Monsieur Honoré had offered to adopt me for at least as long as the war lasted and until their return. I protested that I did not want them to leave me behind.

As the "Final Solution" engulfed Belgium, the population became increasingly sympathetic to its intended victims. Like every country occupied by the Nazis, Belgium had its collaborators, but an effective underground resistance movement, in which Jews participated, came into existence as well. Thanks to it, the Catholic Church headed by Cardinal Jozef-Ernst Van Roey, and the support of the Queen Mother Elizabeth, many Jewish children survived in hiding. Altogether some 25,000 Jews were saved by their Belgian compatriots. It is interesting to compare Belgium and Holland in regard to what happened to their Jewish populations. The two countries are roughly equal in size and population: both consist mainly of plains and are very densely populated and urbanized. Yet, when it came to helping the Jews living among them, the Belgians were by and large more compassionate and effective than the Dutch. Unfairly, the latter were given more credit than they deserved, and the Belgians not enough.

One early summer day my parents and I, along with two of the Lewin brothers, were part of a group of people who departed in the greatest secrecy by train to the French border. We disembarked not far before that border, which we crossed by stealth on foot. What happened next I remember only hazily. Travelling southward, we traversed hundreds of kilometres of the Occupied Zone in curiously diverse ways: now by train or bus, now on foot; I even recall that a man once carried me on a bicycle along a bumpy country path! Of the cities where we briefly stopped I remember Charleville, Belfort and Besançon. A short distance south of the latter city we arrived one evening at an inn in a village named Champagne-sur-Loue situated very near the Demarcation Line, which separated the Occupied Zone from the Free or Unoccupied Zone. This line, drawn at the time of France's surrender two years before, was even more difficult to cross than the international border with Belgium: at every railway station near it, passengers had to detrain and undergo thorough check-ups by German militaries and French policemen, and not all of the passengers would be allowed back on the trains; indeed, some were placed under arrest. There was therefore only one way in which we could cross that line — on foot and led by one of those *passeurs*, smugglers, to whom the illegal refugees entrusted their lives, paying significant sums of money for this service.

As dusk descended on the village of Champagne-sur-Loue, a *passeur* met us at the inn and led us on an arduous trek along country paths and across fields. At one point we even crawled between rows of hops. Eventually, we reached a forest, through which we marched the entire night in silence. Papa sometimes hoisted me on his shoulders. Every now and then the *passeur* motioned to us to lie in a ditch while he scouted the way ahead, until he signalled with his hand that we should move again. Silent on the trail, we conversed in whispers in the ditches, where Papa comforted me and assured me that we would soon be in Marseille and sail from there to Montevideo. We emerged from the forest into the Unoccupied Zone at daybreak, about six in the morning. What happened next befuddles me to this day, for I have no recollection of how we suddenly found ourselves under arrest, sitting at a table in a police station eating porridge! Did the *passeur* betray us, or did we happen upon a patrol, which readily discovered what we were, all the more since some people in our group spoke inadequate French or none at all? We were soon taken under police escort to the city of Poligny in the department of Jura, a few kilometres away from an inaccessible paradise: Switzerland. From Poligny plainclothes policemen accompanied us on a short train ride to the city of Lons-le-Saunier, in the same department, where we were "assigned to residence" — in other words, placed under house arrest.

In France

Upon our arrival in Lons-le-Saunier we were led to a small hotel, I believe the Hôtel Lambert, on a street that ended at the main square of the city. The hotel had been requisitioned by the police for the purpose of temporarily quartering Jewish refugees from Holland, Belgium and Luxembourg under an *assignation à résidence*, or house arrest policy, pending transfer to one of the internment camps in France. The three of us were given a room and, like regular hotel guests, could take our meals in the dining room and move freely about the city, which we did. The only restriction imposed on our movements was that we were not allowed to leave Lons-le-Saunier. My parents reassured me that from now on we would live quietly in this unremarkable city until the end of the war and that, come October, I would be going to school.

Yet Mama evidently had her doubts. One afternoon, as she was attending to some chore in our room, she suddenly told me that she had written to Aunt Fella, her older sister, to come and take me away to live with her in Limoges, for that was where the Domb family had moved from Nancy at the beginning of the war. I protested and cried that I did not want to be separated from her and Papa. She gently remonstrated that this was for my good, that I would lead a more normal life in Limoges, a large and beautiful city, and that we would not be separated for long. But I refused to be persuaded.

The summer of 1942 was, to say the least, an inauspicious time to arrive in the southern zone. It was then becoming well-nigh impossible to leave Europe; the gates to emigration were being shut as much by the bureaucratic chicanery of Vichy as by the dearth of compassion manifested by countries on the other side of the Atlantic — worst of all, it saddens me to say, by Canada, whose prime minister at the time was the infamous William Lyon Mackenzie King. At a time when our tormentors in Europe held a knife at our throats, King and his viscerally antisemitic crony Frederick Blair, then director of immigration, implemented a policy of "none is too many" in regard to Jews desperate for a refuge.

The antisemitic policy of the French government turned violently repressive. The Statut des Juifs, enacted by the Vichy regime in October 1940 within the framework of its National Revolution, featured a definition of who is a Jew that was even more sweeping than the German one. Whereas the German criteria were religious, the French criteria were openly racial: they defined a Jew as any person having three grandparents, or two grandparents and a spouse, of the Jewish "race." Jews were divided into two categories: those who held French citizenship, and refugees and immigrants who had not been naturalized. French Jews were promised the protection of the French government, a protection that did nothing when the Germans chose to challenge it, as happened in December 1942 when several hundred doctors, scientists, intellectuals — all leaders in their professions — were arrested, interned in Compiègne and later deported to German camps. Though decorated veterans and other well-known scholars and leaders had initially been spared, ultimately they too were nabbed and deported. All Jews were to be dismissed from the professions and the military.

As for non-French Jews, they were liable to internment at the discretion of regional police prefects. To supervise the implementation of that infamous statute and "Aryanize" Jewish property, the government created a General Commissariat for Jewish Affairs, whose first head, Xavier Vallat, condescendingly told young SS-*Hauptsturmführer* Dannecker, when he met the latter in Paris, "I am an older anti-semite than you are: I could be your father in this matter."

Yet Vallat was a "moderate" compared with Louis Darquier de Pellepoix, who succeeded him in the post of Commissar for Jewish Affairs in May 1942, at the time of our arrival. A yellow journalist of the lowest stripe, Darquier, whose aristocratic credentials were entirely bogus, had already won notoriety before the war for his antisemitic screeds. As early as 1937 he proffered that the "Jewish problem" must be resolved urgently, either by expelling the Jews from France or by massacring them. Now that he held a government position, Darquier ruled that non-French Jews who had found refuge in the "Free Zone" were to be rounded up and transported back across the Demarcation Line into the hands of the German occupation authorities in Paris. Darquier, who caused the death of thousands of Jews, never paid for his crimes; after the liberation he availed himself of Franco's hospitality and died in Spain.

To measure the extent of the French government's ignominy, one only needs to keep in mind that the Germans allowed France full autonomy over internal affairs in the entire country and that in the Free Zone the French government was the sole governing authority. There was little, if any, pressure applied by the Germans on the French, other than to require that France supply the Wehrmacht with food and industrial products. The *rafles*, as the rounding up of the Jews was called, were carried out in the main by the French police, which was not above refusing assistance from the terror-inspiring navy blue-uniformed and navy blue-bereted *Milice* and the pro-Nazi thugs of the Parti populaire français (PPF) in the discharging of that sinister task. The *rafles*, which began in 1941, at first targeted Jewish men of specific nationalities, who received summons to present themselves at the police commissariat nearest to their place of residence, supposedly for verification of their identity papers; to their shock, these men found themselves trapped and dispatched to the labour camps of Pithiviers and Beaune-la-Rolande near Orléans. Shocking though it may seem, even Jewish men who volunteered to fight and spill their blood for France in 1939 were arrested and handed over to the Germans in 1941.

False pretences such as identity verification were abandoned on July 16–17, 1942, with the advent of *la Grande Rafle*, which targeted entire families. In the pre-dawn hours police vans and requisitioned buses fanned out across Paris: about 13,000 men, women and children, roughly half the number of Jewish immigrants on the police lists, were caught in the net. The Germans ordered that massive roundup and the French obliged: they could have refused, because the Germans did not have the manpower required to stage such a gigantic manhunt. The operation, code-named *Vent printanier*, Spring Wind, was carried out from start to finish by the French police, without the participation of a single German. Worse yet, the Germans had agreed that children below the age of sixteen not be arrested at this stage, since most of them were born in France and were French citizens, but Prime Minister Pierre Laval decided on his own initiative that young children should be arrested nevertheless, on the grounds that it would be cruel to separate them from their parents. Six thousand Jews were sent immediately to the transit camp in Drancy, located in a suburb north of Paris, for deportation from France. Thousands more were crammed into the Vélodrome d'Hiver in sweltering heat, with scarcely any food or water or medical attention. After several days in the hellhole that the Vél d'Hiv had become, the French police transported the tortured victims of their collaborationist zeal to the internment camps of Pithiviers and Beaune-la-Rolande, as well as Drancy. From there they were sent to Auschwitz.

As the police hunted for Jews who had escaped the net, Laval did not even allow for the release of children whose parents had found relatives or strangers willing to take charge of them. Bordeaux police chief Maurice Papon and others of his stamp sent gendarmes to hunt down Jewish children, even toddlers, entrusted to rural families and Catholic institutions. The end result of Laval's "humanitarian" decision was that the children who were rounded up were separated from their parents all the same, interned in Pithiviers or Beaune-la-Rolande after their parents had already left these camps in the Occupied Zone, and sent all alone to Drancy and Auschwitz in separate trains, with no adults to comfort them. It is difficult to imagine the terror that gripped these children, some of whom were mere toddlers, brutalized by French policemen who robbed them of what little they had before packing them into the ghastly trains of death. The French thus willingly and zealously collaborated in the implementation of the "Final Solution."

I shudder at the thought of how close I came to sharing the fate of these children. Our family had sought refuge in the Free Zone precisely at the time when it became the scene of similar *rafles*. On August 26, a manhunt as massive as the one carried out in Paris the previous month swept the Free Zone. The British historian Paul Webster writes in his book *Pétain's Crime* that "the eleven weeks between July 16 and September 30, 1942, were the bleakest period of the war, when 33,000 Jews were sent to their deaths as a result of policies decided by a legitimate French government technically at peace and recognized by democratic nations like the United States."

I don't think that we had been in Lons-le-Saunier longer than two weeks when, early one morning, Mama came into the room where I had stayed overnight with Dutch friends. Roused from my sleep, I was shocked to see her in tears as she ordered me to get up and dress quickly because the police were waiting for us in front of the hotel. She pleaded with me that I should cry, so that perhaps I might soften the heart of the policemen. But strangely enough, I, who had hitherto been something of a crybaby, could not bring myself to shed a tear. I looked at Mama with pleading, frightened eyes, yet felt too numb to cry. Once out on the street we were gathered into a large crowd of Jews who had been collected from our hotel and elsewhere in town. To my further dismay, I discovered that Papa was not with us. He had gone out before the police arrived, perhaps to buy a newspaper, or could it be that he was pursuing a lead to a possible hiding place for us? I shall never know.

Like a lugubrious procession we were marched along the street that led to the railway station. The police chief in charge was a burly brute with a moustache like Stalin's; he swore at us, spouted anti-semitic insults and shoved and bullied our pitiful flock all the way. What awaited us when we reached the square in front of the rail-way station was a veritable *coup de théâtre*, a sudden turn of events: by an unbelievable coincidence Aunt Fella had arrived on the night train from Limoges and happened to walk out of the station at the very moment when we were brought there! I still hear her cry of as-tonishment, "Mon Dieu, qu'est-ce qu'il se passe?" (Oh my God, what is happening?) Then, seeing that I happened to be at the end of the queue and that the police chief had momentarily turned away from it, she pulled me by the hand whispering, "Viens, sauve-toi avec moi!" (Come, run away with me.) But I was too dumbfounded to run. A moment later the police chief turned around; he saw my aunt pull me away and raced after us, slapped my tiny, frail aunt on both cheeks, and violently seized me by the hair and the seat of my trousers. Thus holding me kicking and screaming, that brute ran inside the station and toward the awaiting train on the first platform, past Mama, whom I saw being dragged over the station floor struggling and crying. The entire station was a scene of bedlam, with men, women and children being pulled, shoved and hurled into the train....

Just as the police chief was about to throw me into the train as well, two gendarmes in khaki uniforms appeared in the nick of time to stop him. Without a word he let go of me. One of the two officers took me aside and gently pressed my head to his chest, so that I would see no more of these horrendous scenes. After a moment he turned me around, saying, "Look, your mother is in that window over there waving goodbye to you." The train then moved. That was the last time I saw my mama.

The two gendarmes handed me over to my aunt, who was waiting outside the station. Aunt Fella took me to the home of people she knew who lived nearby. These were friends of hers, who had moved from Nancy to Lons-le-Saunier at the onset of the war. In 1998, Marcel Chagnac, a gentleman who resided in Herzliya, Israel, wrote to me that my aunt had hurried to him that morning very distraught and that, upon learning what was happening, his sister rushed with her back to the station, where a gendarmerie officer named Chastaing, whom they knew, had his office. According to Mr. Chagnac, it is to that officer that I owe my life. It was he who had sent the two gendarmes who saved me. But, had Aunt Fella not acted quickly, the miracle of my being saved would quite likely not have happened. Mr. Chagnac's version of the facts left me with a shade of doubt, though, for between the moment that the police chief seized and ran with me toward the train and the sudden arrival of the gendarmes in khaki, no more than a few minutes could have elapsed; could such intense activity, no matter how rushed, have taken so little time? When, in my adult years, I questioned Aunt Fella about the details of that awful day, it seemed that each time she gave me a different version. (Be that as it may, I deeply reproach myself today for never having properly expressed my gratitude to her.) However, this mystery was solved when I met Marcel Chagnac at his home in Israel in June 2014. He explained to me that he and his family had lived just a stone's throw from the station, on the same side of the tracks.

The host of the house to which Aunt Fella took me, this same Mr. Chagnac whom I met so many years later, gently sought to distract me. He sat me at a desk, placed in front of me pen and paper and, opening an atlas, piqued my curiosity by explaining that Holland was a country made up of three very large cities. Having offered this inaccurate information, he then encouraged me to draw a map of Holland; drawing geographical maps became a hobby of mine.

In the afternoon, Aunt Fella took me to see Papa, who had gone into hiding. I can only wonder who these people were at whose place he stayed. From where did he know them, and how did Aunt Fella know where to find him? However it happened, Papa and I fell in each other's arms and my pent-up distress exploded into sobbing without restraint, until Aunt Fella gently took me by the hand and prompted me to bid Papa adieu.

In the summer of 1992, my wife, Terry, and I visited my cousin Ginette Domb and her husband and sons in Strasbourg. From there we travelled to Avignon on an express train, which, to my surprise, stopped for three minutes in Lons-le-Saunier. The station looked just as it had fifty years before and the streets outside looked unchanged — just as banal and unremarkable, except for the cars crowding them and the shop signs. From my window I stared at the scene with almost suspended breath and watched travellers dragging their luggage, greeting or parting. The thought raced through my mind that probably none of these people, not even the elderly, were aware of the tragedy that had unfolded half a century before where their feet now trod, while I was reliving in my mind memories of that horrible day: the screams of my mother, the intense fear that had gripped me.... After our return home to Vancouver I wrote a letter to the two daily newspapers of Lons-le-Saunier; one acknowledged receipt of my letter, but neither published it. The thick fog of amnesia that for nearly half a century had descended upon the slumbering French memory was not to be disturbed now.

The morning after Mama's arrest, Aunt Fella and I boarded a train for the short ride to Lyon, where we visited with members of our family whom I had not yet met. These were my maternal uncle Paul, his wife, Zilly, and their three children, Ginette, Freddy (Manfred) and Jacques. Present also were the latter's maternal cousins Claude and Armand Olievenstein. The Olievenstein brothers became famous medical doctors three decades later: Claude as the foremost French specialist for drug-addicted youth and director of the psychiatric hospital Marmottan in Paris, Armand as an author of volumes of poetry published under the pen name of Oliven Sten. Like my cousins

Ginette and Freddy, Armand and Claude had been born in Berlin. The Arenstein and Olievenstein families both had left Germany for France after the founding of the Nazi regime. Other than chattering with my male cousins, the only memory I retain of these three days in Lyon was that of riding a streetcar with Aunt Zilly and asking her how old she was. "Forty," she answered, laughing. I found her so kind.

I never heard of my mother again and never met anyone who might have witnessed the final days of her life. On that fateful day of our arrest, the train she was on went to Rivesaltes, north of Perpignan in French Catalonia. Rivesaltes has been described as the worst of the several internment camps set up in the Pyrenees in 1938 by the last government of the Third Republic. It "welcomed" to the land of "Liberty, Equality, Fraternity" Spaniards who had fled from the fascist armies of Franco, now victorious in the three-year-long civil war that they had provoked. Beginning in 1940 these camps housed foreign Jews as well, among them thousands of German Jews who had been driven by the Nazis over the French border. Rivesaltes became known as "the Sahara of the South": it was exposed to blistering heat in summer and icy winds in winter. Internees died in its unheated barracks from malnutrition and disease. Charitable organizations like the Swiss Red Cross, the Quakers and the Œuvre de secours aux enfants (OSE) were at times permitted to bring in relief; the OSE even obtained temporary release for some of the children on the grounds of health. It nursed many of these children back to health in its sanatorium at Palavas-les-Flots, near Montpellier, before transferring them to its children's homes in Creuse.

The historian Gérard Gobitz, who published a book documenting the deportation of Jewish refugees from the Free Zone, informed me in 2002 that he had found the name of my mother on the list of Convoy Number 5, which left Rivesaltes bound for Drancy on September 14, 1942, arriving there the following day. In his monumental *Memorial Book of the Deportation of the Jews of France*, Serge Klarsfeld lists close to 80,000 names and the numbered convoys in which these Jews were transported to Auschwitz. The book also includes correspondence between French and German bureaucrats relevant to these transports. In that correspondence I found a letter addressed by Jean Leguay, the delegate to the Occupied Zone of René Bousquet, secretary-general of the French police, to SS-Obersturmführer Heinz Röthke in Paris, a letter in which that criminal provided the SS chieftain with the list of the unfortunate passengers of Convoy Number 5 and a detailed schedule of the route travelled by that train: time of its departure from Rivesaltes, time of its crossing of the Demarcation Line at Vierzon and time of its arrival at Drancy. From Klarsfeld's volume, I further learned that my mother left Drancy the day following her arrival there, on September 16, by Convoy Number 33, which carried 1,003 Jews to Auschwitz. Of the 407 women who arrived at Birkenau on that train, only 147 were registered and had a number tattooed on their forearm; the others were sent directly to the gas chambers. I can only assume that my mother, being small and frail, was among the latter, unless she died en route because of the atrocious conditions in which the doomed passengers of that train travelled. I never learned for certain what happened to her; there will never be closure for me.

~

From Lyon I travelled with Aunt Fella to Limoges. I have no memory of precisely what happened when we arrived in that city. I only remember that I was hospitalized for what seemed like a long time. When I emerged from hospital I lived with the Domb family, but not for long. Lieutenant Simon Domb had recently participated in saving Vichy from destruction from the air and the refugees camping in its streets from thus being massacred by declaring it an open city, for which the grateful city would award him its Gold Medal in 1967. But after November 1942, when the Germans occupied the southern zone, Simon Domb was a wanted man who joined an armed resistance movement grouped around the underground newspaper

Combat, edited by the writer Albert Camus. The movement's *Maquis* units, rural guerrilla bands of French Resistance fighters, operated in the wooded hilly regions of Limousin and Auvergne.

Uncle David and Aunt Fella always conversed in Yiddish, except when Simon and his wife, Lucienne, who was not Jewish, came to share in the noon-hour meal. Uncle David was a rather strange man and I feared him. If I took a cluster of grapes out of the fruit bowl on the dinner table, he would draw a pair of scissors out of a pocket of his jacket and cut some of that cluster off, or he would spoon some food from my plate onto his, all without a word. His temperament was explosive; whenever he burst out in anger, which was often, he would shout at the top of his lungs at poor Aunt Fella. Sometimes, upon coming home for the noon-hour meal, he would dip his spoon in the soup, declare it too hot or too salty, then immediately grab his long overcoat and hat and rush back into the street, indifferent to Aunt Fella's pitiful pleadings that he should eat something before going out again.

One morning Aunt Fella woke me up at an unusually early hour, when it was still night outside. Upon opening my eyes I saw the back of a strange woman lying next to me. She had arrived during the night and explained to me that she had come to take me with her to some unknown destination. Forced to hurriedly bid adieu to Aunt Fella, I followed the woman along dark pre-dawn streets to the railway station.

The *terra incognita* to which my chaperone took me was Creuse, a gentle, unruffled, laid-back rural region of central France, steeped in tradition. Our destination was the château du Masgelier, situated on a low rise several kilometres away from a village simply called Le Grand-Bourg. Having never seen a French château before, let alone lived in one, I was fascinated by its imposing silhouette and its towers, vast halls and many rooms. The Masgelier was one of three castles acquired by the OSE in Creuse in 1939 to shelter Jewish children whose parents had sent them away from Paris at the onset of the war, or who were otherwise separated from their parents. Some of them were children of Jewish refugees from Germany and Austria, while others had been spirited out of Rivesaltes and other camps.

The OSE was founded in 1912 in St. Petersburg to provide relief and medical assistance to the victims of pogroms in Russia. Transferred to Berlin in 1923, it became an international organization placed under the prestigious presidency of Albert Einstein. Ten years later the OSE was transferred to Paris and in 1940 to Montpellier in the Free Zone, where it could function independently of the Union générale des israélites de France (UGIF), the Judenrat-type organization imposed on the Jews by the Germans and Vichy. Also, in Montpellier the OSE could access financial assistance from the Lisbon office of the American Jewish Joint Distribution, known as the Joint.

One of the other castles operated as a children's home by OSE was situated a few kilometres from the Masgelier in the village of Chabannes, where they were sheltered under the protection of its inhabitants, led by a remarkably kind old gentleman named Félix Chevrier. Its story is the subject of a very moving documentary entitled *The Children of Chabannes,* made on the occasion of the reunion in that village, nearly half a century later, of former hidden children from all over the world. Chevrier was recognized as Righteous Among the Nations in May 1999.

Fascination with castles apart, I did not at all feel happy to live in one that was filled with children. Being an only child who had never benefited from the companionship of siblings, this unexpected insertion in a collective of perhaps two hundred children of various ages shepherded by strangers would, even in normal circumstances, have been a daunting experience. But for me, who had been uprooted, hauled across borders and violently separated from my parents, all in rapid succession, such abrupt change was unsettling in the extreme, in spite of the comforting welcome given me on arrival by the director, Alice Bloch. This lady was the eldest daughter of Marc Bloch, the great historian of feudalism and hero of the Resistance who, less than two years later, in June 1944, would be shot with other hostages by the Germans near Lyon.

In other times and happier circumstances, what could have been more romantic for a child destined to steep himself in history than to grow up in a château? But the Masgelier was no romantic abode in 1942: it was a shelter for children in need of a refuge.

The pedagogy at the Masgelier was secular and progressive. School and other daytime activities took place inside the castle, and there were gymnastics and games outdoors. Physical culture was vigorously promoted by Jewish master sportsman Georges Loinger, a man of foresight whose goal was to develop the endurance of the children, so that in an emergency they could run fast and survive in conditions of great physical hardship and danger. Gardening was another important activity; the children grew the vegetables served at the meals. Alas, I was in no mood to participate in those activities, much as they might have lifted the lid of gloom that weighed down my soul.

The dormitory in which I slept with at least a dozen other boys in two rows of identical little beds was the reconditioned loft of a detached three-storey house situated a short distance downhill from the castle. Every morning Jenny, the young woman who was our *monitrice*, instructor, walked into the dormitory and, at the count of three, shouted, "Vite, vite, vite!" (Quick!) to force us out of bed and get dressed in a hurry. I dreaded that early morning reveille, fearful of being punished if I was not instantly ready to troop down the stairs with the others and hurry up the slope to the castle for breakfast. I felt lonely and unhappy; sometimes I cried myself to sleep. It seems that almost every day I wrote to Aunt Fella in Limoges pleading with her to come and take me away from the château du Masgelier.

Finally, after perhaps not more than two weeks, the day that I feared would never come arrived. One morning as I stood outside on a balcony overlooking the grounds I spotted in the distance a lady marching toward the castle. Soon I was called to the director's office and introduced to the stranger, who ordered me to gather my things and follow her. But it was not to Limoges that she had come to take me, but to some unknown, mysterious destination. Moreover I was not going to travel alone with her, but in the company of several other children.

We travelled into the unknown by bus for what seemed a very long time, perhaps as long as three days. This time, however, the unknown that awaited me at the end of the journey was no mere matter of destination, for I was being uprooted from the Jewish universe in which I had lived hitherto and transplanted into a fearful gentile one. Yet the journey, as I remember it, was not unpleasant. My eyes glued to the bus window, I watched lovely landscapes unfold before me: fields, meadows, forests, villages, castles large and small.

I had always assumed that I owed my early removal from Masgelier to the pleading letters that I wrote to Aunt Fella, but I now wonder whether the cause was not a more serious one. Like other OSE children's homes, Masgelier was occasionally subjected to inspections by police officers searching for Jewish children who did not have French citizenship. The five hundred or so children for whom the OSE had earlier obtained release from Rivesaltes were now being hunted down by the police and returned, sometimes in handcuffs, to Rivesaltes in the name of Laval's policy of "regrouping families" prior to their deportation to the East. As an intended victim who had had a narrow escape by being "left behind" in Lons-le-Saunier, I risked being arrested again and transported to a horrible death in Auschwitz via Rivesaltes and Drancy, if I were not promptly removed from a Jewish children's home that could become a trap.

In the wake of the summer roundups in the Free Zone in which Mama and I had been caught, the national directors of the OSE, Doctors Eugène Minkowski and Joseph Weill, who were keenly aware of the true and terrible meaning of "resettlement in the East" and held no illusions about the fate awaiting all Jews, decided that the OSE homes should be closed as soon as hiding places could be found for the 1,500 children sheltered in them. Priority was given to the many who were not French citizens, since they were the immediate intended victims of the war on children waged by the Germans and Vichy. OSE leader Georges Garel then promptly organized a remarkable network of assistants and social workers, Jewish and non-Jewish, most of them young women, to fan out through the country in search of families and institutions willing to hide Jewish children. The sometimes dangerous tasks assumed by these women included chaperoning the children to places of hiding, visiting them in order to ensure that they were safe and well treated, and paying for their upkeep wherever payment was required. What then became known as the Circuit Garel (Garel circuit) benefited from the invaluable assistance of the saintly archbishop of Toulouse, Cardinal Jules-Gérard Saliège, and several other prelates who broke rank with the church of France and its policy of submission to Marshal Pétain. Helpful also were the prefect of the department of Hérault and a few other obliging officials. When the Germans invaded the Southern Zone in November 1942, saving the children turned into a race against time.

A race against time ... Adam Rayski, the great historian of the Jewish resistance in France, wrote, "On the clock of history, the needles moved faster for the Jews than for the other peoples of occupied Europe. The time of the others was not exactly our time."

Vendœuvres

That memorable journey ended in Vendœuvres-en-Brenne, a *bourg* or large village of about two thousand inhabitants situated in the very heart of Berry, a region which, like Creuse, bore the quintessential charm of deep rural France of yesteryear. There dwelt, seemingly rooted in the land, people whose ancestral way of life seemed little affected by the passage of time. It was the *douce France* — the "sweet France" of Charles Trenet's nostalgic song so popular at the time, a song that began with the words "Douce France, cher pays de mon enfance" (Sweet France, dear land of my childhood…).

Vendœuvres was, however, not one of those many picturesque and lovely villages that are the gems of rural France and so delight the eye of the visitor. Its appearance was rather ordinary, even austere. At one end of the village two roads converged to form the roughly triangular Place Saint-Louis, from which streets led in several directions. One of these two converging roads began in the hamlet of La Barre, a kilometre and a half to the north and became Rue Grande, the main street of Vendœuvres, which led to the church at the other end of the village. From the square that fronted the church, a lane led to the cemetery and a road descended toward the hamlet of Malakoff about two kilometres to the south. The Rue Grande was the natural hub of Vendœuvres. Fronting it were houses large and small; bakeries, groceries, butchers, hairdressers, hardware, clothing and other shops;

shoemaker, saddler and blacksmith workshops. There was also a shirt factory that employed women, while men worked mainly as agricultural labourers, as artisans or in forestry. And there was the *mairie*, town hall, set back slightly from the street. Across from it stood one of the two boys' schools: the public and secular *école communale*, local primary school, and next to it, the religious Catholic *école libre*, free school, which, despite its name, was a private school for which one paid tuition. The *école communale* for girls was around the corner from that of the boys on a side street that led to the tiny railway station. Crossing the railroad tracks one reached a lane that turned left toward a road at the corner, where stood the house of the Lamoureux family, with whom I lived during my first few weeks in Vendœuvres.

Upon our small group's arrival in Vendœuvres we were taken to a house on the Rue Grande, in which lived a Jewish doctor named Bloch (I believe) and his wife, who caringly welcomed us and led us to the families that had accepted the task of hosting Jewish children. Suzanne Lamoureux, who took me into her home, was either a widow or the spouse of one of the more than one million French prisoners of war in Germany. She lived with her elderly mother and her son, Guy, who was a few years older than me, in a modest house with a small garden.

In the evening Suzanne and her mother busied themselves in the kitchen, while Guy and I sat at the table doing our school work. My work done, I remained seated at the table, lost in thoughts, saying little, and watching the needles circle the dial of the clock on the wall, grinding the minutes and even seconds of a seemingly interminable wait for supper to be served, or for bedtime. Guy sometimes summoned me away from my boredom-induced reveries to play in the garden or help him saw firewood for the kitchen stove. He loved to tease me but was a kind boy. There were moments when Guy's mother and grandmother questioned me out of curiosity about my family and where I came from. I never spoke of my Jewish origin but did once innocently inquire of the ladies about eating matzah, the unleavened bread eaten at Passover; they looked puzzled, having never heard of such a food. How easily this childish question could have betrayed me, had I raised it in the presence of people who would not have wished me well!

From the rambunctious little boy prone to mischief that I had once been, I now grew into a timorous child, anxious not to displease anyone: not the teacher at school, not my classmates and least of all, not the kind people who sheltered me. In fact, I was sometimes complimented for being *sage comme une image*, an expression whose nearest English equivalent would be "quiet as a mouse." Yet, to my surprise, I was soon removed from the care of the Lamoureux family to that of a young couple who lived in the hamlet of La Barre: Jean and Fernande Cassaud. The Cassauds lived with their toddler daughter, Jocelyne, in a tiny two-room cottage with a fairly large garden in the back of it, a well in the middle of that garden and, at the end of it, the outhouse. In winter the house was heated by a woodstove. I slept on a folding bed in the kitchen. Before retiring for the night Fernande placed hot water bottles inside the beds. Living out in the country, my hosts were able to procure food beyond what was allowed under the wartime rationing system with its strict government-imposed restrictions. Their garden supplied them with vegetables and fruit, and they raised chickens and rabbits. In addition, Jean, who was a rural labourer, hunted and fished, and also obtained food from farmers in exchange for services.

The hamlet of La Barre was situated at the end of the country road that leads to Vendœuvres where, as I indicated before, it became Vendœuvres' main street, the Rue Grande. As one reached La Barre, that road formed a T-junction with a similarly narrow road that led to the town of Buzançais, ten kilometres to the north. Walking from the junction about half a kilometre in that direction, one reached the home of the Cassauds, which was the first in a line of houses on the left side of the road. The house faced a borderline, dividing meadows to the right from a large and dark forest to the left. The elegant eighteenth-century castle of Lancosme rose at the far end of that borderline. A small river called Claise coursed through the meadows, at the time the hamlet's laundry stood on its banks; local housewives gathered there to do their wash and gossip.

With my removal to the care of Jean and Fernande Cassaud, my life now took a happier turn. I use the word "happy" guardedly, however, for I missed my parents painfully. Besides, my adaptation to a seemingly strange culture and unfamiliar surroundings — a rural milieu that seemed backward compared to the modern life that, even as relatively poor people, we were accustomed to in Luxembourg and Brussels — was not easy. Jean and Fernande were warm-hearted people and attentive to my well-being. When my conduct called for it, they remonstrated with me patiently, but they could also be strict, though perhaps not more than necessary. Fernande taught me proper French manners, such as always saying Monsieur or Madame after "merci," "bonjour," or "au revoir," especially when guests were visiting. If I forgot, Fernande would remind me of that formality by asking rhetorically, "Merci qui? Merci mon chien?" (Thank you, who? Thank you, my dog?) I was also told that if I wished for an extra serving of whatever was on the table during a meal, the proper way to ask was, "Pourrais-je en avoir d'autre, s'il vous plaît?" (Could I have some more, please?)

Jean Cassaud reminisced many years later that my apparently ravenous appetite had made it difficult for Suzanne Lamoureux to feed me and that I was so famished when I was placed in his and his wife's care that the sudden abundance of food made me ill and they had to habituate me gradually to normal meals. Even in a fertile agricultural region like Berry, the impact of rationing was severe due to the paucity of fertilizers and fuel; such shortages, added to the requisitions of the occupation army, dramatically reduced the productivity of the land. Jean and Fernande often expressed surprise at my craving for meat and butter rather than for chocolate and sweets as normal children do. Nonetheless, I dreaded the punishment of being deprived of dessert!

The villagers referred to and even addressed each other as "Father such-and-such" — which was also the title by which one otherwise addressed a priest — and "Mother such-and-such." "Père" Cassaud at times admonished me, saying that if I did not behave as I should, he would take me across the road into the dark forest, where wild boars roamed, and abandon me there. Great was my fear of the boars! One chore that was assigned me, when Jean and Fernande were out, was to "babysit" Jocelyne. It was a task that I found daunting, not knowing how to entertain the toddler so that she would not burst out into loud wailing. On some winter nights after I returned home from school, I was sent to a farm with a jug to fetch milk. To reach that farm, located about a kilometre away in the direction of Buzançais, I had to walk along a stretch of the road that for several hundred metres skirted the forest. I listened fearfully to the sounds of the forest, as the very rustling of the leaves in a gust of wind startled me. One night when I was walking back from the farm, some sound scared me to such a degree that I took to running and dropped the jug of milk!

One afternoon I was drawn to the garden in the back of the house by a commotion: Père Cassaud was helping a neighbour to butcher a pig, without a legal permit to do so. I was so shaken by the horrific scene of the pig being bled and by its writhing and desperate screams that I ran away to the house in tears. Père Cassaud, shaking his finger, warned me that if I so much as uttered one word to anyone about what I had seen, he would take me into the woods and abandon me there to the boars. Needless to say, my discretion was fully assured.

Gradually, I fell into a rhythm of life that was by no means unpleasant. Weeks and months seemed to stretch into very long periods. Whereas from the home of the Lamoureux family school was perhaps not more than a twenty-minute walk away, from La Barre it seemed like a long hike. In winter it was still dark when I rose from bed, gulped down breakfast and hurried on my way. Turning from the T-junction onto the road to Vendœuvres I sometimes ran into other boys from the hamlet, particularly the very friendly Gérard Lamoureux, Guy's cousin.

The *école communale* was a typical French school: its enclosed yard was framed by a stone wall and one entered it through an iron portal that was wide open during the day. In the yard stood a few plane trees and there was a *préau*, a small covered playground, where pupils huddled during recess if it rained or snowed.

The school day was divided by two recesses, morning and mid-afternoon, and by a two-hour lunch period. Boys who, like me, did not return home for the midday meal ate the *déjeuner* in the school canteen. The meal consisted of soup and a main course that were ladled by the teacher into an aluminum plate, which we had to wipe afterwards with a piece of bread and then turn over to receive dessert, usually a tablespoon of jam, on the back of it. Once, when I gulped down an extra spoonful of jam that I had received from another boy in exchange for a portion of my main course, I found myself mocked by the whole assembly with catcalls of "goulu, goulu" (glutton). I felt so humiliated that I ran out crying. The school day ended at about four o'clock and in winter dusk had already descended by the time I reached La Barre.

The school week began with a Monday morning ceremony in front of the town hall. We had to stand at attention as the flag was raised and sing a hymn to Marshal Pétain, which began with the words, "Maréchal, nous voilà, devant toi l'étendard de la France!" (Marshal, here we stand, before thee, the standard bearer of France!) This ridiculous farce over, we had to march, as discipline required, in ranks two abreast, in silence, hands behind our backs, heads up, across the street back to the school. This did not stop the boy who was marching beside me once to whisper into my ear the tune of the initial verse altered to "Maréchal, tête de cheval..." (Marshal, you horse head).

There was no school on Thursdays and since the public schools were secular, parents who so wished could thus send their children to catechism classes held mid-week in churches. I never went to catechism, but I often attended mass on Sunday mornings in the village church, either alone or with Fernande. The flock of the faithful in the church on Sunday mornings was composed largely of women and children, while men for the most socialized in the cafés across the square. At church I occasionally met with one or the other of the Jewish boys or girls who were hidden with me in Vendœuvres, but I did not seek out their company, which, in any case, was not encouraged. I did however sometimes walk over to the house of our neighbours who sheltered a sweet little Jewish girl from Paris whose name was, I think, Arlette. Some Sundays, after mass, I walked with the Cassaud family to the hamlet of Malakoff, where Fernande's parents lived. They welcomed me with genuine grandparental kindness. We would lunch and spend the rest of the day with them in their cottage and on one or two occasions even stayed overnight.

I now spoke "unaccented" French and virtually forgot the languages I had grown up with. Yet, according to Jocelyne and her sister, Jacqueline, their parents were surprised by my ability to speak several languages and by my knowledge of geography, as evidenced by my ability to draw from memory a map of France and pinpoint on it the principal cities. Still, my two years in Flemish school in Brussels counted for nothing, for I had to start elementary school all over again in Vendœuvres, even though I now was two years older than most of my classmates. I remember fondly my teacher, Monsieur Renard, a small, mild-mannered man, so different from the burly teacher of the upper grades, Monsieur Moreau, who was reputed to be brutal and looked it.

During my stay in Vendœuvres I received only two letters from my father. Not long after I saw him in Lons-le-Saunier, he settled in Lyon, to be near our family in that city. His letters to me were written in German: I understood the first one, but the second letter, which came three months later, I could hardly understand, having become nearly unilingual in French in the intervening time. Luckily, Père Cassaud, who had learned some German during his military service in Alsace, helped me decipher Papa's letter. How I missed him and worried about Mama's fate!

Years later, when the vagaries of life carried me to Poland and then to China, I was often seized with a terrible nostalgia for France and felt more French than when I had lived in the country. Whenever, in my dreams or waking hours, a longing to find myself in France again welled in my heart, it came wrapped in visions of Berry, particularly of the countryside around Vendœuvres and La Barre, at least as often as it did in visions of Paris and its abundance of beauty. In my travels around France I had opportunity to admire far more scenic land-scapes than those of the Berry, yet this area, where I lived in a par-ticularly difficult period of my childhood, held a spell over my remi-niscences that no other region could. My imagination often pictured me sauntering along the familiar country road or running through the fields and meadows, past the castle of Lancosme, to the little river Claise and beyond. Visualised through the prism of memory, these surroundings assumed a particularly romantic allure in the chill of winter, when heavy rains left puddles and ponds in the meadows and local people would say that "il tombe de l'eau" (it's falling water). Berry in my mind represented the "real France," the "deep France" so very different from cosmopolitan Paris: parochial perhaps, conserva-tive, exclusive, yet steeped in charm.

Even the school curriculum, set by the Ministry of National Edu-cation in Paris, and the teaching methods had changed little since the early years of the Third Republic in the 1870s. The curriculum, text-books and daily timetable were the same from one end of the country to the other, and even in schools across the French colonial empire. The first class on Monday morning was devoted to morals and civic instruction. The next one featured French and consisted of dictation, grammar, poetry recitation and the weekly written assignment on a given subject called *rédaction* (writing exercise) or *composition fran-çaise* (French essay composition). The hours that followed were de-voted to arithmetic (later mathematics), history, geography, natural science and other subjects. Foreign languages were not taught until secondary school. The French education system of my childhood was rigid and had its faults, but its academic standards were very high — quite a contrast with what passes for education nowadays even in France, especially at the secondary level.

One Sunday as I was walking home from church I suddenly roused myself as if out of a dream, scarcely believing what my eyes perceived: not far ahead, advancing toward me, was my cousin Ginette Domb! She was with a woman I did not know. Overcome with joy, I ran into Ginette's arms. Alas, our time together was to be short, as Ginette had to catch an early train back to Limoges, but she did meet the Cassaud family. That brief encounter made me yearn all the more for my father, but I readily understood that the circumstances of his life in Lyon and the much greater distance separating that city from Vendœuvres did not make a visit feasible.

Vendœuvres may have seemed as though it was slumbering in time, but the world outside decidedly was not. In November 1942 the Germans responded to the Allied landing in North Africa by crossing the Demarcation Line and occupying the Southern Zone, except for the Alpine region and Provence, which were taken over by the Italians. For the next eight months, the Italian occupation zone became a safe haven for the persecuted Jews, a haven that disappeared when Mussolini fell from power and Italy surrendered to the Allies, at which time the Germans invaded Italy and took over the regions of France previously occupied by the Italian army. I have long looked askance at what seems to me a misuse of the word "fascism," which consists in lumping together all populist movements of the extreme right. As evil as Fascism (strictly speaking, an Italian movement) was, it bears no comparison with the ferocity of German Nazism. Though Mussolini did enact antisemitic laws in 1938, these were applied haphazardly. In the part of France it occupied, which included major cities like Grenoble, Annecy, Nice, Cannes and Menton, the Italian army protected the Jews by blocking the French police's attempts to stage roundups.

The German occupation of the Southern Zone dramatically worsened the predicament of the Jews. Ensconced in the peaceful rural surroundings of Vendœuvres, where the descent of winter further slowed down the rhythm of life and no Germans, or even French policemen, were to be seen, I was not at all aware of the catastrophic developments that would force yet another displacement on me. But soon the cocooned life I had enjoyed for several months came to an abrupt end.

I believe that it happened on February 2, 1943, a date that has entered history as the last day of the long drawn-out battle of Stalingrad, which ended with the resounding German defeat that turned the tide of the war. I was sitting in school that morning, when the class was interrupted by the sudden entrance of Père Cassaud, who took Monsieur Renard aside and exchanged a few words with him. The teacher then turned to me and said with a kind smile, "Stand up, René, and say goodbye to all your friends here. You are leaving us and we will miss you." Speechless with astonishment, I followed Père Cassaud out of the classroom. With a smile on his face, he informed me cheerfully that somebody had arrived to take me to Lyon that very afternoon, to be reunited with my father! I was beside myself with joy as I returned home with Père Cassaud for a farewell lunch. The excited anticipation of travelling that afternoon by train to Lyon, the boundless joy at the thought that in less than a day I would see Papa again, more than dispelled the regrets that I felt at the prospect of leaving the loving Cassaud family who had been so good to me.

Great was my amazement when, upon arriving in front of the railway station, I saw all the other Jewish boys and girls who had been sheltered in Vendœuvres gathered around an unknown couple. One of the boys exuberantly announced to me that he was going to be reunited with his parents in Paris. I thought it odd that he and I were to travel on the same train, considering that Paris and Lyon lay in different directions, but then I reasoned that we would likely be transferred to different trains at some station along the way. Soon, we were all on the train: the boys with the gentleman in one compartment, the girls with the lady in another.

The train was not long on its way before I grew disconcerted by the suspicion that we were travelling in a westward direction. Having inherited from my father an almost inborn sense of geography and direction, I turned to our chaperone and asked, "If I am travelling to Lyon, which is in the southeast, and he is going to Paris, which is to the north, how come we are now travelling west?" Surprised and embarrassed by my query, the gentleman then bent down and quietly said, "Listen to me, boys." Then, looking at me and my friend, he continued, saying, "You are not going to Lyon, and you are not going to Paris. We have to hide you all in a place where no undesirable person will be able to find you!" I felt shattered, speechless with hurt.

Before long the train reached Buzançais and we were all ordered off. The gentleman then took us boys onto one train, while the lady took the girls onto another. Of the second leg of that journey I remember nothing, except a sensation of being carried into the unknown on a mystery ride which, with night descending, filled my soul with despairing resignation. The thought that at the end of it Papa would not be there waiting for me plunged me into a pit of anxiety. I paid no further attention to our itinerary. We alighted at the railway station of the small town of Pellevoisin, from where we walked in the dark of night several kilometres along a country road, until some dim lights beckoned to us as we trekked up a small rise, atop which came into view a long stone building, whose austere façade announced that it was a Catholic institution.

Had I not been removed from Vendœuvres, I would likely have been caught in one of the hunts for Jewish children hidden in rural areas staged by the Germans and their French collaborators. Vendœuvres was destined to become less of a calm backwater. After the Allied landing in Normandy, the *Maquis* became active in the department of Indre and staged acts of sabotage against the Germans, which were followed by reprisals and even massacres. During the campaign for its liberation, Châteauroux, the chief city of the department of Indre, changed hands three times.

Les Besses

The austere premises that we entered, which were now to become our shelter from the chaos raging around us, were those of a Roman Catholic convent school for boys called Pensionnat des Besses, Besses Boarding School. We were ushered into its reception hall well past bedtime, and the hundred or so pupils of the school were already asleep in the dormitories. Waiting for us in the dimly lit hall stood several women clad in long grey dresses with pectoral crosses dangling from their necks and grave faces framed by grey headdresses. Their appearance exuded austerity and severity. These women were, however, not *religieuses*, nuns, in the conventional understanding of that French word, but members of some kind of celibate lay order. One did not address them as "ma sœur," as is normally the case with nuns, but as "mademoiselle" followed by their Christian names.

The two "nuns" under whose authority we were placed were Mademoiselle Susanne and Mademoiselle Marie-Renée. The latter made us commit to memory our new identities and promise to reveal to no one our real names and past. Furthermore, we were instructed never to let anyone see our private parts, since in France only Jews were circumcised. From that moment on I was no longer to be René Goldman, born in Luxembourg, but René Garnier, born in Châteauroux. Was it wise, I wonder today, to have assigned to me as birthplace a city situated so near, where I had never set foot, and from where many of the boys in that school originated? But it worked.

Having thus been instructed, the four of us — Hansi Vogel, now Jean Hanzy; Ilik Gandverg, now Georges Gramont; Manfred Freund, whose new name I have forgotten; and I, René Garnier — were led across one large dormitory and up a few steps into another large dormitory, where we were assigned our places in the long rows of uniform little beds. Upon waking up in the cold morning I faced the curious stares of a crowd of roommates who soon pressed around me with questions. Frightened by this alien new world into which I had been dropped and where from now on I was fated to live for only God knew how long, I was on the verge of tears. As soon as we had all dressed and made our beds, we were ordered into ranks and led to the chapel for a brief morning service, following which we marched, in ranks again, to the refectory for breakfast, then, immediately after, to the classroom. We four Jewish boys were later introduced to the headmistress of the school, Mademoiselle Hermance, an affable lady whom we saw only occasionally, as she rarely left her office. She had a deputy, Mademoiselle Berthe, who frequently made the rounds of the place and, in contrast to the severe nuns directly in charge of us, was warm-hearted and showed motherly concern for our well-being.

The routine of existence at the *pensionnat* was steeped in a high degree of religious discipline. We rose daily at seven, dressed quickly, washed our hands and faces, and made our beds under the watchful eyes of Mesdemoiselles Susanne and Marie-Renée, who slept behind a screen in a corner of the dormitory. Then we formed ranks and marched to chapel, refectory and classroom. We recited prayers, crossed ourselves before and after meals and in class before and after lessons, and attended chapel service morning and evening. On Sundays a priest came from Pellevoisin or Heugnes to conduct mass in the chapel, on which occasions one or two boys were called to serve as altar boys and the nuns and some of the boys took communion.

Day in, day out, we were shepherded along a dreary succession of drafty halls with names ending in "oir(e)": *dortoir*, the dormitory; *réfectoire*, the refectory; *parloir*, the reception hall; and *couloir*, the

corridor that connected the main building to the chapel. I was often seized with *désespoir*, despair, especially during the initial period
of my life at Les Besses, and I felt lonely even though I had three
Jewish companions who shared my predicament. Life at the château
du Masgelier would have been paradise in comparison had I stayed
there. My time at that O S E home had left me with the notion that a
place where a large number of children resided must necessarily be a
château, but when at first I referred to my new asylum as "le château
des Besses," this caused a great deal of hilarity on the part of the nuns,
who pointed out to me that the architecture of the Pensionnat des
Besses was not at all that of a castle!

Every boy in the school was given a number, which was sewn on
his clothing and marked on his belongings. My number was thirty-
six, a number of quasi-magical significance to me. The Hebrew language has no written symbols representing numbers, but it assigns
numerical values to the twenty-four letters of the alphabet: when one
adds the values of the letters that make up individual words according to a method called *gematria*, one sometimes comes across amazing and meaningful coincidences. Thus the word *chai*, which means
"living," is composed of two letters: *chet*, which has a value of eight,
and *yud*, which has a value of ten, for a total of eighteen. The number
thirty-six is the double of *chai*, the plural of which, *chayim*, means
"life." Moreover, number thirty-six combines the letters *lamed* and
vav. According to Talmudic lore, there are in each generation thirty-
six hidden saints, just and righteous individuals who are usually ordinary people unknown to one other; by their virtuous conduct these
lamed-vavniks, as they are sometimes known, behold the Divine Presence and it is thanks to them that the world still endures. And, since
the 1960s the ninety-odd departments into which France is divided
have an administrative number, which is affixed to the postal codes
and the vehicle licences: that of the department of the Indre, where I
was given a second life during the war, happens to be thirty-six!

Schooling at Les Besses was at the elementary level. In the classroom boys of different grades sat in separate rows, while preschoolers were in a hall of their own. Mademoiselle Marie-Renée, who taught the upper grades, sat behind a desk on a raised platform. On the wall behind her hung a portrait of Marshal Pétain and a framed copy of his 1940 proclamation "Aux enfants de France" (to the children of France) decorated with the *francisque,* a double-bladed axe, which was the emblem of the regime. Those of us who were in the lower elementary grades had as our teacher Madame S., who was not a "nun," but a lady employed along with her husband, the handyman, by the institution. Seemingly not minding the cold, she wore only a blouse and a knee-length skirt underneath her apron. She sat on a low chair with a rod near at hand. Every time she called on a boy to stand up beside her and recite a memorized text, conjugate a verb or answer some question of grammar or any other subject, she was likely to stimulate a sluggish memory with one or more whacks of the rod on his bare legs. Such was her dexterity at wielding the rod that, whenever a boy was deemed to deserve severe punishment, she would apply "correction" to his bared buttocks. I remember two boys being thus punished for the sacrilegious act of trading "pious images," cards bearing the pictures of saints, the way modern North American boys trade hockey cards.

France is a country richly endowed by nature, but during the war years, when more than a million men were held prisoner in Germany and France had to supply the occupying power with much of its produce, food rationing was stringent, particularly in the cities, where procuring food became a permanent obsession. A boarding school like Les Besses did not seem to have warranted special consideration in this matter, for we, too, endured hunger: breakfast consisted mainly of *bouillie,* a kind of porridge; at lunch and dinner we received small portions of unappetizing food consisting mainly of rutabagas (curiously enough, I've heard these sometimes called "pommes de terre du Canada"), turnips, carrots and dry bread with a spoonful of marmalade, which we munched slowly *pour faire durer le plaisir*, to make the pleasure last.

But at times the daily fare was supplemented by surprise treats, one such occasion being a saint's day, an annual event in life deemed at least as important as a birthday. My own saint's day, "la saint René," happened to fall on November 12 and I remember being presented on that day with half a pear! Nourishing supplements were doled out on important Catholic holy days such as Christmas and Easter, a feast marked by a hunt for painted eggs in the woods below. A particularly exciting festive day, one that all looked forward to was, if my memory serves me right, Mardi Gras. That morning at breakfast time, we were seated as usual on both sides of the long tables of the refectory, our gaze fixed in excited anticipation upon the kitchen door until it suddenly opened and, to shouts of delight, Mademoiselle Marie-Renée and Mademoiselle Susanne marched in carrying trays loaded with huge (probably two feet long) gorgeous brown *galettes de sarrasin*, buckwheat crepes. Each boy received one such crepe topped with a piece of butter and a heaping tablespoon of jam, the idea being to spread these over the surface of the crepe and then roll it.

Yet, in the second year of my life at the school, the morning of Mardi Gras was not one of undiluted joy. Seated across the table from me were two boys, brothers, mild and fearful; one of them, nicknamed Coco, was plagued with the curse of bedwetting. He and others in that predicament were roused every night not long after going to bed, to be led once more to the toilets; mishaps, however, still occurred. On the eve of that Mardi Gras, Coco was warned that if he wet his bed that night he would be severely punished in the morning. Alas, that morning Mademoiselle Marie-Renée rushed with her usual quick steps to his bed and, upon lifting the blankets, found it wet; thereupon, with shouts that rang like a combination of fury and sadistic exultation, she seized a wet towel, rolled it tightly and vigorously spanked him with it. That was, however, not the end of punishment for the poor lad: he sat at the breakfast table with eyes red with tears when the buckwheat crepes were brought in and Mademoiselle Marie-Renée sadistically slid the tray right under his nose and left him with nothing to eat, while others indulged their ravenous hunger. To my shame I admit that, like others at my table, including Coco's brother, I sat with head bent low over the delicious *galette*, not daring to look up at poor Coco. I wonder what might have happened if I, or anyone else at the table, had given him a piece of our crepe. I doubt that our ever-watchful harridan would have observed such breach of discipline without dealing a blow or two.

The discipline of the school, bereft of pedagogy, love and even simple affection, fostered among the boys a spirit of meanness and antagonism. There was little solidarity — whoever suffered punishment faced indifference or, worse yet, derision and cruel mocking. And there were those who sought to become pets of the women who wielded authority over us. One boy at my table astonished me by picking up twigs on our walks to present to Madame S. to use as "correction" rods in class. If any code of honour governed our relationships it may be said that it consisted of a single article: namely, that one must not be a *rapporteur*, tattletale, or *mouchard*, one who "rats" against another, even if that other was a bully who made one's life more miserable than it already was.

The awareness that I had to hide my true identity made anxiety an ever-present feeling. I sensed somehow that there was something about me other than my physical appearance, which was not noticeably Jewish, that must have made me appear "different" in the eyes of the other boys. I was anxious not to displease anyone, not to draw unnecessary attention from either the women or the boys, particularly the big fourteen-year-old bullies who cowed the small and weak into silence. I learned to accept reprimands, mockery and insults, no matter how unjust, without talking back. Mademoiselle Susanne and Mademoiselle Marie-Renée derided my meekness and called me *empoté*, clumsy, *poule mouillée*, a wimp, and other such mocking epithets. My slowness and awkwardness were probably caused as much by the bullying boys as by the intimidating presence of these two nuns.

I believe that the recurring bouts of unrelieved sadness and depression that I suffered years later in my adolescence were caused to no small extent by the silencing of emotions in the painful time when I was a hidden Jewish child. That repression became nearly impossible to overcome later in life. In the *pensionnat* I shed silent tears when alone, as I longed for my parents and also thought nostalgically of the Cassaud family who had given me a home. How I missed them all! I had to be careful not to be caught crying, lest in such a moment I accidentally let down my guard and revealed the circumstances in which I had been separated from my parents and, thereby, divulge my real identity. After all, I did feel like a stranger in a world not my own and was compelled, paradoxically perhaps, to be true to my false identity at all times.

Afternoons were usually the pleasanter part of daily existence at Les Besses. As soon as lunch was over we left the school for long walks chaperoned by Mademoiselle Susanne. We walked along dirt roads and footpaths, across fields or meadows, and through villages, and we stopped at times to visit a farm that supplied the school with some of its provisions. On one such occasion the farmers informed us that their horse was ill and begged us to pray for his recovery, which we did when in chapel; the horse recovered and we were thanked.

I retain the fondest memories of these walks, which slowly awakened in me the first stirrings of an undying attraction to nature, hills and dales and mountains, besides cultivated fields. Never again in my life would a single year seem to me so long a time as to appear in retrospect almost like an entire epoch. I contemplated from day to day the gradual changes wrought upon our surroundings by the slow march of the seasons as they came and went. I delighted at the spectacle of the melting of the snow and the onset of the spring rains that teased the first buds and tender greens out of the wakening trees, till their foliage grew dense in the heat of the summer and generously dispensed the coolness of their shade. And then I marvelled at the spectacle of the farmers gathering in nature's bounty from the fields, as the trees and shrubs turned golden and brown. What a joy it was come autumn to taste fragrant apples and pick walnuts off the ground beneath trees that lined some of the country roads, to eat their rich flesh with our bread. Even the rain-drenched bareness of late autumn held charm, as nature peacefully slid back into slumber and winter returned to bedeck it with a white mantle. I truly found solace in nature.

It was during those leisurely walks, when we did not have to form ranks and could even tarry behind that, early in our sojourn at Les Besses, two of us Jewish boys took to plotting an escape. We found a mentor in a fourteen-year-old boy who, like us, felt unhappy and wanted to run away. With him we made detailed mental notes of the places that we frequently passed on these walks, our object being that one afternoon, while we lingered behind the pack and Mademoiselle Susanne had her back turned, we would surreptitiously run behind some haystack or into an isolated shed and hide there until we could make our way to the railway station at Pellevoisin, where the "big boy" would sneak me aboard a train bound for Lyon! We eventually set a day for our escape, but as that day neared we became increasingly riddled with anxiety. The older boy could bear the anxiety no longer and, unbeknownst to us, reported the whole scheme to Mademoiselle Marie-Renée. One afternoon as we were sitting down to the usual quiet study period that followed the walk, the formidable nun strode down from her desk toward the two of us and summoned us aside for interrogation and a dressing-down such that the idea of running away never crossed our minds again.

In April 1960, I made a return visit to Les Besses and was welcomed there by Mademoiselle Berthe. With her characteristic cheerfulness and affableness, she accompanied me around the premises.

As we conversed about the time when I was hidden at the school, she alluded to the escape that I had plotted and laughed, saying that she hoped that I understood why we had to be severely punished, for had we actually attempted that escape, we would have run into the waiting arms of the Gestapo. She thanked me for my having returned for a visit and warmly shook my hand as I bade her adieu.

I was pleasantly surprised by the changes in the appearance of the *pensionnat* on that visit: the halls were the same but were gaily decorated; there were toys lying around; and French and American flags flew here and there. At the time there was an American military base near Châteauroux and the wives of the officers were generous patrons of Les Besses. Every month these ladies organized a celebration with birthday cake in honour of the boys who had their birthday that month, each of whom received a present. At least here the characteristic American generosity was, I gladly noted, gratefully appreciated.

Sometimes, the afternoon study period was devoted to correspondence with one's parents. The letters had to be written first in draft form, beginning with sterile formulae like "I eat well; I sleep well; I am in good health" and the like. Mademoiselle Marie-Renée, who usually presided over the study period, then read each boy's draft letter, corrected spelling and grammar, and censored it, after which the boy would rewrite the letter in clean and hand it back to our nun for mailing. I wrote to Papa regularly but only very rarely received a letter from him. Once I received a parcel; alas, the clothing that Papa had made for me and enclosed in that parcel were stolen or lost in the postal chaos of the time.

～

The nearby town of Pellevoisin was one of some religious significance, due to the apparition of the Virgin Mary in answer to the prayers of a pious local young woman who was dying of tuberculosis. Apparently, the timely intervention of the Virgin Mary, who appeared to her a number of times, saved her life and the grateful people of the town consecrated a church to Notre-Dame de Pellevoisin. Once a year the statue of Our Lady of Pellevoisin was carried out of the church and borne in solemn procession around the countryside. The clergy led the procession of townspeople and children, a procession that we, the boys of Les Besses, dressed in little blue uniforms, had to join. As we marched we sang a hymn of praise to Mary, of which I remember only the refrain, which went as follows: "Soyez la Madonne qu'on prie à genoux, qui sourit et pardonne, chez nous, chez nous" (Be you the Madonna, to whom we pray on our knees, in our home, in our home, who smiles and forgives).

While the highlight of every Sunday was morning mass in the chapel, we were sometimes doled out supplements of piety by being taken to afternoon vespers and special services at the church in Pellevoisin. In one such service that I remember vividly, but of which I no longer know the occasion, we were lined up single file and ordered to proceed, each boy in turn, to a large crucifix that was laid on a low stool. There we were to kneel and kiss the body of Christ. After each boy had accomplished this act of devotion he was told to move to one side, while Mademoiselle Marie-Renée wiped with a handkerchief the spot which he had just kissed, before signalling to the next boy to step forward, kneel and apply his kiss to the crucifix. Perhaps this ritual was performed during Holy Week, which was a time of intense religious preparation. On the afternoon of Good Friday we were subjected to a truly gruelling spiritual exercise, which consisted in symbolically re-enacting the Via Dolorosa of Jesus: kneeling on the hard floor of the chapel we had to rotate clockwise, a few degrees at a time, to face each and every one of the carved images of the Stations of the Cross that adorned the walls all around us, reciting a prayer at each station until, after perhaps two hours, we had completed a full circle, never rising from our knees. On Easter Sunday we reaped the rewards of our toils when, after the mass celebrating the resurrection of Christ, we were served a better meal than usual, and then sent on the Easter egg hunt.

What a good little Catholic I had become! I found in religion a balm for my emotional distress. As if praying when required at meal and classroom time and in chapel at dawn and at dusk, besides mass on Sunday and other services, was not enough to soothe my soul, I also used idle moments to pace along the corridors, rosary in hand, reciting at each bead the Ave Maria in French: "Je vous salue, Marie, pleine de grâce..." (Hail, Mary, full of grace...). The nuns marvelled at my piety; Mademoiselle Marie-Renée smiled benignly when I once told her that, should I live to be one hundred, I hoped to become a saint and ascend to Heaven to be reunited with my parents, as if in some dark recesses of my heart an inaudible voice was sadly whispering that I might never see them again. I entreated the nuns to allow me a turn at serving as an altar boy during Sunday mass; they assured me that I would, but my turn never came. I have forever been grateful to the nuns of Les Besses that they did not take advantage of the extreme vulnerability of the Jewish boys whom they sheltered to formally baptize us, as happened in Montluçon to Saul Friedländer, who was destined for the priesthood, and Jean-Marie Lustiger, who rose to become archbishop of Paris, a cardinal and primate of France during the pontificate of John Paul II.

To ask whether Saul Friedländer and Jean-Marie Lustiger genuinely wished to convert or were pressured is almost pointless. I suspect that the nuns of Les Besses could have converted me without using much pressure. The aura of mystery that enfolds the rites of the Catholic Church filled me with devotion and a burning faith in the love and protective power of the Holy Mother of God and her divine son, Jesus.

One morning when we were playing or milling about during recess, something extraordinary happened. A steady and loud rumbling overhead made us all suddenly stop in our tracks and raise our eyes to the sky. High, very high over us, untold numbers of bomber aircrafts moved in seemingly slow motion. We all stood there, lost in fascination, when suddenly a dark object detached itself from one of the airplanes and descended in our direction. Shouts resounded everywhere: "A bomb! A bomb!" Seized with panic, the nuns hustled us inside the school building, instead of ordering us to scatter and lie down. Huddled against the entrance door and windows, we excitedly watched the object fall in the field about a hundred metres away from the building. As it happened, it was some piece of equipment, possibly an engine, not a bomb. In the confusion that followed, a rumour soon spread that, just as the object was about to crash into the building, the Virgin Mary had appeared over the roof and with an outstretched arm pushed it away into the field. Eventually, everyone swore to having seen the outstretched arm of Our Lady of Pellevoisin! I dared not challenge the veracity of the miracle that so many claimed to have witnessed. Having been pushed to the back of the pack crowding around the entrance to the building, I had seen nothing.

During another mid-morning recess I happened to stand in front of one of the classroom windows, looking out, when a big bully who often tormented me crept up unnoticed and dropped a wasp or a bee behind my collar. My screams of pain and copious swearing promptly brought Mademoiselle Marie-Renée to the scene. In a school where the utterance of a single swear word, even the innocuous word "merde" (shit), brought swift punishment, the pain of repeated stings made me release a stream of foul language, yet the nun did not even scold me; on the contrary, she instantly grasped what had happened and vigorously slapped the bully on both cheeks. This richly deserved punishment permanently released me from his unwanted attentions.

I no longer remember whether the most painful period of my life at Les Besses happened before or after that incident with the bully. At the time a strange fad had taken hold of some of the boys: during afternoon playtime in the fields and in the wood they cut small limbs from shrubs or trees and used pocket knives to carve them into pointed javelins. They then competed in throwing these javelins as far as they could. One afternoon I happened to be standing nearby, shivering in the late autumn cold, when a pointed javelin thrust from seemingly nowhere planted itself into the lower part of my right leg. The pain was excruciating. Mademoiselle Marie-Renée, who was standing nearby, solicitously bent down, inquiring whether I was hurt but, fearful of being mocked as a "crybaby," I pretended that nothing grave had happened and stemmed the bleeding with a handkerchief.

The pain, however, didn't go away; not only was the hole in my leg noticeable, but it became infected and the whole leg began to swell. The nuns grew alarmed and called in a doctor, who found the matter serious enough. Without his timely arrival and prompt treatment, the consequences could have been dire indeed. My leg was heavily bandaged and tied to a board to keep it immobile. I spent the whole winter thus immobilized, sprawled on a bench placed in the kindergarten hall, where there was little to occupy my attention other than the activities of the preschoolers and the comings and goings of the schoolboys on their way to play or to our usual chores (such as the periodic outdoor latrine cleaning or the picking of Colorado beetles in the potato field) or to chapel. I now had friends who showed me attention and sympathy, and the doctor repeatedly came to check on the progress of my recovery. At bedtime I was carried upstairs to the dormitory, my leg steadied by the board to which it was tied, and in the morning brought down in like manner to the refectory and the kindergarten. A fire might have been lit in the preschool hall every now and then, but most of the time I felt cold and the enforced immobility caused my toes to develop chilblains. I think it took about three months before I became fully mobile again.

In the wake of my long infirmity I found my situation in the school markedly improved. I was particularly touched by the motherly attention given me by Mademoiselle Berthe, who was after all the most important person in the school next to headmistress Mademoiselle Hermance. Her appearances were like rays of sunshine. One day she took me aside to tell me, as she repressed a smile of connivance, that an unknown well-wisher had paid for me to receive every day a supplement of food in the form of an egg that I was to swallow raw, right in the kitchen, where no one was to see me go in. Deep down I suspected that the well-wisher was none other than Mademoiselle Berthe herself. The dearth of calcium in the food that we received had caused my fingernails to turn white. Although we were all from time to time given a small square of ersatz chocolate said to contain vitamins, this candy (of which we were asked to save the foil wrap) did not suffice to ensure good health for growing boys.

The spring of 1944 brought two surprising visits by a strange lady, who each time left with one of my Jewish companions. Needless to say, these utterly unexpected visits left me in a state of suspense and anxious anticipation that perhaps the lady might soon return for me. She did! One afternoon, the stranger (or perhaps it was not the same lady) returned and, after conferring with the nuns, called for me. She excitedly informed me that she was going to take me to Lyon to be reunited with my father and made me promptly gather my belongings and bid adieu to my hostesses. This time it was true: my long confinement at the convent school was suddenly brought to an end and the next day I would be in Lyon! My happiness knew no bounds. Accompanied by the cheerful stranger I walked for the last time down the alley between the woods and the fields and cast an almost nostalgic backward glance at the school, before it disappeared from sight. The lady and I walked to Pellevoisin, where we boarded a train bound for Châteauroux. There we spent several hours, or perhaps even a night in a hotel room, before setting out for a long train ride to Lyon.

I have often wondered why I and the other Jewish boys were removed from a place that seemed such a safe haven, when the occupation and the war were by no means over yet, in order to be, in my case, placed at risk in Lyon. As for the unknown lady who removed me from Les Besses, I wonder whether she was Pierrette Poirier, one of the heroic conveyors of Jewish children to their places of hiding mentioned by French historian of the Shoah Sabine Zeitoun in her book *Ces enfants qu'il fallait sauver* (*Those Children Who Had to Be Saved*). Pierrette, who was not Jewish, was then thirty-two years old and the mother of a little girl. A devout Catholic, she heard a mystic call that she believed came from God asking her to go and save Jewish children. She then spent the summer of 1942 prospecting Catholic colleges, convents and boarding schools in and around Châteauroux; Les Besses must have been one of her "finds." Pierrette won the backing of Monseigneur Lefèbvre, bishop of Bourges, a righteous prelate who formally forbade the conversion of Jewish children without the consent of their parents. It is estimated that Pierrette saved about a hundred children, possibly including me. May she be remembered for a blessing.

Lyon

The train rolled in a southerly direction along the scenic Rhône valley. I was sitting near a window with eyes fixed on the panorama, when the first houses and streets of Lyon came into view. It was a sunny morning, and my heart filled with excitement and wonderment at the vistas that flashed in rapid succession before me: the bridges on the Rhône, the eastern slope of the Croix-Rousse hill with its jumble of narrow streets winding up and down every which way, and then, on the side of the river along which our train travelled, avenues lined with elegant multi-storeyed buildings along which coursed streetcars and automobiles, and people everywhere. Not since we left Brussels had I seen such a large city, with several railway stations. I could almost hear my heart thumping as the train rolled through the Lyon-Saint-Clair and Lyon-Brotteaux stations and crossed a bridge over the Rhône before slowing down and coming to a final halt at Lyon's central station, Perrache. Stepping down from the train I peered with trepidation into the crowds, hoping to spot my father. My chaperone led me by the hand through the multitude pressing along the main platform until suddenly we came upon my cousin Ginette! She gave me a warm welcoming hug as she exchanged a few words with the chaperone, who then said goodbye.

At the time, Ginette was a seventeen-year-old *lycéenne* (high school student), quite small in stature. With a beaming smile and hugs and kisses, she led me out of the station and assured me that I would find my papa at home when we got there. After a long streetcar ride we arrived at our address: Number 20 of Rue Pouteau, a grey, sooty old stone building on a steep street, which one negotiated up or down successive flights of wide steps between rows of similarly grey stone buildings. Our family lived in a tiny flat at the end of a dark corridor of the top floor, which may have been the sixth or seventh floor depending on how one counts them. In France the ground floor never counts as a first floor: it is the *rez-de-chaussée*, or ground floor; then, in Lyon's old buildings the floor above the ground floor is called *entresol*; what is called first floor would be the second or even third floor by North American reckoning. There were no elevators in those old buildings and if any light was to be had in the stairways, they were of the *minuterie* (timer) kind: one pressed a button on the wall, and depending on how fast one climbed the stairs, the light lasted long enough to reach one or two floors higher before one had to press a button again.

As soon as Ginette opened the door of the flat, my eye caught sight of Papa seated in a corner. He barely managed to rise from his chair before I fell into his arms! Aunt Zilly and Uncle Paul took me in turn in their arms. No words can describe these moments of new-found happiness: I was now at home in the womb of my family, after what had seemed like a never-ending succession of months hidden here and there. I sat on Papa's knees and combed my hand over the dark hair that partially covered his forehead; his deep dark eyes seemed to smile. If only Mama could be with us…. There was nothing more in the world I could have wished for at that moment, except perhaps also the presence of my other two cousins, Ginette's brothers Freddy and Jacqui, who had found refuge in Switzerland through the efforts of Uncle David Domb.

With my arrival, we now were four or five persons living in a single room that served as kitchen, sitting room and bedroom. There was no bathroom: we washed at the sink. The toilets were of the squatting kind, in dark cubbyholes located between the floors, each serving the needs of half a dozen apartments. Papa often slept in a different place, perhaps less because of the cramped space in which we lived than because of his underground activity in the Resistance. He worked by day in a large tailoring workshop on Rue d'Algérie, off the Place des Terreaux, a beautiful square adorned with a statue and a fountain in front of the elegant eighteenth-century city hall. He carried a false identity card under the name of Jean-Pierre Thierry, born in Oyonnax, a town north of Lyon in the department of Ain. The workshop was only a half-hour's walking distance from home; I often dropped in on Papa and was always cheerfully greeted by the several men who worked with him and their employer Monsieur Mounier, or Monier.

I was soon taught the precautionary measures to be observed. The flat was, after all, our hiding place. We needed to observe certain precautions, such as the agreed-upon signal when returning home: a rhythmic pattern of knocks at the door. We froze into silence whenever we heard footsteps in the corridor and did not open until after the agreed-upon knocks were heard. Also, during air raids we dared not descend into the nearby underground shelter, for fear that someone might become excessively curious about us.

During the day Papa and Uncle Paul went to work and Ginette to the *lycée* where she studied. I usually remained alone with Aunt Zilly but was also often outside exploring the surroundings. Having grown accustomed to walking several kilometres a day I spent hours jaunting about that great city of Lyon, which held me in fascination with the diversity of its parts. Lyon's most striking geographical feature is that so much of the city, including its central sections, is enclosed within a peninsula shaped by two great rivers, the Rhône and the Saône, both spanned by many bridges; their confluence forms the southern tip of the metropolis. Heading north from the *hôtel-de-ville*, city hall, on Place des Terreaux, the peninsula widens immensely as it slopes sharply upward toward the plateau of Croix-Rousse, which is the upper part of the city. The street where we lived was on that slope.

On the west bank of the Saône lies the old Lyon with its five-hundred-year-old cathedral of Saint-Jean; further west, alleys and lanes wend up toward the plateau of Fourvières, which is crowned with an ugly *fin de siècle*, end of the century, basilica and a miniature Eiffel Tower. The spot commands a breathtaking panorama of Lyon and its two rivers and, on exceptionally clear days, the snow-capped silhouette of the Alps lines the distant horizon.

Wandering about aimlessly, I admired the stately buildings of the city's thoroughfares and the grandeur of squares like the Place des Terreaux and the Place Bellecour, a vast tree-framed rectangle with flower parterres to one side and an imposing equestrian statue of King Louis XIV in the middle. Sometimes I set out with a destination in mind, only to be led in a different direction on a whim or by some unusual sight that I happened on. I was never lost, no matter how far I wandered away from Rue Pouteau. If the afternoon turned late I knew that it was time to walk back home. I never rode the streetcars, unless accompanied by Papa or Aunt Zilly. Perhaps that had been enjoined on me as a precaution as well. If I saw uniformed Germans or, worse yet, the vile *Milice* I gave them a wide berth. The Southern Zone, even under German occupation, was at any rate a less dangerous place than the Northern Zone or Belgium. For one thing, the wearing of the yellow star was never imposed in the South and there were no "Jews not admitted" signs at the entrance to cinemas and public gardens. Besides, I did not have "Semitic" features, even though I was red-haired like my mother. In France, unlike in Poland, that particular trait did not in itself raise the suspicion that one was a Jew, since many non-Jews, particularly the Celtic Bretons, have red hair as well.

Being careful also required that I conduct myself politely with inquisitive strangers. That was a lesson Aunt Zilly drove home to me one afternoon, when she gave me a small bag of cherries to nibble on while I ambled about town. Since she did not tell me where she bought the cherries, she need not have recommended, as she did, that if anyone saw me eating and asked where I got them that I should not tell. References to a mysterious "black market" cropped up time and again in adult conversations and I imagined it to be a market installed under black canvas covers, whose location a child was not supposed to know or even ask about. As luck would have it that afternoon, I happened to cross the Place des Cordeliers in the city centre, when a lady became curious and approached me asking where "my mammy" bought these cherries. Instead of politely telling the truth, that I did not know, I rudely answered that it was none of her business. The lady was exceedingly angry; she shouted that I was an ill-bred brat and I promptly ran away from her in a burst of indignation. Back home I was anxious to prove to Aunt Zilly that I had obeyed her order not to tell strangers where she bought the cherries. To my surprise she furiously reprimanded me for my insolence!

One of my haunts was the Croix-Rousse plateau, particularly its wide boulevard, where markets and fairs were held. I was fascinated by the merry-go-rounds of the fair but rarely had enough money to indulge in more than a single ride or a few *berlingots*, pyramid-shaped hard candies, from the mouth-watering candy stands. Eventually, Aunt Zilly ordered me not to hang around the fair area, lest someone approach me inquiring why I was not in school at that time of the day.

When I recollect this brief period that I spent in Lyon in the spring of 1944, it amazes me that my family allowed me to thus saunter about the streets by myself. But I never felt so happy as when I went on outings with Papa on his days off. On such days we visited friends or acquaintances and also places of interest and amusement. On at least two occasions he took me to the vast and beautiful Parc de la Tête d'Or in the middle of which is a lake; there, he rented a boat and taught me how to row, besides strongly urging me to learn to swim. I hung on his arm or held his hand, chatting incessantly. Acquaintances who met us laughingly chided me for being a veritable chatterbox and for clinging to my father and chiming over and over again, "mon papa."

Papa endearingly called me "Fissie," a funny diminutive of his own invention, in which he added the German ending "ie" to the French word for "son," *fils*. It was as if after two years of enforced separation and near silence, I was overcome with an irrepressible urge to talk. Papa good-humouredly answered my innumerable questions or told me stories; he was a fine narrator who knew how to hold my attention. We now naturally conversed in French. Papa spoke the language fluently, although with a "certain accent," as the French would say, while I had largely forgotten the languages in which I grew up. He was patient with me to the point of tolerating my Catholicism, accepting that I could not be expected to shake that religion off so soon after having been immersed in it. I remember one Sunday morning when we happened to walk past the cathedral of Saint-Nizier and, upon hearing the sound of prayer and singing echoing from inside, I begged to go in and he obligingly sat with me through part of the mass.

These were our golden moments during the several weeks that I was in Lyon. Even on days when work and his underground activities absorbed his time, Papa usually managed to come up to the flat at bedtime to spend a few moments with me, before heading out again into the night. Lying in bed I pressed him with anguished questions, such as when would the Allies land and the war end. He comforted me with the promise that the Allies would land very soon and that the war would be over not long after; Mama would then come back to us and we would live happily together as a family again, and I would get a little sister. To have a little sister was perhaps my most cherished wish, one which I had already expressed when we lived in Brussels and to which my parents responded at the time by promising that it would happen after the war. Papa and I also talked about where we would live after the war: he did not seem to envisage returning to Luxembourg or Brussels; rather his imagination led him to fantasize about us living in Norway, near one of its romantic fjords, or in England, curiously enough, in the city of Folkestone. One evening when

I must have felt particularly anguished I told Papa, as he was about to bid me goodnight that, should he happen to die I would go to his grave and die there myself. How troubled he must have felt by this utterance of mine.

Two of Papa's friends lived on Montée de la Grande Côte, an astonishingly long and steep street that connects the lower reaches of the city with the Croix-Rousse plateau. One was Monsieur Kasriel, who provided Papa with a nook where he slept, the other a gentleman who lived with his wife above his tailoring shop and was known to me simply as "le grand Jacques." He was indeed a tall man and was always cheerful and playful with me. One afternoon when I happened to be standing in front of his shop, which faced the Rue Vieille-Monnaie, I spotted Papa, wearing his long raincoat, in the distance, upon which I ran the entire length of the street into his waiting arms. That seemingly insignificant moment remains a memory that I cherish with intense emotion.

That Rue Vieille-Monnaie, today Rue René-Leynaud, has a special significance in my remembrance of things past. In a nook-like courtyard near the middle of that street lived a couple surnamed Pfeffer, whom we visited from time to time. The man, whose name was Léon, had a hollow cheek and his deep, dark eyes bore a hauntingly sad expression. A hero of the Resistance, he was tortured to death shortly before the liberation of Lyon. On that same street, at Number 12, lived the most important persons among Papa's friends — Irma Meyer and her son, Pierre. Their apartment was on the second floor of a grimy building, but then, all the buildings of Lyon were grimy at that time: the city acquired a new and decidedly more beautiful appearance in the late twentieth century, when the accumulated grime was washed away and the washing, to the surprise of many, revealed façades of various colours. One walked into Number 12 through a short tunnel-like entrance, which led into a courtyard like a well; on the ground level, in a flat that faced the courtyard, lived another Jewish family, named Najman, who were also in the underground resistance movement. Pierre and his mother lived on the second floor of the wing, separated from the street-side building by the courtyard.

Pierre, who was one year my senior, acted almost like an elder brother to me and we often hung out together. His father was estranged from his mother and lived elsewhere in the city. The Meyer family came originally from Hamburg, where Pierre was born. Both parents spoke fluent French but with a German accent. Pierre evoked for me the comings and goings and secret meetings that were held in the apartment — Papa and Irma Meyer belonged to the same cell or group of the Jewish section of the underground resistance movement Main-d'œuvre immigrée (MOI), a cell that Irma later remembered as being composed largely of Polish Jews. When I interviewed her in Sydney, Australia, in 1994, she also told me that my father "just lived for the Communist Party" and was known in their cell as a good speaker.

The MOI was one of the mass organizations created by the French Communist Party (PCF) in the 1920s to spread its influence to people of all walks of life. Its function was to draw under the PCF umbrella the hundreds of thousands of mostly working-class immigrants streaming into France at the time. The MOI was divided into ethnic sections: Jewish, Armenian, Polish, Romanian, Italian and others. Each of these sections was led by its own native communists, who received their instructions from the Central Committee of the PCF. Soon after the beginning of the German occupation, the MOI was converted into an underground resistance organization with an elaborate structure of cells engaged in propaganda or welfare activities, and combat groups. The movement was so compartmentalized that most members rarely knew more than two of their comrades. Partly for that reason I was, alas, unable to gather much information about my father's activities, other than that he distributed leaflets and in 1944 pasted the walls of buildings with stickers bearing the caption "Dernier été sous les boches!"(Last summer under the *boches*!)

The Jewish section of the MOI was the largest and most dy-

namic. It had a particularly strong presence in Paris and in Lyon. Its
secret printing shops published newspapers and leaflets in Yiddish
and French, and its women organized the hiding of Jewish children.
Combat groups, trained by veterans of the international brigades of
the Spanish Civil War, engaged in sabotage activities against the enemy and occasionally executed denunciators of Jews. The September
1943 execution in broad daylight of Julius Ritter, Eichmann's representative in Paris, by twenty-year-old Marcel Rayman and others under the leadership of the Armenian poet Missak Manouchian, can be
counted among the most brilliant actions of the MOI combat groups.

Sometimes Papa and I would meet up with Pierre and his mother
for meals and walks together. I remember one such outing on a Sunday afternoon, when we walked along a narrow lane that led up the
hill of Fourvières and unexpectedly found ourselves in the midst of
a procession headed for the esplanade in front of the ugly basilica
where, from what Papa explained, Cardinal Pierre-Marie Gerlier was
to conduct a religious service. We did not attempt to enter the crowded sanctuary but walked around the esplanade and ascended the little
metallic Eiffel-style tower to delight in the panorama of the city.

Cardinal Gerlier was then the archbishop of Lyon and Primate
of the Gauls (the official title of the head of the Church of France).
Who would have imagined, in those dark years, that less than half
a century later the incumbent of that exalted post would be Monseigneur Jean-Marie Lustiger, whose Jewish mother had been killed
in Auschwitz in 1943! Monseigneur Gerlier was a pillar of the Vichy
regime; in his public utterances he never failed to praise "the Marshal," but his antisemitism was not of the virulent kind. He blamed
the financial ruin of his family in 1934 on a financial scandal of which
the chief culprit was a certain Alexandre Stavisky, but protested to
Pétain against the violation of basic human rights in the application
of the regime's anti-Jewish laws. During the roundups of the summer
of 1942 in the Southern Zone, the Catholic resistance group Amitié
chrétienne, led by the philosemitic Jesuit Father Pierre Chaillet and

the Jewish-born priest Alexandre Glasberg, managed to spirit eighty-four Jewish children out of a fort in the suburb of Vénissieux, where they were interned and about to be transported with their parents to Drancy. These children were brought to a Jewish Boy Scouts of France building in a former convent pending their dispersal among different locations, an operation for which the cardinal provided cover. Lyon's prefect of police demanded of Monseigneur Gerlier that the children be returned to the authorities, but the cardinal refused to reveal their whereabouts.

Lyon, as a major industrial and communication centre, was often the target of Allied air raids. I soon grew accustomed to the alternatively rising and descending wails of the sirens and I don't remember being afraid of them. Most of the alerts were false, but some of them were real enough. After a true alert, several minutes, sometimes a quarter of an hour or even more, would elapse before the ominously heavy sound of approaching bomber aircraft was heard, soon followed by explosions. The usual targets were the industries that supplied the German military and were for the most part concentrated in the suburbs of Vénissieux and Saint-Fons. Precision could not, however, be expected, particularly at night when the blackout rendered the city invisible from the air, and civilian objectives often suffered what we nowadays euphemistically call "collateral damage." Air-raid alerts sometimes woke us up at night; Uncle Paul would then listen intently, trying to guess how far from where we lived the raid was taking place. Since, in any case, there was little likelihood of our part of the city being targeted, we refrained from going down to the neighbourhood shelter, lest we drew the attention of some Jew-hunters who might denounce us.

Small neighbourhood barbershops often functioned like informal political forums in which the barber arbitrated the debates. One morning when I was awaiting my turn in the shop one street below us, I listened to men commenting about the relative merits of different air forces: the British and Canadian bombers were held in high regard because they dared to brave the German anti-aircraft guns by flying low in order to strike at their targets without inflicting much damage on the population, whereas the Americans were reviled for dropping their bombs from altitudes of seven or eight thousand metres, a strategy which they called "high altitude precision bombing." Feelings ran particularly high in the aftermath of the devastating raids of May 26, 1944.

That night I was sleeping over at Pierre's place. Around midnight we were jolted out of bed by sounds of bombs exploding at the very same moment as the sirens howled. The alert stations had failed to detect the approach of aircraft. Pierre's mother hurried the two of us down the stairways, across the courtyard and the gate into the street, where we joined panic-stricken crowds racing toward a tunnel under construction on Montée Saint-Sébastien (the tunnel in which a metro line runs nowadays). As we were running, I looked in fascination up into the skies, where flares illuminated the silhouettes of countless bombers while explosions were heard some distance away. It was about two in the morning when the sirens announced the end of the raid and we emerged from the tunnel. Pierre and I were sleeping in that morning when, at about ten o'clock, another air raid, this one announced by the wail of the sirens, roused us out of bed again. This time, however, we did not run for shelter but, instead, like other residents of the building, stood watch by the window, listening to the reports of the inhabitants of the top floor, who shouted down for all to hear where the raid was taking place. The chief targets were at almost opposite ends of the city: they included the Perrache railway terminal, the connecting bridges over the two rivers and the river station and docks on the Saône in Vaise.

During that long raid four hundred American bombers dropped huge numbers of bombs from an altitude of seven thousand metres, razing entire blocks of the city and killing and wounding more than 1,800 people. Yet the Perrache railway station suffered little damage other than smashed windows, and the railway bridges remained standing as well. The only significant damage inflicted on the Germans was the destruction of the building containing the archive section at the Gestapo headquarters. I remember that the next day the newspapers carried a list of casualties that covered three pages. The population was understandably indignant while the enemy's propaganda machine, which included Radio-Paris and the collaborating newspapers, benefited from this colossal blunder. Pétain visited Lyon to offer his sympathy to the population.

To keep abreast of events, particularly of the military situation, required inquisitive, explorative reading, since the legal media served the Germans and Vichy. The leaflets and underground papers disseminated by the Resistance, notably the clandestine Yiddish newspaper *Unzer Vort*, Our Word, published by the MOI, were sources of information. The most dependable source, however, was the BBC's French-language program, but anyone reported or caught listening to the London radio courted danger. We often listened in our flat, ear bent close to the radio set, the volume turned low, particularly at night when the sound was clearer. I still remember the opening signals: a four-beat drumming repeated several times, followed by a voice announcing: "Ici Londres, les Français parlent aux Français" (This is London: Frenchmen are speaking to Frenchmen). Next heard was the news, followed by coded messages understandable only to the particular units or fighters of the Resistance for whom they were intended. The London broadcasts also included entertainment consisting of ditties or songs lampooning Radio-Paris and the strident oratory of its editorialist Philippe Henriot. The rhyming refrain intoned was "Radio-Paris ment, Radio-Paris ment, Radio-Paris est allemand," a refrain that was then repeated by substituting the name of Philippe Henriot for the station name "Radio-Paris."(Radio-Paris lies…Radio-Paris is German; Philippe Henriot lies, Philippe Henriot is German). I remember hearing Philippe Henriot's last rant soon after the D-Day landing in Normandy: a few weeks later, that overwrought loudmouth of a collaborator was executed by the Resistance in his suite in the ministry of information building.

June 6, the long-yearned for "D-Day" — also called *le débarquement*, the landing — was a day I will remember as long as I live! The happy news burst on me that morning as soon as Uncle Paul set the radio dial on London. Delirious with joy I ignored Aunt and Uncle's attempts to restrain me and ran out the door, raced down the many floors of our building, down the wide flights of steps of our street and of the passage leading further down from it to the Rue Vieille-Monnaie, and from there all the way to Place des Terreaux. I arrived out of breath in Papa's workshop and cried out the exciting news. Shouts of joy welcomed the news and me, their bearer. Monsieur Mounier decreed time off and invited everybody to the small café around the corner, where he ordered a glass of wine for all his employees and a glass of grape juice for me and led us in drinking a toast to victory!

June 6, 1944: Could anyone alive in those dramatic times in Europe not remember that morning that saw the dawn of our liberation? The memory of it is so deeply engraved in my heart that on its anniversary dates, and at other times too, it brings forth feelings of gratitude for the thousands of young men — Canadians, Americans, British — who crossed the Atlantic Ocean and the English Channel to end the torment-filled nightmare that held us in its grip for so long. But it also inspires in me sadness for the thousands of them who laid down their lives on the beaches of Normandy. Thoughts of their sacrifice also rouse in me anger at the gratuitous anti-Americanism of so many French people today, who forget that America came to the rescue of their country in both world wars and then, through the agency of the Marshall Plan, helped France back on her feet after World War II. I think it was actually Pétain who once quipped that the French have a short memory.

Even though liberation loomed on the horizon, hard times still lay ahead. If anything, the Germans became more erratic and violent.

They contemptuously ignored Vichy's feeble protests against their encroachments on its sovereignty and, as they retreated, they took Pétain captive to Germany. In the meantime they unleashed the thugs of the *Milice* as never before — they and other dregs of French society roamed the streets for prey, kidnapping some Jews and murdering them even after the ransoms demanded for their release were paid. In one incident in December 1943, a hand grenade attack ended the religious services held at the great synagogue of Lyon; eight worshippers were injured and the perpetrators were never identified. Six months later, the *Milice* arrested all present in the same synagogue and sent them to Drancy, from where they were deported to Auschwitz. Also in June 1944, a group of seven Jews was arrested and subsequently murdered by the *Milice*. Implicated in all of these events was the notorious Paul Touvier, who headed the *Milice* in Lyon. Touvier managed to dodge justice for forty years, thanks to the complicity of certain Catholic priests, who hid him in a succession of monasteries.

For Jewish men the streets of Lyon were rendered ever more dangerous by the presence in the crowds of gangs of "physiognomists," who would suddenly surround someone who to them looked Jewish and force him inside the entrance of a building, where they would pull down his trousers for the purpose of verification. This exposed the MOI Resistance fighters to accrued dangers and forced women to engage in actions hitherto shouldered by men. I heard the word "Gestapo" crop up in adult conversations, and although no one cared to explain to me its meaning, I could sense the dread that the mere utterance of it inspired. I no longer remember where I happened to be one morning when I was warned somehow not to return home: the Gestapo had come up to our flat and, finding no one home, sealed its door. Aunt and Uncle went into hiding and Ginette was sheltered by one of her classmates. Under the circumstances, Papa and Irma Meyer, understandably, decided that it was not wise to keep me and Pierre in the city. They took us to Chozeau, a village in the department of Isère, not far from Lyon, where they paid a peasant farming family to board us.

Meanwhile, in the rural areas of the Southern Zone, guerrilla activity by the *Maquis* rose dramatically in the wake of D-Day. In the foothills of the Alps, the heroic *Maquisards* established a veritable liberated area, which encompassed the plateaus of Vercors and Glières between Grenoble and Valence. To show that they still wielded clout, the Germans surrounded the area and launched a vigorous military operation to recapture these highlands. The *Maquisards* had counted on the anticipated Allied landing in Provence and the dropping of supplies from the air, but the landing was unexpectedly delayed and the dropping of supplies by air did not work out. The Vercors chapter of the French Resistance ended in tragedy. At the same time, in the hills of the Massif Central and the plateau of the Limousin, of which Limoges is the chief urban centre, *Maquis* units combined into large detachments and rushed into action to prevent German reinforcements from reaching the Normandy front. My cousin Simon Domb commanded one of these detachments, engaging the SS Das Reich division in fierce combat in order to keep it from reaching the Normandy front. His brigade was then integrated into the reconstituted French army and took part in the liberation of Alsace. As a reward for his distinguished service, Simon was promoted to captain and awarded both the *croix de guerre* and the knighthood of the Legion of Honour.

On June 10, the Das Reich division, harassed by guerrilla activity on its march north, vented its frustration on the peaceful village of Oradour-sur-Glane, which was not a centre of resistance. They surrounded that village, burnt it down and massacred 642 people.

When Pierre and I settled in the village of Chozeau, that region was also becoming an area of *Maquis* activity, but not on the scale of the organized operations taking place in the foothills of the Alps and the Limousin plateau.

The Last Summer

I had enjoyed for only a few weeks the comforting companionship of my father after a long and painful separation when fate now parted us again. Yet again I was sent into the unknown to live with strangers. The house to which they brought us was that of the Réboz family farm. I vividly remember the moment of our arrival in Chozeau when we stood at the door of the farmhouse kitchen and Papa handed the farmer's wife some money, after which he and Irma left us, promising that, Lyon not being far, they would visit us from time to time and we could visit them.

The Réboz family now sheltered, besides Pierre and me, two or three other boys from Lyon who were not Jewish. It was a common practice during the war for city people to board their children with peasant farmers, in order to keep them away from air raids and afford them better nourishment. Our hosts were a couple about sixty years old; they expected us to address them as if they were our grandparents by calling them "Pépé" and "Mémé," which I was reluctant to do. Pépé Réboz was a quiet, rather subdued man; the authority figure for us boys was Mémé Réboz. The couple had eight children, all of them adults, most of them married with homes of their own in the village. We addressed them by their first name preceded by the title "Tonton" or "Tatan," the diminutives for uncle and aunt in that region. The youngest, Tonton Gérard, was twenty-five years old and lived with his parents; it was whispered that he was a member of the *Maquis*.

Although I had lived in rural areas in Vendœuvres and at Les Besses, it was not until that summer of 1944 in Chozeau that I lived with a peasant family and experienced true rural life. Pépé was a well-to-do farmer who owned several fields scattered outside the village. He grew grain and vegetables and owned cattle and sheep. Like true peasants, the Réboz couple conversed among themselves and with their neighbours in the local patois, which we city boys could not understand.

I attended school in Chozeau for perhaps not more than two or three weeks before the school year was over. The school year in France used to begin on the first of October and end near the eve of the national holiday of July 14, the anniversary date of the storming of the Bastille prison fortress by the people of Paris in 1789. This holiday may not have been celebrated under the anti-Republic government of Pétain, but that would not have altered the school calendar. While I treasure such vivid memories of my school days in other places, before and after the summer of 1944, I retain from the school in Chozeau only the faintest of images. Likewise, I remember very little of what the village of Chozeau looked like and don't remember the church at all. The oddity of this failure of my memory to register clearly a place where I lived for at least three months surprises me. Memory can be so curiously selective.

With the coming of summer we boys had to sometimes give a hand on the farm by leading the sheep and goats to meadows, where we socialized with some of the village boys. They were rough and their language was crude, but on the whole we got along. They seemed to take pleasure in shocking our sensitivities. It was from them that at the age of ten I learned, in the bluntest and crudest manner imaginable, the mystery of how children come into the world. The sexual act bore in their eyes no association with love and the finer things of life. I was further shocked to discover that country folks had no feeling for animals, not even their dogs and cats. A particularly brutal scene that remains indelibly engraved in my memory is of the manner in which the unwanted kittens of the farm cat were disposed of. We children were made to watch Tonton Gérard seize the tiny felines one after the other and from a distance toss them against the wall of the stable. Unable to bear the shrill cries of the kittens and the sight of their poor broken and bloodied little bodies lying on the ground, I ran away in tears, sick to my stomach.

On at least two occasions Pierre and I were able to escape for a couple of days to Lyon. Oh, how excited we were in anticipation of these visits with our parents! With what gusto we marched the five kilometres to the little railway station in Crémieu, singing rhythmically the two-line refrain "un kilomètre à pied, ça use, ça use; un kilomètre à pied, ça use les souliers!" (One kilometre on foot wears out, wears out; one kilometre on foot, wears out the shoes). Then we'd go on to "two kilometres on foot, wears out...", "three kilometres...," and so on! The repetition ad infinitum of that refrain, occasionally interrupted with animated conversation, ensured a vigorous pace. The train ride from Crémieu to Lyon was short and, almost before we knew it, we found ourselves in the waiting arms of Papa and Irma Meyer. These were, alas, mere moments of bliss and all too soon we found ourselves back in Chozeau.

Papa and Irma came once or perhaps even twice to see us there. We walked with them around the village and led them to farms where they could buy eggs, little round white cheeses, and some butter as well. From Pépé Réboz they might have bought one of the large round loaves of rye bread that he baked every week. The peasants were experts at concealing food from the authorities; what they did not consume themselves they sold to visiting city people anxious to supplement their meagre rations with some healthy farm products. The dreaded *Ravitaillement général*, the food supply authorities, obligated the farmers to deliver large quantities of grains, meats and produce to feed the urban population and, more importantly, the occupation army. Traditionally mistrustful of government, the peasants were bound by a certain degree of solidarity, any breach of which could invite dire consequences on the culprits. We heard that one farmer in the village, said to have collaborated too eagerly with the authorities, suffered to see one of his fields burned down by the *Maquis*.

I witnessed peasant solidarity also at work in a different way. The farmers of Chozeau had a tradition of cooperation during harvest time. Pépé Réboz and some of his neighbours would come together to gather the harvests of every member of their group in turn. For several days men came at dawn to the Réboz farm to work with Pépé in his fields, leaving at night. While they laboured in the fields, their womenfolk busied themselves in Mémé's kitchen cooking up gargantuan meals. I was astonished at the vast quantities of food served at the long table in the crowded kitchen, at noon as well as in the evening, meals that included several kinds of meat. What a contrast with the meagre diet I had grown accustomed to before I came to Chozeau! The peasants shouted louder and louder as they ate, drinking bottle after bottle of their own wines and sometimes getting drunk, especially in the evening, when they imbibed without restraint. I remember one supper at which the usually subdued Pépé became so drunk that he picked a violent quarrel with his wife, loudly shouting and cursing with no regard for the ears of us children seated at the table. That outburst ended with Pépé throwing a heavy iron key at Mémé and bellowing that he would rather sleep with his mare than with her, upon which he staggered outside to spend the night in the stable! After about a week of working on Pépé Réboz's fields the rambunctious company, including our hosts, moved on to perform the same operation on the fields and farms of whoever's turn came next.

Some time during the summer, Pierre and I were separated for reasons that remain unclear. By then we had been told not to travel to Lyon anymore and even to desist from all communication with our parents "for the time being." As the Allied armies marched from Normandy to Paris and progressed from Provence northwards, the Germans, sensing that defeat was in the air, acted like cornered beasts with all the ferocity that Nazi fanaticism could command. They wildly lashed out in all directions, stepping up repression of the Resistance and the hunt for Jews to a feverish pitch. Nowhere perhaps was this ferocity more evident than in Lyon, where the Gestapo enlisted the assistance of the *Milice* and assorted dregs of society. They even fired indiscriminately at passersby in the streets. As the summer progressed its streets became veritable battlefields, with almost daily attacks against Germans and their collaborators, spectacular acts of sabotage and random roundups of hostages followed by atrocious tortures and summary executions in the "butcher of Lyon" Klaus Barbie's cellars on avenue Berthelot. Lyon truly deserved the recognition it won as "the capital of the Resistance." Alas, even as Paris was about to be liberated, Barbie hurriedly filled up one last train with victims destined for the concentration camps, a train that the Resistance vainly sought to derail or otherwise prevent from reaching its destination. That train that left Lyon on August 11 included more than 600 prisoners, Jews and resistance fighters, who had been held at the sinister fort of Montluc. Decades later I learned that my beloved Papa had been among them....

Meanwhile in Chozeau I felt forlorn, cut off from contact with Papa and with Pierre. I relieved my anguish by indulging my penchant for escapism. Whenever there were no chores to do at the farm I went on long walks, letting curiosity lead me to explore villages in different directions. I walked alone, seemingly unaware of possible danger until, one afternoon, following a riverbank in the vicinity of Chozeau, I came upon three yokels, who stared and jeered at me, since I clearly did not look like a local boy. They then set upon giving me a real fright. One of them betted that I was a little Jew and the others echoed his bet by proposing to pull down my shorts and find out. "Déculottage," as this practice was known, was no mere harmless invasion of privacy and infliction of humiliation. In a country where only Jewish males were circumcised, this could spell death. In any event, I outran my pursuers, or else they gave up the chase.

Then, slowly, almost imperceptibly, hope germinated in my heart, as rumours spread that the Allied forces were approaching our area. I heard Mémé Réboz shout in patois to one of the neighbours that the Americans were in Grenoble! One late August mid-morning, as we children were loitering in the farmyard, one of the adults peered over the stone wall and excitedly shouted to all to come and see. From the haze-enveloped horizon in which lay Crémieu, a dense cloud of dust slowly surged toward our village until in the midst of it we gradually made out the turrets and guns of a column of tanks moving along the road. We were seized with terror. Suddenly, one adult shouted, "Those tanks are not German! The Americans, the Americans are coming!" We all became delirious with joy.

Soon GIs made their appearance near the first houses of the village and from all sides people ran to them. As the day progressed, more and more soldiers arrived to bivouac and pitch their tents between the net-covered artillery and tanks parked in the fields. We boys wandered all over the fields gawking at those imposing soldiers, many of them uncommonly tall, who gave us chocolate bars, colourful candies and chewing gum. Their uniforms looked so smart, so unlike the dreary *feldgrau*, field grey, of the Germans! And we marvelled at what they ate: one sight that caused no end of comments was that of American soldiers devouring large round orange-coloured cheeses, each bite they took being as big as the entire pieces of cheese that we were given to eat together with chunks of bread; our custom was to bite a small morsel or even only a tiny nibble of the cheese at a time and swallow it with a mouthful of bread.

The villagers spoke no English and the GIs spoke no French, but all conversed amicably with signs and smiles. GIs wandered around the village meeting the people. Sometimes two or three soldiers would walk into the kitchen of the Réboz farm and unload from their heavy knapsacks on the table a veritable cornucopia of foods, most of them canned, which to us were strange and exotic, like pineapples in slices, peanut butter, corned beef, chewing gum, and whatnot. These they presented in exchange for fresh eggs, fresh butter, cheese and whatever else the farm could offer at the moment.

I no longer remember how long the Americans stayed in Chozeau, perhaps only a few days. They then resumed their advance on Lyon. In the wake of their departure, villagers, both adults and children, who went into the nearby woods to pick mushrooms, found themselves unexpectedly engaged in a treasure hunt for things discarded by the Americans, including such items as soiled underwear in good condition, which needed only laundering.

Lyon was liberated on September 3, 1944, following an offensive in which units of the former underground participated alongside the Free French Forces and the American army. The underground fighters had previously engaged in street combat that began in the suburb of Villeurbanne, but unlike the insurrectionary forces in Paris, did not succeed in forcing the Germans to surrender. Before they fled the city, the Germans dynamited almost all the bridges on both rivers, an act of malice and futile vandalism that did not effectively slow down the Allied advance.

As these dramatic events were unfolding I remained without news from Papa or anyone else of my family. Expecting to see them, or at least hear from them, was like a never-ending wait. Mémé Réboz, who in the early weeks of my stay at the farm seemed to have liked me, turned hostile for reasons I could not grasp. Was it because payments for my care had long ceased, I wonder? She took to mocking and humiliating me. One day, for no reason that I can remember, she grew so angry that she came at me with a whip and called me a "dirty little Jew." Dodging a lash from her whip I shouted at her, "Vieille garce" (old bitch)! Needless to say, after that row I could no longer live under her roof. Fortunately, one of her sons took me in; he and his wife and children lived in a small house at the intersection of the main road and the lane on which the farm was situated, a mere couple of hundred metres away. The daughter-in-law, whom I called Tatan Mimi, was kind and understanding and I lived with that young family for some time. I saw the old couple when I was called upon to help with the gathering of the grapes and the felling of the walnuts, both of which were enjoyable activities.

Then, one autumn day, who should appear on our doorstep but Aunt Zilly! What a joy to see a member of my family again at long last and to learn that my exile in Chozeau was over and that in a matter of hours I would be in Lyon! I anxiously inquired about Papa. Aunt Zilly explained to me that he had joined the Free French Forces at the time of the liberation and assured me that he would return to us when the war was over, which, it was anticipated, would happen soon. In the meantime I was to live with her, Uncle Paul and Ginette. Her explanations filled me with disappointment and excitement at the same time: disappointment that I would not see Papa yet, but excitement and pride at the knowledge that he now was a soldier fighting the Germans.

Alas, I would later learn otherwise.

Liberation and Change

I was so happy to be back in Lyon, liberated and reunited with family. But that joy was dimmed by the absence of Papa. I drew a measure of comfort from the knowledge that he was a soldier fighting to bring about this so fervently hoped-for day of *la fin de la guerre*, the end of the war. And I was so proud of my father, my hero! At the same time I hoped almost against hope that Mama would likewise return, even if some prescient feeling whispered to me that she was no more.

Aunt and Uncle had now moved from Lyon proper to Villeurbanne, a suburb that was in fact a city of more than 82,000 inhabitants contiguous with Lyon, with which it shared a common public transit system. The main street of Villeurbanne stands as a well-known example of that cold and insipid Art Deco architecture of the interwar period. It is lined with *gratte-ciel*, skyscrapers, as these ten- to twelve-storey-high edifices were boastfully called, and ends on a square across which stands the city hall with its ugly rectangular tower in the middle. My family rented an apartment in one of these "skyscrapers." Bright, sunny and modern, the apartment had a dining room and two or three bedrooms, and the building had an elevator. To me this seemed like the ultimate luxury! Such a contrast with the cavernous stone buildings of old Lyon.

The city, due to the recent violence, had been left a shambles, cut into three segments. A few hurriedly raised wooden bridges made it possible to cross the rivers into the downtown peninsula from the

east or the west, but these temporary bridges were not strong enough
to support the weight of streetcars, the rails of which now reached
no further than the river banks. As a result, commuters had to walk
across to catch connections. Throughout the winter, German prisoners of war were put to work rebuilding some of the stone bridges.

In October, I went back to school. The neighbourhood boys'
school was only a fifteen- to twenty-minute walk from the skyscrapers and it was a school that I enjoyed attending. I was accepted in the
first year of the *Cours moyen*, the equivalent of Grade 4. The classroom teacher, the bespectacled Monsieur Servy, was tall and austere
in appearance in his long grey lab coat, strict but not unkind. He had
a knack for teaching history in so captivating a manner that during
the mid-morning and mid-afternoon recesses, the school playground
became the theatre of a re-enactment of the Napoleonic Wars. But the
boys who took on the names of Napoleon's marshals were rather too
many and our childish version of the *Grande Armée* was one of "more
chiefs than Indians." One dominant boy, however, was acknowledged
by all to be the emperor. He assigned and alternated the roles that we
were to play: to be this or that marshal, or better yet, to be English,
Prussians, Austrians or Russians, lest there be no rivals to battle. And
the fighting at times could turn rough. Taller boys became horses
with smaller boys on their backs or shoulders. These pairs then raced
at similarly mounted enemies and grappled with them. I still see myself riding the shoulders of a classmate running at and then wrestling
with one of the "enemy" mounts, until one of us was unseated. I have
no recollection of anyone suffering real injury falling down. Monsieur Servy saw to that in any case; he kept a watchful, amused eye
and amiably answered questions put to him in regard to details of the
battles that had convulsed Europe a century and a half before.

Though I now went under my real surname again, I encountered
no manifestation of antisemitism in that school. In the eyes of my
classmates I was a Belgian boy and some called me jokingly *chou de
Bruxelles*, Brussels sprout. They were mildly curious about me and

sometimes asked questions about the country from where I had migrated into France. I was in any case not the only "ethnic" specimen in the school — there were a few other Jewish boys and a number of Armenians. I once had a run-in with some Armenian boys on our skyscraper-lined street; one of them hit me with a piece of metal on the elbow and I ran away from that gang in pain. When Aunt Zilly discovered the bloodied bruise on my arm she scolded me for playing with Armenians, claiming that they were *voyous*, hoodlums. I did not accept that generalization, since one of my friends in class was a very gentle Armenian. The relationship between Jews and Armenians in Lyon seems to me in retrospect to have been on the whole one of mutual sympathy between two peoples who suffered genocide and poured by the thousands as refugees into France. Uncle Paul, who made his living by selling clothes at street markets and in later years owned a small clothing store, usually gave priority to Armenian wholesalers if there was any merchandise he could not obtain from Jewish wholesalers.

After the Liberation, for the first time in my life, I became involved in Jewish social activities. One warm autumn day, Pierre Meyer and his mother took me along on a train excursion organized by the communist Union de la jeunesse juive (UJJ, Union of Jewish Youth). To my surprise, the site of the picnic was a meadow outside the town of Crémieu. The food brought by the many participants was put together and shared in one common meal. There was singing and games, and a happy afternoon was had by all. In the wake of that picnic I was encouraged to participate in the *patronage* activities organized by the UJJ for children in its locale of the Croix-Rousse.

I should clarify that the several meanings of the word *patronage* do not always overlap in French and in English. The word *patron* in French means "boss," "employer," and also "pattern," while *patronage*, in addition to indicating honorary sponsors of an event, refers to a drop-in centre where recreational activities are organized for children. Since in France in those days there was no school on Thursdays, churches held catechism classes, while secular Jewish organizations established *patronages* to occupy schoolchildren in the afternoon (and sometimes Sundays as well) with activities such as group games; Yiddish or Hebrew lessons; learning songs in Yiddish, Hebrew and French; storytelling; talks on subjects of interest; artwork or handicrafts; and cultural outings and picnics. Orthodox Jews educated their children in Jewish "free schools," in which Thursday was a regular school day and students were released for the Sabbath. In Jewish schools Hebrew and Jewish subjects were taught in addition to the state-prescribed curriculum.

Unlike Pierre, I did not find the *patronage* of the communist UJJ attractive and instead became a regular member of the *patronage* of the socialist Arbeter Ring, Workman's Circle, located in a building on the Place des Terreaux, diagonally across from Lyon's city hall. The walls of the room were attractively decorated, and a banner posted on one of them proclaimed "Le socialisme vaincra!" (Socialism shall triumph!) I became a regular of the *patronage* of the Arbeter Ring, which was directed by a very dynamic and warm-hearted woman. We played games or sat in circles listening to talks, readings or narrations, holding discussions and singing Yiddish songs. I found the activities of that *patronage* so stimulating and culturally enriching that each week I looked forward with excited anticipation to Thursday afternoon and persuaded one of my Jewish friends at school to come along, an initiative for which his mother thanked me profusely.

My other source of delight at the time was the cinema. In the age before television, cinema was the common passion of children and adults, a passion most people could afford to enjoy only once a week. I saved every penny of the pocket money I obtained from my aunt and uncle to treat myself, usually on a Sunday afternoon, to a cinema program, which I went to with one or more school friends. American films ruled the screens and excited us to no end, particularly the hilarious Laurel and Hardy movies, the classics of Charlie Chaplin (nicknamed Charlot), and Westerns, *les films de cowboys*, as they were known to us. No other films could attract boys of my age. At the time, cinemas used to change their programs once a week and a common reaction of boys, upon discovering that the subject of the film playing in a particular cinema that week was love, was to shrug and sneer contemptuously, "Bah, c'est de l'amour!" (It's love!) Sometimes my aunt and uncle took me along with Ginette to a cinema for an evening show that featured the wonderful child actress Shirley Temple, then at the height of her popularity.

But the months following the Liberation were not altogether carefree. The winter of 1944–1945 was exceptionally harsh: it snowed heavily and ice floated down the Rhône. Clutching the money and ration cards entrusted to me by Aunt Zilly, I would go on Thursday mornings to procure bread. The queues in front of the bakeries were often long and it even happened that when my turn came there was no bread left, in which case I had to walk or run to another bakery, and another, and stand in line again and again. Ordered to save money, I was rarely allowed to ride the streetcars. On at least one occasion I walked several kilometres in search of bread. I had become accustomed to walking great distances and the fact of not having clothing that was adequate for the winter toughened me for life, I think. There were shortages of everything and Aunt Zilly and Ginette did their share of standing in queues to obtain necessities. News of the setbacks suffered by the Allies in the Battle of the Bulge in the Ardennes and in Holland snuffed out hopes for an early end of the war. That unanticipated delay caused the Allies heavy losses, while thousands more victims, my father among them, perished in the Nazi camps.

I intensely yearned for the return of my male cousins Jacqui and Freddy from Switzerland, but that return was, to my chagrin, constantly deferred. Then, one Thursday afternoon, the lady who ran the Arbeter Ring *patronage* informed me that my cousins were in a group whose return was announced for the end of that week. I excitedly brought the news back home with me and we were all thrilled. But our expectation was fulfilled only by half: Freddy returned from

Switzerland alone; Jacqui was recovering from a ski accident and was not to return until much later. I was disappointed but nevertheless delighted to have the companionship of Freddy, two years my senior, who teased me and played with me as with a little brother.

Unfortunately, by the time Jacqui was about to return, I had to go. Uncle Paul and Aunt Zilly had three children of their own and found it difficult to care for me as well. They sent me to a colony recently opened by the Zionist organization Dror or L'œuvre de protection des enfants juifs (OPEJ) in the town of Bourg-d'Oisans in the foothills of the Alps, about fifty kilometres northeast of Grenoble. A gentle young Italian lady who was a counsellor in that home met me and a few others in Grenoble, from where we journeyed for hours to Bourg-d'Oisans in a rickety old train, which was so slow and made so many stops that it seemed like one could almost follow it on foot.

Bourg-d'Oisans was a fairly attractive mountain town set against a distant background of snow-capped peaks. The colony numbered some thirty or forty boys and girls chaperoned by a director and two or three counsellors. It occupied a small hotel situated on the main street and managed by its owners. The children attended the local public school and received, in addition, a vigorous Zionist education that included a smattering of Hebrew in order to prepare us for aliyah, immigration to Palestine, then still under the British Mandate. In addition to "Hatikvah," the future national anthem of Israel, we learned pioneering songs, one of which proclaimed, "Nous irons en Érets et nous bâtirons, en Érets, en Érets, en Érets Israël" (We shall go to the Land of Israel and build).

In the spring of 1945, with the approach of Passover, a rabbi visited the home in order to teach a few boys, whom he judged apt and eager to learn quickly, enough Hebrew to enable us to read passages from the Haggadah. I was one of them, but unfortunately, we received only two or three lessons and then the rabbi came no more. My knowledge of the divine tongue dwindled thereafter to only a few letters, a few words and the present tense conjugation of the verb *shamar*, to guard, watch over or keep. It was not until thirty-five years later, during a sabbatical leave from the University of British Columbia in Vancouver, a leave during which I spent several months as a visiting scholar at the Truman Institute of the Hebrew University of Jerusalem, that I undertook a systematic, intensive study of Hebrew at the *ulpan* of the School for Overseas Students.

My initial feelings about the Dror colony were favourable, thanks to the leadership of a dynamic and lovely young couple named Aryeh and Roujka. Unfortunately, very soon after my arrival, they made aliyah to Palestine and after their departure the atmosphere in the home deteriorated. The new director, whom we called Jacques, was a strict disciplinarian and not at all engaging, while the two young lady counsellors, one Italian, the other Dutch, were so gentle and kind that, unless Jacques stepped in with harsh punishment, they were taken advantage of, especially by the rough Algerian Jewish boys from Lyon's industrial suburbs of Saint-Fons and Vénissieux.

These Algerian Jews were in the majority, at least among the boys. Though not all of them were of violent temper, there was a chasm between them and us, the small number of Ashkenazim who had been torn from our parents and were particularly sensitive to any mark of brutality. Lording over the Algerian boys were two or three big fellows who were truly intimidating and violent. They acted like chieftains and sometimes marshalled their small troops of hangers-on on the sidewalk in front of the hotel. The worst among them was a fourteen-year-old tough named Isaac, who ruled with his fists and was not above threatening others with a switchblade knife. Whenever they did not want us, the Ashkenazim, to understand, the Algerians conversed in their Maghrebian Arabic dialect.

It sometimes happened that US army trucks loaded with supplies rode through the town, usually after dark. Isaac and his like waited in hiding for the last truck to pass in front of the hotel and then ran and jumped into the back of it. With incredible speed and without anyone noticing, they pushed crates of canned foods out of the truck and onto the pavement. These they managed to gather up and hide in their rooms, where they stored equipment to open the cans and cook up a hasty meal, which they shared with hurriedly contacted others, boys or girls, sometimes in the middle of the night. I reckon that, notwithstanding the antagonism between Algerians and Ashkenazim, peer solidarity included all children where food was concerned. The most reprehensible form of punishment that Jacques inflicted was to send children to their room without dinner, or even without food altogether for a day. When anyone was thus punished, his origin became inconsequential: whispers went quietly around the dining room during mealtime, and even though we sat around several tables, pieces of bread and other bits of food passed from hand to hand and whatever was collected under the tables was then discreetly taken upstairs to the culprit's room.

The village school of Bourg-d'Oisans was not one that I attended with pleasure. Antisemitism hung in the air, and neither children nor teachers held us in high regard. Isaac and his group were anything but studious, which did not improve matters. We indulged in the misdemeanour of missing school fairly frequently, offering excuses to the teachers that ranged from feeling unwell to not having shoes. Curiously enough, it seems that no teacher ever contested these excuses or required a written justification from our director. On sunny days the mountains beckoned and I vividly remember a many-kilometre hike I indulged in one beautiful afternoon with three or four others up the nearby Alpe d'Huez, and how careful we were not to be seen by either teacher or counsellor when we walked back to the hotel just before suppertime.

Perhaps because of overcrowding in the main school building, my class was moved to a detached classroom in a very small building at one end of the village, near a path that led toward the mountains. That isolated location and the fact that we were only one small class there under the tutorship of a kind and caring woman made me like school again.

One afternoon, however, the congenial ambiance of that class-room was spoiled, after I had asked the teacher for permission to go to the toilet, which was an outhouse. Just as class was being dismissed at the end of that afternoon, a man walked in to inform the teacher that a swastika had been painted on the outhouse. The teacher then turned to me and angrily accused me of having committed that misdeed, since I was the only one in the class to have gone outside that afternoon. Deaf to my protestations, she underlined her accusation, shouting that one would never have expected that "one of those children" who had suffered from the Nazis could commit such an act. Exploding with rage at this unjust and absurd accusation, I stormed out and refused to return to school until, days later, to my amazement, the teacher walked into my bedroom and, taking me into her arms, she apologized profusely and kissed me.

Returning from school one afternoon, we saw flags hanging at half-mast and were informed that President Roosevelt had died. The town mourned the passing of the great American leader and my heart filled with deep sadness. At the time Roosevelt was to me a much revered figure; it was not until decades later that I learned of his callous indifference to the martyrdom of my people. One evening not long after Roosevelt's death, news reached Bourg-d'Oisans that Germany had capitulated and that the war in Europe was over. The town was delirious with joy, with people drinking and holding hands in long chains as they danced in and out of the cafés onto the streets until morning. Alas, that following morning the rejoicing ended rather abruptly, when news came in that the announcement of the end of the war had been premature!

About a week after this mishap, on May 8, a new report arrived that the German high command had signed the act of surrender the night before. The reaction to this new report was understandably cautious: many remained skeptical until the afternoon when the entire population was called upon to gather in front of the city hall in order to hear a broadcast over the public address system of General

Charles de Gaulle's victory speech to the nation! Such was the relief and joy felt by everybody that it defies description.

With peace returned, at long last it seemed that one could finally look forward to the future. Looking to the future for me, as for so many Jewish children who had survived the greatest calamity in the tragedy-filled history of our people, meant asking ourselves whether and when our missing parents would return and whether we would be blessed with family life again. In the days and weeks after the end of the war, those of us in the Bourg-d'Oisans home whose parents were absent began our anxiety-filled wait. Daily I hung around the little railway station after school hours, sometimes alone, sometimes with others, scrutinizing the passengers who came off the afternoon train from Grenoble in the vain hope that Papa might turn up among them. I had, after all, been assured by Uncle Paul and Aunt Zilly that he would return a victorious soldier after the war. But about Mama's possible fate I heard nothing but rumours, mostly of a frightening nature.

I no longer remember whether it was before or after the end of the war that we, the children of the Dror home, were taken by train to a meeting at the office of the Jewish community in Grenoble. There we listened to speeches and watched the director raise a toast to the health of us children. The meeting over, the doors of neighbouring rooms were opened and all present were invited to view what was perhaps the first photographic exhibition on the Shoah held in Grenoble. I felt my head spinning with shock and disbelief as I stared at the photographs of emaciated, skeletal-looking *déportés*, deportees, in striped uniforms; of heaps of corpses stacked like cordwood; and of the gas chambers and crematoria, in which millions were burnt to ashes. Suddenly, in the crowd that milled around me a woman uttered a chilling cry and fainted. We were hurried out of the exhibition rooms and were told that the woman had recognized in one of the photographs of the dead a member of her own family.

Such was my first confrontation with the unbelievably atrocious reality of the Shoah, and it left me dazed, speechless. The mind-numbing photos that I had stared at and what I found out from them that afternoon, and much more afterwards, about mass murder by asphyxiation and cremation in places whose very names — Auschwitz, Buchenwald, Dachau, Treblinka, Majdanek, Sobibór, Bełžec, Chełmno, to mention only a few — bespoke the ultimate in horror. They so shook me that visions of them haunted my musings by day and my sleep at night. "Is that what happened to Mama?" was the dreaded question that gnawed at me as doubts mounted that I would ever see her again.

The French Jewish author Rabi wrote in his book *Anatomie du judaïsme français* that "liberation was not for us a day of joy. We searched for traces of survivors and we counted the dead. Liberation was not for us a day of joy: it was the day of truth. Yes, the death camps did exist, yes, the gas chambers did exist. All that was true." How true, alas…. While the French nation rejoiced without reservation, our minds filled with anguished questions about those who were absent. Children coming out of hiding were waiting for their parents and wondering whether they would see them again. Parents were searching for their children. Some Catholic institutions lied to parents who came to inquire and denied harbouring their children, whom they had converted and moved to other places. Altogether 11,450 Jewish children of France had perished; seven thousand survived in hiding without their parents.

During the summer our Dror colony moved out of the small hotel in Bourg-d'Oisans, where I had written that single-page first attempt at an autobiography alluded to in the first chapter of this memoir. After a brief stay in temporary quarters in Grenoble we settled into a new abode in the village of Cessieu near the town of La Tour-du-Pin, still in the department of Isère. About the cause of the move I can only surmise that the owners of the hotel in Bourg-d'Oisans ordered us out as a consequence of the rowdy behaviour and damage to property caused by the likes of Isaac, or that OPEJ had acquired ownership of a property. Nonetheless, in Cessieu we enjoyed more space and freedom and had a congenial director. We lived in a large country house with a garden in the back, bound by a narrow river with a small island in its midst. It being summer, we enjoyed games in the garden, country hikes and outings to the public swimming pool in La Tour-du-Pin.

One morning as I sat in my room absorbed in my favourite pastime, copying maps of various countries from an atlas, I heard my name being called from outside. Who should I see when I looked out the window but Aunt Zilly and Aunt Fella standing in the garden! My aunts scolded me for sitting in my room on a beautiful sunny morning when other children were playing outdoors. I had not seen Aunt Zilly since I left Lyon at the beginning of the year, and Aunt Fella since I lived with her in Limoges. My aunts had come for me and it was with great joy that I prepared to return with them to Lyon. I suspect that Aunt Zilly was probably not elated to care for me again. She questioned me at length but could not comprehend why I was not happy to live in a community of children that was, after all, Jewish, not Christian.

By then Uncle Paul and Aunt Zilly had moved from Villeurbanne back into the centre of Lyon, into an apartment situated on the fifth floor of an old stone building at 13 Rue des Augustins, a mere few hundred metres from the Place des Terreaux. We were rather cramped in that apartment, where I had to share a bed with my cousin Jacqui. One afternoon I went with Aunt and Uncle to the Parc de la Tête-d'Or to a rally presided over by Maurice Thorez, the secretary-general of the French Communist Party, recently returned from his wartime refuge in the Soviet Union.

One memory that intrigues me to this day was the presence in Lyon of a detachment of Soviet soldiers. I sometimes passed small groups of them in the streets and called to them in the first word of Russian that I learned, "Zdravstvuyte" (greetings)! What puzzles me is that nobody — neither cousins, nor acquaintances, nor even a historian of Lyon, whom I queried in recent years — could clarify for me the reason for the presence of Soviet soldiers in Lyon in 1945. My aunt and uncle passed away more than thirty years ago and I wish that I had asked them about this matter, since I clearly remember them hosting three of these soldiers for supper one evening in the dining room of the apartment on Rue des Augustins. One of the soldiers told us that his home was in Dniepropetrovsk, a name which neither of my cousins could pronounce, but I could. He was probably Ukrainian, and he understood Aunt Zilly's broken Polish.

This time my stay with the family was brief, as my life was about to take a new and truly major turn. One morning in July, Aunt Zilly took me to the seat of the Union des juifs pour la résistance et l'entraide (Jewish Resistance and Mutual Aid Union). Founded in 1943 in the underground, the UJRE had emerged out of the Jewish section of the MOI; it was led by seasoned communists, who drew Jews of diverse orientations under their umbrella. After the liberation of Lyon, the local branch of the UJRE established its offices in the building that had housed the German consulate! Of the social services run by the UJRE the most important was the Commission centrale de l'enfance (CCE), the Central Commission for Children, which grew out of the special underground committee that had busied itself with the hiding of Jewish children during the occupation and now strove to retrieve these children in order to reunite them with surviving relatives or adopt them if they were orphaned. For the latter purpose the CCE acquired properties in which it founded group homes. The director of the CCE in Lyon was Sophie Micnik, who at the time went by the name Sophie Schwartz. Sophie had distinguished herself under the occupation as one of the founding leaders of the MOI Jewish communist resistance movement in Paris and in Lyon. Her activities included the operation of secret printing shops for the dissemination of leaflets and the underground press, in addition to the hiding of Jewish children among gentile families or Catholic and Protestant institutions.

On the morning that Aunt Zilly took me to the office of the CCE, we were received by Sophie herself. What immediately struck me about this lady was the radiance of her presence, which readily inspired trust. She spoke to me with such warmth and affection that any misgivings I might have felt about being sent to a children's colony again were soon overcome. Little could I have anticipated on that auspicious morning that before long she would become simply "Sophie" for me and that a lifelong bond would grow between us. The matter was readily settled between my aunt and Sophie: I was adopted by the CCE and would be sent to the first children's home it operated in Montreuil, a suburb of Paris. But, first, my head had to be shaved because of lice, a rather common plague at the time. Alas, that was when I lost the red hair that I'd inherited from my mother; when it grew back its colour had changed to light brown. A day or two after the first interview I was brought back to Sophie's office and was met there by a kind and cordial man named Marcel Baruch, a Romanian Jew who eventually became Sophie's companion. Marcel took me to his home to spend the rest of the day with his wife and young son, Simon, who was destined to become, many years later, a journalist associated with the irreverently satirical weekly *Le Canard Enchaîné*. After supper I was introduced to Dr. Joseph Minc, the general-secretary of the UJRE, just as he arrived to take me with him on the night train to Paris.

To Paris and Beyond

I was filled with excitement at the prospect of going to live in Paris, the city of my dreams. Dr. Joseph Minc was travelling to the capital to assume the post of secretary-general of the CCE, in which capacity he was to supervise the acquisition of homes for the children adopted by the organization. Dr. Minc, a veteran of the Resistance, was a dentist by profession and father of the future well-known public intellectual Alain Minc; he died in 2010 at the age of 103.

The train on which Dr. Minc rode with me did not reach Paris until mid-morning. Because of the difficulties of the immediate post-war period, among them shortages of coal, trains travelled slowly and made many stops. Apart from a few streets glimpsed from the window when the train glided into the Gare de Lyon, one of the several immense railway stations connecting the capital with the different regions of France and Europe, my introduction to Paris began below ground with a ride on the famed metro to the end of one of its many lines: the station Mairie de Montreuil. The elegant city hall of Montreuil, a suburb of Paris, was the first building that came into view when Dr. Minc and I emerged from the underground into the light of day. From the square in front of that *mairie*, city hall, we walked up two intersecting sloping streets until, after fifteen or twenty minutes, we reached the portal of a house on Rue Dombasle: that was the first "children's home" opened by the CCE to shelter orphans of the Shoah.

Maisons d'enfants, children's houses, was what the CCE chose to call its institutions, in place of the conventional name of *orphelinats*, orphanages, a name that once conveyed sad images of cold halls and dormitories, rigid discipline, uniforms, adults whom one addressed formally, and so on. The generous intent of the directors and educators of the CCE was to give traumatized children who had survived the Shoah a progressive education in an extended family-like environment, a warm home-like milieu. Indeed, the *maisons* were also called *foyers d'enfants*, children's shelters, and even *homes d'enfants*, children's homes. Since these homes were destined for children whose parents had either been deported to the death camps or shot as heroes of the Resistance or as hostages, the full official designation given them was Maisons d'enfants de déportés et fusillés (houses for the children of the deported and shot).

The children's home of Montreuil was installed in a typical *pavillon de banlieue*, a suburban house or villa with a garden, fenced off from the street and neighbouring properties by a stone wall with a wrought-iron portal through which one stepped into an inner yard. The entrance to the house fronted that yard, and if one walked past the façade one reached a large *jardin potager*, a vegetable garden with a few fruit trees. At the time of my arrival, this three-storey house accommodated about twenty children. A couple of years later it became the CCE's *maison des jeunes* or youth home — that is, a home for working boys in their late teens or early twenties.

I was warmly welcomed by the woman in charge and introduced to the other children as their new companion. I soon began to feel at home, a feeling I had never experienced in a community of children before. We played in the yard, shared chores or puttered in the garden. On market days some of us accompanied our house mother, or *monitrice*, to the square in front of the *mairie*. It was on one such market day, in August 1945, that my attention was unexpectedly drawn to photographs of a mushroom-shaped column of smoke and sensational headlines in the newspapers on display — the city of Hiroshima had been destroyed by a new and most terrifying weapon: the atom bomb. Three days later, the same fate befell Nagasaki.

Japan had finally been brought to its knees by America's might, and it was in that hour of its debacle that the Soviet Union violated a treaty of non-aggression signed in 1940 and entered the war against it. Marshal Malinovsky's troops raped and plundered their way down Manchuria and claimed the northern half of Korea for a prize. But in August 1945 what mattered was that World War II was at long last over, that the world had been delivered from the scourge of fascism. Few in those heady days were aware that another totalitarian tyranny cast its ominous shadow over the world: that of communism. As children who were being brought up in the communist ideology by adults whom we respected and loved, we looked to the Soviet Union as a kind of paradise on Earth and the harbinger of a new dawn for mankind.

It was in those final days of the war in East Asia that several of us children from Montreuil were attached to a large convoy of mostly non-Jewish Parisian children for a night-long train ride to the Landes, a wooded region of southwestern France. In mid-morning on a luminous sunny day the train rolled into the resort town of Mimizan-Plage and the deep blue infinite expanse of the Atlantic Ocean came into view. Oh, what a thrill that was! I had never before in my life beheld such a seemingly limitless expanse of water. And so blue, blue, blue….

It was an unforgettable summer. I spent over a month in the Colonie du Pylône. The colony consisted of two or three wooden houses standing near the edge of a vast expanse of sand dunes. I vaguely recall that there was a pylon in the vicinity, which explains the colony's name. We daily walked to the astonishingly wide sandy beaches, following marked trails through the dunes. We were not allowed to step aside for even one foot from these trails, as the dunes still hid land mines placed there by the Germans. Ironically perhaps, German prisoners of war were being employed to uncover and detonate the mines. Every now and then we heard the sounds of distant explosions and became so used to them that we scarcely paid attention. We were, however, asked not to mention the mines in our letters. One child broke that rule, writing excitedly that we frequently heard the sound of exploding mines. His family did not take that information lightly and wrote to the director of the colony, demanding that the child be sent home to Paris immediately or they would travel down to fetch him. As a consequence of that indiscretion, our letters from then on were censored.

The arrival of the postman bearing letters and parcels, usually around lunch time, was always a suspense-loaded moment of the day. The word *colis*, parcel, was on every child's mind; for me and others who had no parents, it was painful to watch the joy of those who received parcels containing sweets, chocolates, cakes and other delicacies from home. Some children received one parcel, or even more, every week. One girl in particular received a parcel almost daily and when one day she received two, Monsieur Daniel decided to act and wrote to her family demanding that they desist from thus spoiling their children, who were already fed adequately by the colony. For me even receiving a letter was a rare joy; I did, however, once receive a parcel from Pierre Meyer's mother, Irma.

Apart from our daily wanderings off to the immense sandy beaches where we bathed and frolicked in the sun, we partook of activities such as picnics, walks in the town of Mimizan, sightseeing excursions in the region and long hikes in the nearby pine forests — those immense, fragrant pine forests of the Landes, famed for the rich resin extracted from their trees. There was no undergrowth: the trees grew out of the sand and attached to them were small clay pots for collecting the resin. One day we visited a nearby paper mill. We marched to the rousing rhythms and words of scouting songs; my favourite one, a song that I sing to myself on my walks to this day, began with the wake-up call, "Le ciel est bleu, réveille-toi, c'est un jour nouveau qui commence…"(The sky is blue, wake up, a new day is beginning…). The lyrics of that song then proclaim how lovely it is to be our age (ten, twelve or whatever), to walk through the villages and behold the beauty of all the regions of France in all the seasons. There was also a song about the colony; its refrain began with the words "Pylôni, Pylônia, Pylôni-lôni-lônia!"

Once a week the girls were charged with the task of washing the hair of the boys. Several of them would then compete as to which one would have the pleasure of washing my hair, which, since my head was shaven, had not yet grown back!

Next door to the colony, mere steps away from the house in which we took our meals, was a barbed wire fence, behind which German prisoners of war were held. They looked like a rather dejected lot and the director and the counsellors strictly forbade us from going near that fence and staring or shouting at the prisoners, something we itched to do! Monsieur Daniel, a Pole, was a strict disciplinarian and his very appearance inspired fear. When he was displeased, he loudly raised his voice but rarely his hand. Early in the term he encouraged all children to get a suntan and promised that the child with the best tan at the end of the summer would be rewarded by being taken to an ice cream parlour in Mimizan. Eating an ice cream was a rare indulgence at that time; the mere prospect of being treated to one made our mouths water! I consequently applied myself to bathing alternatively in the ocean and in the sun with such determination that on the day of the competition I was one of the few selected to stand in a row to face the director. Next to me stood a girl with a much darker tan; Monsieur Daniel ruled her out immediately for the sake of fairness, because she was native of Morocco and he judged her tan to be "un-European." Next, he looked at me and observed that my tan was so much darker than the ones sported by the two or three others selected for the competition, that in "fairness" to them he ruled me *hors concours*, disqualified! I was so angry, so upset by such brazen injustice, that I cried and barely held myself from cursing him.

In September I was back in Paris and Montreuil, but not for long, for the children of the small home on rue Dombasle were now directed to a considerably larger and truly fabulous haven: the manoir de Denouval in Andrésy. That manor was the crown jewel of the CCE network, which comprised five children's homes in the vicinity of Paris, one in Aix-les-Bains in the Alps and one at Sainte-Maxime on the French Riviera. But, prior to the transfer, I had to be seen at the seat of the CCE, then situated at 120 rue Vieille-du-Temple. There I met two sisters who were destined to become my companions in Andrésy: Marguerite and Henriette Élias. The sisters were accompanied by their mother; at the time the CCE accepted also children who had lost "only" one parent in the Shoah, and Marguerite and Henriette had tragically lost their adored father. In her delightful book, *Cachée* (*In Hiding*), which she illustrated herself, Marguerite recalls that I politely introduced myself to them, asked for their names and said to them when I left, "à notre prochaine réunion!" (Until we meet again!)

And so, one sunny autumn afternoon I was in the first group of children to be settled in that *manoir enchanté*, enchanted manor, as some had already baptized it. The small town of Andrésy, situated about forty kilometres west of Paris in the then department of Seine-et-Oise (now Yvelines), stretched for about three kilometres along the river Seine. A short distance away from the southern end of the town, a country road gently ascended to the portal of the manor. An immense park surrounded the manor and on the east side of it, the grounds sloped all the way down to the banks of the Seine. The setting was a dream-like one: elegant alleys meandered between vast lawns, flower beds and groves to the crescent-shaped front steps of the manor, to outbuildings scattered around the grounds, to sport fields and to a water tower. Also, there was a fountain and there were places where one could seek solitude. The property had been purchased in 1904 by Sarah Hershey Marsh, a prominent member of the American community in Paris; she hired one of France's leading architects to design and build the grand manor destined to become her residence. The most striking feature of the manor was its slender turret with glass panes in its upper part, which provided a wide-ranging panoramic view of the region. Unfortunately, Ms. Marsh did not get to enjoy her residence for long; she died in 1911 and was buried in a secluded part of the grounds. During the war the property was requisitioned by the Wehrmacht and for a time occupied by Field Marshal Rommel.

As far as I know, the CCE purchased the property after the war with funds from various sources, notably the American left-wing trade union Jewish People's Fraternal Order, the South African Jewish community, and the world-famous painter Marc Chagall, who, I heard, made a substantial donation. In the summer immediately preceding its opening as a children's home, the manor served as a vacation camp for the Cadets, the youth organization operated by the UJRE in Paris; it seems that it was they who baptized it *le manoir enchanté*. I believe that the funds for the upkeep of the children in the CCE homes came in large part from the American Jewish aid organization the Joint, the Jewish business community of Paris and the French government's Ministry of Veterans and Victims of the War.

For us, the more than one hundred children housed in the manor in the autumn of 1945, it was a place of enchantment indeed. The front steps led up to the lobby, from where one entered the awe-inspiring central hall with its eight-metre-high glass ceiling, an organ and glass doors that opened to a wide veranda overhanging the grassy slope that descended to the river Seine. It was in that hall that we held our gatherings, notably the Saturday evening *veillées*, vigils. The way the week was structured in French schools, with Thursday being the day off other than Sunday, we could not observe the Jewish Sabbath. To the CCE this must have mattered little, since it was a secular communist organization.

On Saturdays we returned from school as usual between four and five o'clock in the afternoon, ate the traditional after-school *goûter*, a snack consisting of bread and butter, sometimes biscuits, and a cup of hot chocolate, and then headed downstairs to the basement, boys and girls in separate groups, for our weekly shower. Then we lined up in front of a counter, behind which the washer women handed each one of us a pile of clean clothing for the new week, each item in the pile bearing our individual identification number sewn on it; mine was, as at Les Besses, number 36! As soon as we got into our clean clothes we rushed to the dining room in a mood of mounting excitement at the thought of the *veillée*, the evening gathering that was to follow the supper.

After dinner, we moved the stools and benches to the great hall, where we placed them in a wide circle for an evening of happy and creative entertainment consisting of games, sing-a-longs, reading, storytelling and play acting. Perhaps our most uproarious game was the one in which one child volunteered to walk on all fours around the inside of the circle in which we sat, stopping at random to mew pitifully like a pussycat at the feet of others, who had to respond by patting him or her on the head and saying "pauvre petit chat" (poor little kitty) without laughing! If the child in front of whom the "cat" mewed laughed, it would then be his or her turn to go down on all fours and become the pussycat. All too soon bedtime beckoned, at which point the counsellors, or *moniteurs* as they were called, led us in singing calming songs, among them one that began with the words, "C'est la nuit: tout s'éteint sur la plaine, la montagne, la forêt…la paix vient." (Night has come: light wanes over the plain, the mountain, the forest…peace descends). We were then asked to quietly climb up the stairs that led to the bedrooms on the upper floors.

We were over a hundred boys and girls ranging in age from pre-schoolers to fourteen- or fifteen-year-olds, and were organized into four groups in order of age, each with a name and its own *moniteur* or *monitrice*. I belonged to the third group, that of the ten- to twelve-year-olds, which adopted the name "Avenir" (future). The chief *moniteurs* of the home were Henri Goldberg, a young Alsatian Jew whom everybody called "Heini," and his future wife, Hanka, a native of Warsaw. Those two were a most dynamic duo. Heini was an excellent educator, very imaginative and gifted, a good musician who played the flute and led us in choral singing; he also programmed the *veillées*.

The other principal *moniteurs* were Lazare Warszawski, his wife, Simone, and Mathilde Seibald. All were young, in their twenties. Lazare, who was in charge of the fourth group (the oldest children), was an ardent sportsman who vigorously enticed all to the playing fields to practise soccer, basketball and volleyball. I did not enjoy sports and dodged these games as best I could, by hiding if necessary. Lazare rarely succeeded in luring me to the sports fields. I was hopeless at catching or throwing a ball; other boys mocked me for my clumsiness and I would leave the field in tears. Simone had charge of the second age group, and Mathilde of the first group, the little ones.

Mathilde was the only professional pedagogue. She had, before the war, worked as a young intern under the direction of Janusz Korczak in one of the two orphanages that this world-famous progressive pedagogue and author of books for children ran in Warsaw. In 1942, Christian friends offered Dr. Korczak an opportunity to save himself, but he chose instead to travel with the children of the Warsaw ghetto orphanage under his care to the death camp of Treblinka in order to comfort them in the atrocious last moments of their lives. The other educators of the CCE were characterized by Katy Hazan, author of a major study of the postwar Jewish children's homes, as "always devoted and generous, but more militants than pedagogues...."

There were also temporary counsellors who did not seem to be charged with responsibility. One of them was a tall, handsome and wonderfully friendly young Bulgarian named Arnold Araf. I remember him walking from table to table during mealtimes to chat and amaze us with skilful feats, such as tossing an empty bowl up into the air and then, slipping his hands in and out of his pockets, catching the bowl as it came down. It may have been at Arnold's suggestion that one of the novels I read at the time was about an adolescent boy in a

French provincial boarding school who becomes attached to one of his professors, an exiled Bulgarian prince named Ivan Nikolov. Having also read some works of Alexander Pushkin, I very much wanted to learn Russian, but there was no one around who knew that language, except for Boris, nicknamed "Shuster," an endearing dwarfish and crude cobbler, who taught me juicy Russian swear words. Arnold offered to teach me Bulgarian, which is related to Russian and written with the same Cyrillic alphabet, but I was not keen on that language and gave up after a few lessons. For reasons that I never discovered (possibly an "illicit" relationship with a *monitrice*), Arnold was dismissed and left Andrésy; this angered me and several others who loved him. We even staged a protest demonstration down the corridor in front of the director's office!

The other "counsellor-at-large" was Georges Walter, a twenty-five-year-old playwright, who in later times became an announcer on French television. The subject in which I excelled at school was French composition and my ambition was to become a writer, a goal that Georges encouraged me, twelve-year old thespian that I was, to pursue. But it was a forty-year-old woman who lived with us for several months as a resident writer who most stimulated my literary ambitions. Her pen name was Juliette Pary and she was the author of a book entitled *Mes 126 gosses* (*My 126 Kids*), about a summer colony that she operated in 1936. The book seemed to have won wide acclaim. Juliette lived in a flat above our infirmary, which was located in one of the outbuildings of the manor. She was of Russian origin and with her encouragement I undertook to write a novel about Russian revolutionaries exiled in Siberia under the tsars. Juliette secretly led me to a spacious attic, where a small writing desk stood next to a wide wooden door. That attic became my abode, known only to Juliette and me; there I hid for a couple of hours after school or on days off. As it neighboured Juliette's flat, I could readily seek her advice. She befriended me and did not seem to mind spending time conversing with me.

I was enthralled with the "enchanted manor." It nourished in me a fascination with mystery, as I explored it for hidden nooks and ventured up the narrow winding steps that led to the turret, sometimes even in the dark of night! This I did for a while with a couple of fellow conspirators. We played at stealthily placing scary yet funny anonymous messages signed with the initials "P.H.," an idea that came to us after an outing to a cinema in the nearby town of Conflans, where we watched a film entitled *P.H. contre Gestapo.* Our messages were addressed mainly to girls and we hid them where they could readily find them. One night I even crept into a room where two pig-tailed girls slept in adjacent beds. I tied the right pigtail of one to the left pigtail of the other and attached to the string a message signed P.H. And I did it without waking the girls! At breakfast the next morning I suppressed a guffaw as I listened to the two girls telling others how scared they were when they woke up.

School, naturally, occupied the major part of our days, including a two-hour break for lunch. Our arrival in Andrésy considerably augmented the population of both the boys' school and the girls' school. The schools were situated roughly two kilometres from the manor, at the other end of the village. The boys' school was located in the same building as the town hall and faced the tree-lined bank of the Seine. The girls' school was a short walk up a lane from the boys' school and the canteen was located on its grounds. That was where we headed during the lunch break. After the meal there was usually time enough left to sit in a covered part of the yard, or play among ourselves, and even with the girls, whenever any could be found who were willing.

I still see us marching to school along the main streets of Andrésy, in clusters that did not always bear a semblance of order, chattering or singing children's songs as well as, unfortunately, revolutionary communist songs that had been taught to us, such as the one entitled "Amis, frères, prolétaires de tous les pays unissez-vous!" (Friends, brothers, workers of all countries unite!) What were the adult villagers thinking, I wonder, when on that cool October first day of school, they first beheld our motley procession of children from "somewhere else," clad for the most part in the school outfits provided by the Ministry of Veterans and Victims of the War: side-buttoned blue smocks for most of the boys, pink smocks for most of the girls. How happily I looked forward now to normal, uninterrupted, schooling! Before long our twice-daily march through the town became a regular scene of its life.

There were five of us boys, "children of the manor," as people knew us, in the second year of the *Cours moyen* (which corresponds to a combination of Grades 5 and 6). Our classroom teacher, Monsieur Fraysse, was a true model of the *instituteur républicain*, a teacher who raised his charges in the cherished ideals of the French Republic, ideals rooted in the principles enunciated by the great revolution of 1789 — namely, that all men are born free and equal before the law, and that citizenship confers upon them rights but also obligations. Then and throughout his long life, Lucien Fraysse forcefully championed the inclusive secularism of the French public education system.

My friend Bernard Ebenstein was one of our little band in Lucien Fraysse's class. Nearly half a century after our year in Andrésy, Bernard and I renewed our contact and had a reunion in Limoges, a city he has served for many years as deputy mayor in charge of finances. One beautiful day in March 2005, the two of us drove down to visit Lucien Fraysse, who was living in retirement in the picturesque nearby city of Brive-la-Gaillarde. Prior to that day, I had exchanged a few letters with our old teacher and his companion, Germaine. Lucien invariably signed his letters with the words, "Vive l'école laïque!" (Long live the secular school!) We spent a delightful afternoon in their garden and were amazed at Lucien's vitality, which belied his ninety-four years. Germaine told us how he would proudly inform people that one of his favourite former pupils lived in Canada, another one in London (Bernard Masson), while yet another, Bernard Ebenstein, was deputy mayor of Limoges!

The vagaries of life in that first decade of the twenty-first century led me also to a reunion with Bernard Masson, the other just-mentioned former pupil of Lucien Fraysse and a native of Andrésy, whose brother Philippe shared a desk in class with me. Bernard and his wife, Monique, live in London, where my wife and I visited with them. In fact I owe it to both my friends named Bernard to have reconnected with our old teacher and to have found an opportunity to pay him a visit in 2005, for in the following year Lucien Fraysse passed away.

Even though I think back fondly to the only school year that I spent in Andrésy, it did not pass without some difficult moments. At the beginning we confronted a degree of antisemitism from some of the boys of the village. During recess, which we spent in the schoolyard, and when it rained or snowed in the covered area, the *préau*, we were many a time provoked into fist fights. Accepting that "boys will be boys," the teachers kept a benign yet watchful eye a short distance away, intervening only if they thought someone could get seriously hurt. I was not of a pugnacious temperament, yet I had to fight, sometimes one against two or three of the village boys, my fists flying in all directions. Having concluded that we fought well, the village boys ended up respecting us and we became the best of friends, to the extent that on some Thursdays we invited them to the manor to share our *goûter*, while some of us were even invited to their homes.

Sometime in the spring of 1946 one incident brought to light a degree of bravery that arose from our situation with the village boys. My teacher had to absent himself for a week and was replaced during that time by a swarthy little man who spoke with a strong southern accent that caused pupils to mock him behind his back. That replacement teacher seemingly knew no way to handle discipline problems other than by dealing blows. On the day of the said incident, the morning classes had just ended and we were in the yard forming ranks in preparation for marching up the hill to the girls' school for the noon-hour meal. Momentarily forgetful of the rule that we should not speak when standing in ranks, I was chatting with the boy with whom I had been paired when, unnoticed by us, the replacement teacher surged from behind and violently slapped me. My friend protested and was also slapped, upon which he broke rank and ran out the school gate, shouting that he would return with his father. Chaos broke out and the swarthy little man lost control of the situation; he retreated and, with his back pressed against a tree, faced a mob of boys circling around him shouting, "SS! Nazi! Kapo!" That evening at the manor, our *moniteur* Maurice, in a thundering voice, gave me a verbal lashing, mockingly calling me a "hero." The following Monday, Monsieur Fraysse returned and sermonized the entire class over our misconduct!

My favourite subjects at school were history, geography and French. History in elementary school meant the history of France only, and as yet no foreign languages were taught. The daily French classes consisted of dictation, reading aloud for effect, recitation of poems learned by heart, and exercises of grammar. Once a week we had to write a French composition on an assigned topic, which the teacher graded for presentation and style, spelling and wealth of vocabulary — we had to avoid repetition of nouns and adjectives and evidence ability to use synonyms, images, metaphors. At the age of twelve I had become an avid reader of novels and poetry; my favourites at the time were Russian authors, whom I read in translation. Maxim Gorky made a particularly deep impression on me. I could almost palpably make mine the pain and anguish he suffered in his orphaned childhood in Nizhny Novgorod. I loved the poetry of Victor Hugo and, later in my adolescent years, even more the impressionist poetry of Baudelaire, Verlaine and Rimbaud. Yet, the lyrical verses of Pushkin, even in translation (eventually, by the age of eighteen, I was able to read him in the Russian original) enthralled me most of all.

At the home I was nicknamed "the Poet"; that is how I am to this day remembered by companions with whom I renewed contact in recent years. Unfortunately, the poems that I wrote at the time, one of which was a ballad about a Jewish child left orphaned by the Shoah and another entitled "1946: year of hope," have all been lost, including the one or two that appeared in print in the bulletin published periodically by the cce. Otherwise I wrote articles or poems by hand for our *journal mural*, wall newspaper, of which I was, along with Georges Walter or another counsellor, one of the editors. The editorial work consisted of inviting submissions in the form of articles and drawings or paintings, correcting the articles for spelling and grammar, and having them copied in clean with margins left for illustrations. Last came the *mise en page*, the layout and pinning of that treasure trove of our creativity onto a large board affixed to a wall. We endeavoured to post a new issue every month. At one time Bernard Ebenstein and I even attempted to put out a "real" newspaper with political pieces studded with sonorous words gleaned from adults or our readings. We set up "office" in the coach house by the gate, but unable to solve the problem of printing, proceeded to imitate print in handwriting. Needless to say, we soon gave up that exercise in futility!

Thursdays and Sundays, which were free from school, were filled with extracurricular activities, including workshops and sports. There were occasional outings to the cinema in Conflans and cultural events in Paris. At the beginning of 1946, the schools took us to a sports event held in Paris's infamous Vélodrome d'Hiver (winter cycling track), or "Vél d'Hiv," as it was popularly known. The program featured a bicycle race around the oval and a "catch" wrestling match between two sumo-size champions, one of them being the popular Rigoulot.

At the time I was not aware of the horror that had filled the Vélodrome d'Hiver less than four years before. Every time I think back to that outing, anger surges at the thoughtlessness of the school principals and, what is truly reprehensible, the insensitivity of our educators, who surely knew of what had taken place there so very recently. I can find no justification for their allowing us to participate in that school outing. The decent thing to do would have been to refuse our inclusion in it, at the risk of causing us disappointment, and explain to us the reasons for their refusal.

Unfortunately, our educators misguidedly believed that we should and could turn the page without regard for the terrible past that was still so recent. Rather than allow our thoughts to dwell on the fate of our murdered parents and the six million Jewish victims, they exhorted us to draw inspiration from heroes of the French Communist Resistance such as Colonel Fabien, Gabriel Péri, Lucien Sampaix, the young Jewish fighters Marcel Rayman and Valentin Feldman, and those who had fallen in the Warsaw Ghetto Uprising. They also held up for us the examples of Soviet heroes who had died fighting the Nazis, like Zoya Kosmodemyanskaya, and Oleg Koshevoy and his Young Guard.

Thoughts of the death camps, the gas chambers, the crematoria and the ghastly tortures that the Gestapo inflicted on the heroes of the Resistance whom we revered were never far from our minds. Among the survivors of the catastrophe (which was then not yet known as the "Holocaust" or "Shoah") who arrived from Eastern Europe and spoke no French were children who, regardless of their age, had in the death camps ceased to be children. Several of these were brought to Andrésy and proved, understandably, difficult to manage. In the presence of these children, and of adult survivors, we were made to feel that we had not really suffered, or that what we had suffered simply bore no comparison to the horrors that they had miraculously survived. After all, the surroundings in which we lived in hiding in those terrible years were rural landscapes and city streets; we were not starved and beaten, and we did not gaze at the smoke of the crematoria every waking moment. In view of these facts our *moniteurs* did not want us to talk about what we had been through and felt. Indeed, our traumas at times seemed so paltry to us that we would have felt embarrassed to dwell on them. Child psychology was still in its infancy in those years and the adults who brought us up believed that we should look to the future, when the advent of socialism would supposedly free humankind from the scourge of racism and antisemitism.

Our sufferings as children who endured the Shoah in France went unrecognized, and as I grew into my adolescent years I even asked myself whether I had a right to be happy when most of my family had perished. A measure of clarification about my parents' fate, but not closure, came decades later with the discovery of the Jewish files of the police for that period and the aforementioned publication in 1978 of the *Memorial Book of the Deportation of the Jews of France*, compiled by Serge Klarsfeld. Other than that, there was nothing that could have brought us closure, no formal confirmation of the loss of those who were most precious to us, no tombstones, no ceremonies at which one wears black armbands or ribbons on the lapel of a coat. In response to queries submitted by the CCE after the war, the police pretended to have no record of my parents' presence in France.

It was not until the 1980s, when the flight of time brought my generation within sight of our senior years, that child survivors of the Shoah, among them "Hidden Children," won recognition as a distinct group bearing their own psychological burdens, different from those of survivors who had been adults at the time. One of my fellow orphans of Andrésy, Marcel Dorembus, did not live to see the coming of a time when his trauma would have been recognized and help to overcome it would have been at hand. In 1962 he wandered onto the grounds of the momentarily abandoned manor of Denouval and there committed suicide.

Notwithstanding their failings, the leaders of the CCE were caring: they visited us quite often and even shared in our activities of the moment. Sophie was a frequent visitor, as was Szmulek Farber, whose nephew was one of us. Szmulek was a tall, gaunt man, a hardened communist fighter who had been expelled by the British from Palestine in the 1930s, and had become one of the leaders of the MOI Jewish resistance in Lyon. He often accompanied delegations of visitors. If there was one word that was on everyone's lips on Sunday mornings, it was the word "delegation." We anticipated with especial excitement the coming of delegations of American Jews, whom we entertained and who brought us cakes, chocolates and whatnot. A few of the children were even adopted by American families. Our most distinguished visitor was the great painter Marc Chagall.

There was a different kind of visitor whom we all yearned, often against hope, to behold. The Hôtel Lutetia in Paris served as a reception centre for survivors returning from "deportation" and Jewish people searching for missing relatives. Every now and then, usually on a Sunday, it seemed, a stranger would make an unexpected appearance on the grounds of the manor, and that person would be someone's father or mother or other relative who had miraculously survived. One morning during school recess, I saw a tall handsome man in military uniform walk into the schoolyard. Everyone's eyes were on him as he spoke to Monsieur Fraysse, who called out "Bernard!" The soldier was Bernard Ebenstein's father, who had fought in Syria and was presumed dead! Unfortunately for Bernard, his parents were separated and never lived together again. Those of us who witnessed such tearful reunions felt happy for the child who was no longer alone in the world, but also envious and, as a result, even more desolate.

If by day, when school and other activities occupied us, we seemed to behave like normal children, such was not the case at night when, lying in bed, our longings came to haunt us. By day I was assertive and sometimes thought and acted older than my age, but that was my unconscious defence mechanism: deep down I passionately desired to be a young child, perhaps nine years old, instead of a twelve-year-old political animal. Every spectacle of a child being reunited with a parent brought me to tears as soon as the lights were turned off for the night. I cried silently until sleep overwhelmed me. Will anyone ever come for me, I mused in my anguish. I had been told that my mother had undoubtedly perished, but since Aunt Zilly and Uncle Paul had said that my father had joined the Free French Forces at the time of the liberation of Lyon, I wondered why he had not come back yet, now that months had passed since the end of the war.

I persisted nevertheless in passionately picturing in my mind scenes of reunion with my parents, of finding one or the other or, better yet, both of them waiting for me upon my return from school on a beautiful day, or suddenly appearing on a Sunday. I then pictured myself leaving the children's home holding hands with my parents and us living together again in a luminous home, perhaps in Brussels, our family augmented by the arrival of a little sister. But week followed upon week, month followed upon month as longing tore my heart apart, yet no one came for me. I clung for dear life to my dream of a reunion, even though hope grew fainter with each passing day. I did not want to mourn yet, not yet, not yet....

One afternoon upon my return from school, our director informed me that my cousin Simon Domb had visited that morning and inquired after me. I was upset that, having come in the middle of what he must have known was a school day, he had not bothered to wait for a few hours. I felt let down, and as I received no word from Simon in the days that followed, and as my expectation that surely one Sunday he would return did not materialize, I angrily wondered why he had bothered travelling to Andrésy and teased me so cruelly.

In my childhood I simply could not imagine that children reunited with one or the other of their parents could not but be happy forever after. It was not until well into my adult years that I learned that such was not always the case, that many a mother or father returned from the camps so distressed and traumatized by unendurable sufferings that he or she could no longer function as a parent and that the family that once was could not be recreated. Single mothers in particular found, as a rule, only low-pay employment. Many a parent remarried with a partner who was not congenial to the child or, worse yet, founded a new family in which there was no room for the child from a previous marriage. We who remained in the children's homes were perhaps happier than some of our companions who went on to live with surviving parents who, in some cases, kept them from continuing their studies because of material difficulties.

The sisters Marguerite and Henriette Élias, with whom I became acquainted at the headquarters of the CCE before being brought with them to Andrésy, had a difficult childhood after they left the "enchanted manor" at the end of that first school year. I was very fond of those two cherub-faced girls, who sang with such cheerful and melodic voices. Some of their songs I remember to this day. Because they were two or three years younger than me, the sisters belonged to another group, but we still sought each other out.

In the late 1980s, thanks to Mathilde Seibald, Marguerite and I found each other again in Canada. I had unfortunately not known that Marguerite had spent the year 1967 in Vancouver with her husband Abdul (Doudou), who was a visiting scholar at the University of British Columbia, where I then taught in the department of Asian studies. Thereafter Doudou was offered a position at McGill University in Montreal and the couple settled in Longueuil, a suburb on the south shore of the St. Lawrence River. Because of the distance, I see Marguerite only rarely, usually at intervals of years, but we correspond with each other like brother and sister.

Mathilde was at no time my *monitrice* in the CCE homes and therefore played no significant role in my upbringing. Yet it was thanks to her that contact was renewed between me and several of my childhood companions, with whom lifelong ties of friendship grew as a result. So radiant and luminous was Mathilde's personality, with brown eyes sparkling in her deeply lined face, that I could not imagine anyone not readily loving her. She never married and had no children of her own, yet until she breathed her last at the age of ninety she endeavoured to watch, almost like a mother, over us, "her" children: *les anciens des maisons de la* CCE, the former children of the CCE houses, as we identified ourselves. Whenever I happened to be in Paris, she was one of the very first persons whom I rushed to call and visit. In the summer of 1986 Mathilde stayed with me in Vancouver, which was then hosting a spectacular world fair.

While living in Andrésy, I occasionally spent a day or two in Paris, whenever an opportunity presented itself to travel there by train with an adult. I would then visit the Olievenstein family: Tante Leni, who was Tante Zilly's sister, her husband, Moniek, and their sons, Armand and Claude. One winter afternoon, Sophie invited me to meet her at rue de Paradis after her office hours. She wanted to take me to a bookstore on Place de la République to present me with a book of my choice. We had an adventure that evening: we were only steps away from the bookstore when in lightning succession we saw a commotion — crowds were running, shots were fired. Sophie pulled me behind a kiosk just as an individual who was being chased by police and a crowd fired in our direction! The crowd caught up with the individual and I fleetingly saw him being punched to the ground before police dragged him away. We were told that the man was a wanted Nazi collaborator.

The CCE organized events that offered occasion to collectively travel to Paris; one such event was the annual *kermesse*, a fair of sorts, at which displays informed the visiting public about the activities of the organization and solicited funds. Then there were the parades organized by the communist and socialist parties on May First, International Labour Day, and July 14, the national holiday of France, in which we marched, carrying banners and flags. I vividly remember how, on July 14, 1946, we marched in the parade from Place de la Bastille to Place de la République, where the leaders of the Communist Party sat on a reviewing stand: as we marched past, carrying a large sign identifying us as *enfants de déportés et fusillés*, Secretary-General Maurice Thorez and his deputy, Jacques Duclos, rose to applaud us. We were so proud. Georges Walter teased me afterwards, saying that I looked so solemn, carrying a banner as though it were a sacrament in a church procession.

We were excessively politicized for our ages and some of us were more susceptible to this indoctrination than others. I was, unfortunately, one of these. Once I even took the initiative of co-writing with a couple of other boys a letter to Maurice Thorez, inviting him to visit our home. Thorez wrote back most amiably, explaining that it would please him to visit us, but he could see no opportunity to do so at the moment. After mildly reproving me for not consulting him first before writing to the party secretary-general, Heini read his letter aloud to us in the great assembly hall.

One initiative that I was proud of, after it was enthusiastically accepted by our *moniteurs*, was to transform a vast lawn behind the manor into a vegetable garden. A professional gardener planted a variety of vegetables and children were encouraged to give him a hand when time permitted. Watching the plants grow, watering them and carrying some of the ready vegetables to the kitchen gave me the additional pleasure of chatting with the two Spanish cooks, Severino Leiva and Pedro. Both had fought on the side of the republic during the Spanish Civil War; the struggle against Franco was a cause dear to my heart and I fantasized that my father had briefly joined the International Brigades, which was not the case. Leiva continued as our cook in the home of Livry-Gargan, where I lived later. He was loved by all. We sometimes teased him by suddenly barging into the kitchen to mimic his Spanish accent, upon which he would assume an angry countenance, seize a dish towel and chase us out, hurling his favourite insult, which was *chiffonnier*, ragman. Having found the Spanish translation of that epithet, we teased him all the more by quickly opening the kitchen door, calling out *trapero*, and running as he pursued us, dish towel held up menacingly in the air.

In summer, a chance to fulfill my father's wish that I should learn to swim presented itself. Since classes lasted until mid-July, we were ferried after school hours to a swimming area on the opposite bank of the river. There, a lifeguard attended to us and I explained to him that, having barely learned to swim, I dared not yet venture into the deep end. He offered to teach me and one afternoon, as he held me by the waist while I moved my hands and feet the way he taught me, he let go of me. Then, as I swam on, he quietly informed me that I was now in the deep end! I was elated. How I wished that Papa were there to watch me swim in the Seine!

Amid the joy brought by the arrival of the summer vacations, my heart filled with excitement when I was informed that I would be included in a small group of children from the CCE homes chosen to vacation for four weeks in England! I was thrilled at the prospect, since Papa had once told me at bedtime that we might go to live there after the war. That prospect dimmed the sad reflections to which I had grown prone. I was all the more proud to have been selected, as the majority of the children were to remain in France and vacation in the CCE-run summer colony at Tarnos, on the southwest Atlantic coast, a short distance below Mimizan Plage, where I had vacationed the previous summer. In the summer colonies of the CCE, wards of the children's homes vacationed together with children of the *patronages*, those after-school clubs run by the CCE for Jewish working-class children in Paris. In these colonies the children were well fed and occupied with sports, outings and cultural activities. At the end of the summer, when the time came to part, it was not uncommon for the children of the *patronages* to envy the orphans of the "homes," for the families to which they were returning were often poor, their condition made more difficult by postwar rationing and scarcities. Still, vacationing in one of those colonies was decidedly not as exciting for me as being sent abroad!

Soon before the date set for the departure to England, those of us who were selected for the trip were called to a brief information meeting by the director of the home, a German Jew named Ernst. He spoke of England in glowing terms, telling us how brave its people had been during the Blitz and what a progressive socialist country it had become, thanks to the Labour Party government headed by Prime Minister Clement Attlee. The latter remark struck me as odd, considering that Heini, Lazare, and other *moniteurs* not only taught us that the Soviet Union was the "Fatherland of Socialism," but that England was, like the United States and France, a capitalist country and that, besides, its government leaders Clement Attlee and Ernest Bevin were as good as fascists. Ernst was probably not a communist and I don't think he remained in Andrésy for long.

The excitement-filled journey to London lasted the better part of the day, beginning with the short train ride from nearby Poissy to the Saint-Lazare station in Paris, where we transferred to a train bound for the port of Dieppe, where so many brave Canadian soldiers had lost their lives in Lord Mountbatten's futile expedition of 1942. Next came the four-hour crossing of the Channel aboard a small ship named *Worthing*, a truly thrilling experience for me as I had never travelled at sea. Before long the coast of France disappeared from sight and then the coast of England slowly emerged from the haze. How thrilled I felt when we came in view of the white cliffs of Newhaven and alighted from the ship! From Newhaven it was a two-hour train ride through the verdant countryside of England to London's Victoria station.

Our destination was a summer vacation camp near Hemel Hempstead in Hertfordshire. An amiable gentleman, who introduced himself as Major Eddy (it seemed to me that he pronounced his name like the French word *idée*), must have been the owner of the camp, for he lived in a house on the grounds. The CCE chaperone in charge of our group was a forceful but caring lady named Hadassah. We were lodged in wooden huts where we slept on bunk beds. The three weeks that we spent in the camp were enlivened with a variety of activities, including sightseeing excursions. I particularly remember a one-day outing to the miniature village of Beaconsfield and the Whipsnade Zoo, where the enclosures were so spacious that the animals almost seemed to run free in nature. Some of the outings were to London. I particularly remember a long boat ride down the Thames arranged for us by the Baroness de Rothschild. It was a thrill-filled afternoon during which a highlander entertained us on his bagpipe, and we were served ice cream, a joy in that time of postwar rationing.

On one truly peculiar excursion we were taken to the Grand Palais, London's Jewish theatre on Commercial Road in Whitechapel, to watch an afternoon performance of Shakespeare's *The Merchant of Venice*. While in France that play was banned because of its anti-semitic slant, here in London we watched it performed in Yiddish!

If only I had been older when I was exposed to that spectacle, and my Yiddish had been fluent enough, I might have grasped the particular manner in which the Jewish theatre director interpreted that tragedy. I now know that the Yiddish translation of *The Merchant of Venice* was the work of David Hofstein who, like other Jewish writers and theatre directors in the USSR, was murdered on Stalin's orders in 1952.

The best part of our sojourn in England that summer was the final week, when we were placed with Jewish families in London. I had the exceptionally good fortune of being hosted by a young and attractive couple in their twenties, Sonia and Montague (Monty) Richardson. Sonia was a graduate of the London School of Economics and Monty of Cambridge, which is where the two met during the war. The couple lived in a small flat on Falloden Way in the Hampstead Garden Suburb. It was on my rides into town with my hosts that I began to learn the English language, although Monty and Sonia spoke tolerable French and we had no difficulty communicating.

English food, and the manner in which English people held a knife and fork, which I thought very elegant, likewise surprised me. I was introduced to breakfast cereals, notably corn flakes, and afternoon teas served with biscuits, dainty little sandwiches, sweet buns or cakes, and have enjoyed these ever since. English dinner foods, however, did not make a very favourable impression on me. After our return to France some of my companions, who had been made to eat lamb with mint sauce, recounted with disgust that the English ate meat with jam!

Sonia and Monty made me feel even more at home by introducing me to their families. Sonia's father was a doctor, who with his wife and two sons, Alan and Ian, lived in a comfortable middle-class house. Alan was then about to be inducted into the Royal Air Force. Ian was a schoolboy two years my junior, who took me swimming in a nearby public swimming pool. Sonia also had a sister named June who, at the beginning of the twenty-first century, was awarded an MBE in recognition of her distinguished public service. Monty had two sisters, one of whom was his twin. Unfortunately, over the years I saw them only on rare occasions. Monty's parents lived in a more modest house in Edgware and welcomed me warmly whenever I visited with Monty and Sonia.

I caused much consternation when, on my first evening with them, I unwittingly stirred up a political debate. In the late 1940s the communists supported the Jewish struggle for Palestine, and my indignation with the violence perpetrated by the British to keep our people out of the Promised Land caused me to call Clement Attlee and Ernest Bevin, respectively prime minister and foreign secretary, "fascists." Monty reacted with some heat to that brazen statement, protesting that Attlee and Bevin were socialists, not fascists. After enumerating to me the benefits that the Labour Party government had brought to working people in Britain, he pointedly assured me that in England twelve-year-olds did not discuss politics and wondered whether in France they commonly did. That was a question to which I would not respond in the affirmative, aware as I was of how exceptionally politicized we were in the CCE homes.

I can now well understand the conflicting feelings so many British Jews must have held toward the Labour government: the Jewish passion for justice compelled them to applaud its enlightened social policies, yet as Jews they were dismayed by the wickedness of its policy in the Middle East. I vividly remember a heated exchange I witnessed one Sunday at Speakers' Corner in Hyde Park. That was in 1948, when the newly founded state of Israel was fighting for its survival; a Zionist activist stood on a ladder holding the flag of Israel, and members of the crowd surrounding him, including a few Jews, strenuously objected to his badmouthing of Britain.

Monty and Sonia also introduced me to Brady's, a Jewish boys' club on Durward Street in the East End of London, which in 1946 celebrated its fiftieth anniversary. At that time, descendants of the Jews who had fled the pogroms of Russia in the late Victorian era still lived mainly in the rundown tenements of Whitechapel and other parts of the East End. Gradually, however, those who, like Monty's family, had risen to middle-class status, were moving north to Golders Green ("Goldberg's Green," as some wits later were to call the area), Hendon, and beyond. Back in the 1890s a group of prominent British Jews, among them Lord Rothschild, concerned with the wretched living conditions in which the children of recent Jewish immigrants were growing up and the dismal future they faced, decided to found a club in which boys would engage in a variety of creative and sportive activities, receive professional and spiritual guidance, and otherwise become "civilized British subjects," as could be read in the minutes of one of their meetings. Fifty years later, the grandchildren of the Yiddish-speaking immigrants had become as English as we, their peers in France, had become French. Eventually, a Brady's girls' club was founded as well, in which Sonia was active, while Monty was one of the directors of the boys' club.

Brady's Boys' Club was housed in a brown multi-storey building where in after-school hours lads ranging in age from about ten to young adulthood were occupied in manual workshops, the reading room, arts, music or gymnastics. The club was open until late evening hours, and there was a snack bar in which those still present at closing time would gather for a short Hebrew prayer service. Brady's owned a country house in Kent, called Skeet Hill House. Monty and Sonia took me there, along with about twenty boys, for a weekend filled with country walks, after-dinner games and singing, and cricket. Everybody sought to draw me into this, to me unfathomable, English sport. One boy even clutched an English-French pocket dictionary in his hand and, leafing through its pages, earnestly — and futilely — strained to explain to me the rules of the game. As could be expected, after a few minutes he gave up!

I returned to France, my head brimming with fond memories and thrilled with the Richardson family's invitation to return to England the following summer to spend a full month with them. I remember that I was next sent, for two weeks, to the CCE summer colony at Lacroix-Saint-Ouen, near Compiègne, north of Paris. That colony was intended primarily for adolescents. The area was a flat wooded region and the colony was housed in the château du Bac, a small castle set in a large park overlooking the River Oise. Some of the boys slept in large tents. The days were filled with sports, walks, sing-songs and theatricals. I vacationed at the château du Bac again in 1948 and 1950. When the two weeks I spent there after my return from England in 1946 were over, I was dismayed to learn that I would not return to Andrésy. Instead, I was transferred to one of the CCE's two small homes in Le Raincy, a suburb of Paris: the one known as Le Raincy-Côteaux, which was intended for adolescents, as distinguished from Le Raincy-Plateau, several streets up the hill, which was intended for small children. The reason given for my transfer and that of my friend Émile was that we were now entering secondary school. In vain did I protest that I could equally well attend secondary school in Poissy or Conflans, towns that were only a short distance farther from the manor than the elementary schools of Andrésy.

There were essentially two kinds of secondary schools in France at that time: the elite *lycées* and the popular *Cours complémentaires*. *Lycée* studies lasted seven years, at the end of which students submitted to the first part of a series of rigorous examinations called *baccalauréat* (*le bachot* in popular parlance), followed by a final year during which students enrolled in a specialized section: philosophy and letters or mathematics and sciences, and submitted to the second part of the *baccalauréat*. The *Cours complémentaire* was an extension of elementary school: it lasted only four years, which constituted the "first cycle" of secondary schooling; at the end of that cycle students submitted to a series of examinations called *le Brevet*. In a *Cours complémentaire* teachers addressed students using the familiar *tu*, as was the practice in elementary schools, whereas in the *lycées*, where one paid for textbooks and supplies, teachers addressed students using the adult *vous*.

The city of Le Raincy had a *lycée*, which was a co-educational branch of the Lycée Charlemagne of Paris. Having failed the *lycée* entrance examination, I was, instead, registered in the city's *Cours complémentaire de Thiers*. It annoyed me that the school, like the roundabout plaza on which it fronted, was named after Adolphe Thiers, the first president of the Third Republic. My reason for loathing Thiers was that he had drowned in blood the popular uprising of 1871 known as the "Paris Commune."

Although we were only about forty children at Le Raincy-Côteaux and in the next home in Livry-Gargan, to which we moved in 1948, I was never again happy the way I had been, in spite of the after-effects of the war from which I suffered, at the "enchanted manor" of Denouval in Andrésy. The separation had been sudden and I was not even afforded a farewell visit there. In the years that followed, I clung to memories of Andrésy and in my musings and daydreams held onto visions of still living in that little paradise, enjoying its varied activities and going to school in the area.

It was not until October 1959 that I found an opportunity to revisit Andrésy and the manor, but by then the children's home had long ceased to exist. Instead the manor of Denouval had become a seminary of the Salesian Order of Don Bosco. I was received there by the father superior, who asked a very friendly young seminarian to show me around the grounds. The visit concluded, I returned to the office to bid *au revoir* and thank the father superior, who blessed me.

Contrary to expectations, the manoir de Denouval ceased to be a children's home in 1949. That year, the CCE sold the property and placed the municipality of Andrésy in a financial quandary. I read in the minutes of the October 29, 1949, meeting of the school commission, that the year before, the municipality had been assured that the manor would in the foreseeable future not only continue to function as a Jewish children's home, but that moreover, the CCE would move to it orphans from the smaller homes of the department of Seine-et-Oise, which it planned to close, these not being as well equipped as the manor. Upon these assurances, the municipality had proceeded to enlarge both schools and equip them to accommodate over 120 additional pupils. The CCE's unexpected change of plans now compelled the school commission to close down newly built classrooms and suppress one teacher's position in the boys' school and possibly one position in the girls' school as well.

The last of the CCE homes closed in 1958, and I understand that Mathilde was very critical of the organization's failure thereafter to provide follow-up support to its former wards as they entered adult life with all its challenges. Perhaps this is one of the major reasons why so many of the *anciens* remained resentful of the CCE and so few participate in the annual gatherings of their association. I think this is unfortunate: time has thinned our ranks pitilessly and I myself contemplate my past in the homes of the CCE with serenity and the mistakes of our educators with indulgence. Sometimes it saddens me to live so far away that I am unable to involve myself in the activities of the association. On the rare occasions that I happen to be in Paris, either alone or with my wife, I stay with "the other René" of the home in Livry-Gargan — René Knoll. My relationship with him and his wife, Micheline, and their daughter, Anne, and son, Marc, has been so warmly sustained over several decades that they are as dear as family to me.

Years after the closing of the seminary, the manor and the park surrounding it became a subdivision of luxurious condominiums. The manor with its striking turret is still standing, but its interior has been remade into apartments. In 1994, a professor of the Hebrew University of Jerusalem, who as a girl of nine had survived the Warsaw Ghetto and was after the war brought to our home, revisited Andrésy. As she searched for the manor, she encountered the deputy-mayor, a young aristocrat named Daniel de Gueroult d'Aublay, who learned from her what the place had been nearly half a century before. De Gueroult was so moved by our story that, at his initiative, a plaque was unveiled on the gate of the park in memory of our parents. Since then, every year on May 8, the anniversary date of the end of the war, after the ceremony in memory of Andrésy's war dead in front of the city hall, a ceremony is also held before that plaque.

English Interlude

The school year had barely begun when I was already counting the months, the weeks and then the days before I would cross the Channel again. English was one of the subjects in the curriculum, and I invested all my enthusiasm into learning it, in the ardent desire to acquire the ability to communicate with my kind hosts and the boys of Brady's in their own language. When the long-awaited happy moment arrived, I went with a CCE group again, but only for the duration of the travel. Once in London I was released into the care of the Richardson family and given a contact address so that I could participate in some of the outings organized for the CCE children.

The highlight of that second summer in England was the fortnight that I spent with Sonia and Monty in the summer camp of Brady's Boys' Club on the Isle of Wight. We travelled there by train from London to the port of Lymington, where we embarked for a short ferry crossing. The camp was situated not far from the town of Freshwater and occupied a stretch of several green acres. Near the gate stood two halls, where we gathered for meals and social activities. We slept in rows of large army tents: senior boys on cots, six to a tent, and junior boys below the age of fourteen crowded a dozen to a tent, in sleeping bags on the ground. I slept in one of the junior tents. Although I was no longer "speechless," my English in the summer of 1947 was still a long way from fluency. To make matters worse, the boys in my tent were East End Cockneys and I understood too little of what they said to be able to participate in their rough and tumble. In any case, I felt ill at ease, a lone stranger among more than a hundred young campers. At age thirteen I had become a loner, burdened with sad thoughts about not belonging anywhere and having no parents. The suffering inflicted on me by the Shoah seemed like something Jewish boys brought up in England and sheltered by parents could not imagine, even if some of them had lived in London during the Blitz.

There were two francophones among the campers whose companionship I sought occasionally. One was a Belgian boy of my age, who had immigrated to England with his parents after the war; the other was a Canadian from Winnipeg, a veteran of the campaign of Italy who spoke colloquial French and whose presence in the camp mystified me, since he was at least twice my age and neither a "boy" nor a "manager," as the counsellors were called. I sometimes walked outside the camp with him and listened in disbelief to the tales of amorous adventures he claimed that he and fellow soldiers had engaged in while in Italy. Monty disapproved of my associating with the Winnipegger, while the latter spoke disparagingly of the English in general and of Monty in particular. This put me in an uncomfortable situation and I ceased to associate with him.

The day at camp began with the sounding of reveille. As is the wont of young boys, we allowed ourselves a few more minutes of sleep before the camp director made the round of the tents. Eventually someone would lift a flap and, upon spotting the khaki knee socks-clad legs of the director advancing toward our tent, frantically shout, "Mr. Freedman is coming, Mr. Freedman!" Thereupon all would pull themselves out of their sleeping bags, and I would be shaken to shouts of "Get up, Froggie!" Vexed by their rudeness, I weakly protested that I had a name and that they should stop calling me "Froggie" or "Frenchie," but to no avail. In any event we had to hurriedly assemble in front of the flagpole and stand at attention as the Union Jack and the blue-and-white flag of the soon-to-be-founded state of

Israel were raised, at which moment we intoned "God Save the King," followed by "Hatikvah."

All then filed to the great hall for breakfast, during which the day's program of various activities and excursions was announced. One outing that I remember vividly was of a visit to Carisbrooke Castle, where poor King Charles I was held prisoner before he was beheaded. That visit was followed by a tea reception with the mayor of the town of Cowes. Another outing that I much enjoyed was one to which I was invited by a "manager." We went to Freshwater where we visited the house of the great poet Alfred Tennyson and had tea there in the library.

One manager who particularly befriended me was Charles Spencer, who was soon to become director of Brady's. Like Monty (but not Sonia who hailed from Newcastle), he was born in London's East End into a family of Jewish refugees from Russia. In 1944 he served in the Jewish Relief Unit that entered Germany in the vanguard of the British Army and was appointed to the Allied military government in Berlin. Charles encouraged me to dispense with formality and to simply call him by his first name. His being a bachelor somehow made that easy; otherwise, I hesitated to address adults by their first name, even though such was the practice in the CCE children's homes. Charles was a short young man with a cheerful, bespectacled round face. I would eventually see a great deal of him during the summer of the following year, 1948, when Monty and Sonia invited me again to spend a month with them. By then I was already bravely writing letters in rather broken English to several persons, notably my hosts, one Brady boy, and a young American woman in Chicago named Shirley Schwartz, who sent me parcels.

On my third visit to England in 1948, instead of travelling with a group of fellow CCE children, I was attached to a group organized by the rival organization: the OSE, in a few of whose outings I would participate while in London. On arrival in London the group was met by a short, club-footed woman who handed each one of us a large blue five-pound banknote to spend as we pleased during that month, along with a printed letter in which she gave her address and invited any of us wanting to take a break while wandering around central London to drop in "for a good English cup of tea or a bad English cup of coffee." As on the two previous visits, I spent time with Monty and Sonia at Brady's club house on Durward Street, and also spent a weekend at the country house in Kent.

That summer of 1948 London hosted the first postwar Olympic Games. Since I could not obtain tickets to the competitions held at Wembley Stadium, I caught glimpses of them as reported in cinema newsreels, or even on television, for that was the year when for the first time in my life I saw television. Sonia's parents, Dr. and Mrs. Caller, owned a set that was a large piece of furniture with a small screen! Many a time I stopped at their home to watch television with Sonia's brothers and the beautiful *au pair* girl from Finland, Sirkka Manninen, who lived with the family. Besides Sirkka, I also sought out the company of Sonia's twenty-year-old cousin Mona, who must have been mightily amused at being courted by a fourteen-year-old boy, who, though tall for his age, was nevertheless still a boy!

I met Charles Spencer whenever he visited with Monty and Sonia, or at Brady's. One day he invited me to lunch with him *en tête-à-tête*, for a private talk, at Bianchi's, an Italian restaurant near Piccadilly Circus. In the course of that lunch he shared with me his love of Italy, where he vacationed at the time. He taught me the lyrics of "Santa Lucia," "O sole mio" and "Il ponte del Rialto" in the original Italian, a language I fell in love with forever after. Charles then took me to a performance of Ram Gopal's Indian ballet company at a theatre on Shaftesbury Avenue. The following year he called me up when he visited with artist friends of his in Paris. Then I saw him no more, until fifteen years later, when I returned to England for the first time in my adult years. In the intervening time he had established himself as an art critic of renown, who contributed to leading art magazines, authored books on Nijinsky's Ballets Russes and painters like Erté and Bakst, travelled a great deal giving lectures, and for some time owned an art gallery off Oxford Street. When I stayed with him in the summer of 1965, he was living in St. John's Wood in an amazing studio that had been designed and long inhabited by the Dutch painter Lawrence Alma-Tadema. Charles led this amazingly active life until his death, a few months short of his ninetieth birthday in 2010. He had invited me to the birthday celebration that was not to be.

During the school year 1946–1947, when I lived in the children's home of Le Raincy-Côteaux, one of my good friends, René Herskovitz, was adopted by an uncle who lived in London and brought him over to live with him in a small building at 25 Baker Street, where he operated a furrier's workshop and also resided. That location in central London was so convenient that I frequently dropped in on my friend and "fellow René" to spend a few jolly moments together, go for walks, or whatever. In 1948 food was still rationed and, as the uncle and his employees were not particularly fond of chocolate, they gladly handed over to us all the chocolate they had in exchange for René's tobacco ration coupons (he was already sixteen and therefore allowed to smoke).

Like so many others released by the C C E from its children's homes into the hands of surviving relatives, René was not afforded the opportunity to complete his secondary education. After less than a year of English schooling, his uncle put him to work in his fur business. This was clearly not my friend's calling in life: he eventually left his uncle and joined a kibbutz in Israel. Unfortunately, I lost track of him and we never met again. My cousin Jacques in Lyon acted likewise when, at age sixteen, his parents interrupted his studies at the Lycée Ampère: he left home and joined a Hashomer Hatzair training camp in Italy. There he met his future wife, Didi, and hebraicized his personal name to Yehuda. The young couple then settled at Bar'am, a model kibbutz situated a mere three hundred metres from the Lebanese border.

All too soon the day to depart from England for the return journey to France arrived. That morning Sonia accompanied me on the long bus ride to Victoria Station. We were engaged in a desultory conversation on no particular subject, when she suddenly asked whether I would like to live in England. Taken aback, I waited in excited suspense for Sonia to explain what she had in mind that could change the direction of my life. The truth was that I dreamt of some magical escape from what destiny might hold in store for me at the time; I loved England and would have fancied living in that country. Alas, Sonia let the matter rest there and said no more on the subject.

Le Raincy and Livry-Gargan

The CCE home where I lived through the fall and winter of 1946 and all of 1947 was, like the home in Montreuil, a *pavillon de banlieue*, a house in the suburbs of Paris. The director of the home was Hélène Hercman; with her we were on formal terms, using the pronoun *vous* and calling her "Madame Hélène." A rather distant person, she did not directly concern herself with our upbringing; her domain was administration. Her son Georges, nicknamed Jojo, was one of us; he was a born leader whose prestige rested in his intellectual prominence and, to a small extent, in the authority of his widowed mother. For several months the educator in charge of us was Paula, a Romanian woman who was authoritarian in a motherly way and whose husband, "Bubi," was a practising medical doctor. We knew both from Andrésy, from where they had been transferred.

Paula was succeeded by Albert Edelman, whom everyone casually called "Sergent" (sergeant), probably on account of the non-commissioned officer rank he had once held in the French army. He treated us like adults and was unusually permissive. Our movements would in any case have been difficult to control, since we lived in an urban milieu so different from the semi-rural surroundings of Andrésy and, moreover, attended a diversity of schools: elementary, secondary or vocational. With Sergent in charge we needed not even ask permission to wander about the streets of Le Raincy and neighbouring towns, or even to ride the bus and the metro into Paris on Thursdays or Sundays.

Next to reading or writing, exploring the surroundings in which I lived, whether by wandering along country roads and byways, or along city streets and lanes, was perhaps my favourite pastime. At thirteen, I could now indulge wanderlust to my heart's content and delight in the sights of my beloved Paris: the animation of the boulevards, children at play in the garden-like squares, housewives carrying their provisions in baskets, men sipping wine or liqueurs in the cafés, market hawkers, street peddlers, and so on. Paris was a city made for casual rambling in this now long-gone age when automobiles were rare and whoever was not on foot or riding the metro or a bus, rode a bicycle or a motorcycle.

Alas, the Paris that fascinated me in my childhood, the Paris sung by Edith Piaf or Georges Brassens, who composed lyrical songs with crude words, is no more. The names are still there: Belleville, Ménilmontant, la Villette, but they are no longer the *quartiers populaires*, neighbourhoods, populated by street urchins the like of Gavroche, celebrated by the great Victor Hugo in *Les Misérables*, and the spirited working-class people, who time and again rushed to the barricades to fight despotism and social injustice, and in August 1944 to drive out the Nazis. Belleville and Ménilmontant retained their character even when in the first half of the twentieth century poor Jewish immigrants from Eastern Europe became part of their population. Alas, that character was lost toward the end of the century. Some streets became gentrified, while one side of Rue de Belleville became a Chinatown and the other an Arab quarter.

There were only about forty of us at Le Raincy-Côteaux, which made for a degree of intimacy — and friction — not possible in a large community of children like Andrésy. I met Evelyne, the other poet of the CCE children's homes, whom I had wanted so much to meet when I resided in Andrésy. Now that we lived in the same home, I was disappointed to discover that she looked not at all like the romantic image I had formed of her in my imagination but was a rather standoffish, scrawny black-haired girl. Another girl was Elsa Zilberbogen, of dignified and elegant bearing already then. Through Mathilde, I met Elsa again in the 1970s in Ottawa, where she worked for a time in the French archives of Parliament. The following decade she and I reunited with Marguerite in Montreal. Our friendship unfortunately ended on a misunderstanding, with Elsa not wishing to see Marguerite and me again. Then there was Eliane Gourevitch, a shy, gentle girl who became a paraplegic and met an early death.

I began my secondary studies at the École Thiers in Le Raincy. From that school I remember with particular fondness my teacher of French, Jean Bondu, who, like Lucien Fraysse in Andrésy, made a lasting impression on me. Whenever he had something important to announce or wanted to convey some moral instruction, he would stand in the doorway separating the two Grade 6 classes and call out, "Les yeux vers moi dans les deux classes!" (All eyes toward me in both classes!) If our own classroom teacher, Madame Proust, encountered a serious problem of discipline, she walked up to that doorway and called on Monsieur Bondu, who immediately strode in and dealt with the unruly in a firm verbal manner.

It was probably Monsieur Bondu who, in the spring of 1947, inspired me and Henri Moreno, a Sephardic boy from the home, two years my senior, who excelled at French composition, to undertake a research project on the city of Le Raincy. In his Monday morning civic instruction lessons, he had exhorted his pupils to learn about government, how a city is administered and other such matters. Henri and I visited the *hôtel-de-ville*, where an assistant to the mayor advised us, following which we spent many an afternoon exploring the streets and discovering diverse neighbourhoods, scenic alleys, buildings of noteworthy architecture and churches. We called on prominent persons, such as businessmen, Catholic priests and the Lutheran pastor. To our surprise we discovered that there was a synagogue in the city;

we visited it but, unable to meet the rabbi, contented ourselves with interviewing the *shamash* (warden), who wore a curious Napoleonic bicorn. Our educators in the home had never mentioned the presence of a Jewish community in Le Raincy. Years later I occasionally corresponded with Monsieur Bondu and had the pleasure of meeting him again during my return stay in France in 1960, by which time he had, to my disappointment, become a militant communist.

Another mentor of mine at the École Thiers whom I wish to remember is Mademoiselle Leborday, our music teacher. A kind lady who took a liking to me, she offered to give me private violin lessons at no cost and loaned me one of her instruments. Unfortunately, there was no place in our Livry-Gargan home where I could practise without disturbing others. Besides, fourteen is perhaps too late an age to begin learning to play the violin. I therefore returned the instrument to my teacher with regret and a feeling of humiliation. I have loved classical music with a passion since my childhood, but early resigned myself to the reality that I would never become a musician.

I was by now allowed to travel alone to visit my family in Lyon during Christmas and Easter vacations, when my aunt and uncle invited me and sent me the money to buy train tickets. Once communications returned to normal, it took little more than five hours to travel from Paris to Lyon by express. During the Christmas vacation of 1946 I had perhaps been in Lyon for not more than two days when Uncle Paul announced that I was to travel with him to visit the Domb family, who had moved from Limoges back to their pre-war home in Nancy. Though happy at the prospect of seeing Aunt Fella again, I felt apprehensive about that first family reunion since the war. When our train reached Nancy after a day-long journey, we were met at the station by Uncle David. He shook hands and exchanged a few words in Yiddish with Uncle Paul and gave me no more than a passing glance. When we entered the apartment on Place des Vosges Aunt Fella embraced me effusively, but Uncle David still ignored me. However, supper was no sooner over when he abruptly turned to me and spoke his mind. Though no public authority had placed me in his care, he informed me that he had decided that I was not to return to Lyon with Uncle Paul but would, instead, stay to live with him and Aunt Fella until my schooling was completed, at which time he would send me to Palestine! He did not ask what I thought of the idea, and the tone in which he presented it brooked no objection.

I was dumbfounded and feebly protested that I could not act in so hasty a manner, that I wanted to return to Lyon to spend the rest of the vacation with Aunt Zilly and my cousins and then to Le Raincy in time for the resumption of school. I added that I should ask permission from the CCE to leave the children's home and gather my belongings. Uncle David countered my arguments by stating that he would give me money so that I could pick up my belongings and, some morning pretend to go to school as usual and, without asking for permission and bidding adieu, take a train to Nancy! It was not acceptable to him, a fierce anti-communist, that I should live in a CCE-run home. The dishonesty of what he proposed unnerved me. Luckily, Uncle Paul had rented a hotel room and, to my relief, we did not have to spend the night at the Dombs. The following day Uncle Paul took me on visits to acquaintances but, alas, we had to return to the Dombs for supper. Uncle David repeated his attempts to sway me. I felt so miserable that I could not even take delight in seeing Ginette again and meeting her husband, Jacques, and their toddler son, Claude, who were now settled in Strasbourg, Jacques's pre-war home.

Emotionally oppressed, but relieved to leave Nancy, Uncle Paul and I travelled back to Lyon on a night train. He was glum and visibly displeased, and I blamed myself for causing him pain. We arrived home before daybreak and Aunt Zilly rose from bed to greet us. Uncle gave her a brief account of what had happened and left the room, upon which Aunt warmly hugged and kissed me, laughingly assuring me that she was proud of me for having stood up to the man, whom she nicknamed *der alter meshugener*, the old madman. Years later, she told me how, not long before my unfortunate trip, she had gone with Uncle Paul to Nancy and how, when he met them at the railway platform, Uncle David had found nothing better to say to her than, "Di bist oich gekumen?" (You have come, too?), instead of rejoicing that they had all survived the Shoah. The rudeness of the "old madman" was likely not the only cause of the chill that descended on the relationship between the Arensteins and the Dombs. They never met again and ignored even weddings, births and deaths. It was left to me to occasionally inform my cousins in Lyon of the doings of our relatives in Nancy and Strasbourg and also Paris, where Simon Domb and his wife, Lucienne, lived.

Easter 1947 brought the prospect of happier vacations. I received a letter from my parents' old friends the Lewin family, inviting me to spend the two-week school vacation with them in Luxembourg and entrusting me to a young couple in Paris who chaperoned me there. I remember that during the train ride, my chaperones were mightily surprised to find me reading Tolstoy's *War and Peace*.

The visit to Luxembourg occurred shortly after I turned thirteen, but I was, alas, not honoured with a bar mitzvah, the traditional celebration of a Jewish boy's coming of age. My aunt and uncle in Lyon did not include me in the joint bar mitzvah celebration they held for their sons, Jacques (Yehuda), who was also thirteen, and Freddy who was fifteen. Needless to say, bar mitzvahs were not part of our upbringing in the homes of the CCE.

Max Lewin owned a small chocolate factory that employed a dozen people, among them a delightfully funny girl who called me "mon petit chou," my little pet. I dropped in at the factory daily and marvelled at the production process, from the mixing of the ingredients to the pouring into moulds and wrapping in brand-name packaging. Chocolate was still scarce in France, but by 1947 Luxembourg and Belgium no longer suffered from postwar rationing; besides, I was told, the Luxembourgeois ate well, as most city people had relatives living on farms. I ate my fill of the delicious chocolate, but it did not take many days before I lost my craving for it. Still, when I left Luxembourg I accepted the several tablets that Max Lewin gave me to share with my roommates, in keeping with the practice taught us in Andrésy that a child who received sweet things should share them. The chocolate factory was not the Lewin family's only source of delights: Joseph, the eldest son, owned an impressive candy store near the railway station.

That postwar reunion with the Lewin family was the last one that I was to enjoy with them before the family scattered. The elderly parents had survived in hiding in Belgium, their children in France, except for Adi, the youngest son, who was caught and perished. The mother had, unfortunately, become blind.

While in Luxembourg I was taken out by the wife of the Communist Party leader, and I also met old friends of my parents, notably Mr. Shupak, a businessman who already owned a car and drove me to Esch-sur-Alzette, where he fitted me with a suit. On leaving Luxembourg I was provided with the addresses of pre-war friends of my parents who belonged to the group that had met on Sundays on the lawns of Gantenbeinsmühle and now lived in Paris. Among them was Mr. Hartstark, of whom I possess a romantic photo showing him standing in a natural setting with his wife, who perished in the Shoah. Hartstark introduced me to the Golub family, whom we happened to come across in a metro station. These lovely people sometimes invited me on Sundays to share their noon-hour meal and spend the afternoon with them. I should also mention a couple named Rotbard and their son, Georges, who were close friends of Papa in Lyon and, likewise, hosted me many a time during the postwar years. I deeply regret that I let the contact with these kind people lapse and wish to express my gratitude to them here and to honour their memory.

～

In 1947 I underwent an unprecedented spurt of physical growth: as much as fourteen centimetres. I was emotionally restless, torn by conflicting wishes. While in my dreaming moments I longed to be a child and be taken care of, in my waking hours I acted almost adult-like, wishing to grow facial hair, so that I could sport long sideburns, which were decidedly not in fashion in the 1940s. For, every now and then, I fantasized about living in the nineteenth century in the days of Dickens and Flaubert, two of my favourite authors at the time.

Yet, at the same time, the communist indoctrination caused me to passionately yearn to see the Soviet Union and even live there. I subscribed to the glossy magazine *France-URSS* and a weekly newspaper called *Vie soviétique* published, I believe, by the Soviet embassy. One day I visited the office of the organization *France-URSS* to meet its president, who connected me with a pen pal in Moscow, with whom I exchanged only one letter. In addition, I read *L'Humanité*, the central organ of the French Communist Party, which was delivered daily to our home. I once even walked into the Soviet embassy, which was situated near the residence of Simon Domb; the gentleman who received me seemed understandably puzzled as he bid me to sit across a desk from him and offered me a cigarette! There was little conversation and I left after a few minutes.

Simon Domb was now a taxation controller in the ministry of finance. He remained, however, loyal to his origins; as I recall, he served for years as president of the Zionist Federation of France. He lived with Lucienne, his wife, in an eighteenth-century aristocratic apartment on Rue de Bellechasse, in a district of ministries and embassies. The several rooms of that vast apartment were each furnished in a different period style, with every piece of furniture, statue or painting an authentic museum piece. I was occasionally my cousin's guest at their Sunday noon-hour *déjeuner*, which was served by a maid. The atmosphere of the place was intimidating and Madame Domb made little effort to put me at ease. Simon and Lucienne owned a secondary residence, a manor in Normandy called Fresne-l'Archevêque, where I was invited only once in their lifetime: at Christmas 1959.

The files of the former children of the homes were held in the archives of the CCE and opened to us in the 1990s. The personal records that these files contain, which we were allowed to copy, include appraisals made by Mademoiselle Jousselin, the psychiatrist hired by the CCE. Some of the *anciens* were mightily angered when they read what that lady noted about them, observations they found erroneous and even demeaning. One should, however, perhaps make allowance for the fact that, sixty years ago, psychiatry and psychology were still in their infancy. I wonder what intrigued the psychiatrist about me that she made me visit her once every month through the spring of 1947 to subject me to Rorschach tests and interviews. I did not mind these consultations, since they provided me with opportunities to ride into Paris and visit Sophie or Mathilde in their office. On May 8, 1947, on the second anniversary of the end of the war, Mademoiselle Jousselin drafted a summary in which she noted that I evidenced "a spiritual maturity well above his age, which contrasts with certain still very childish traits," a "very intense internal life," a rich vocabulary that enabled me to express abstract ideas, and ambition. Attached to this evaluation was a one-page statement that I wrote on that date about how I envisioned my future. I wrote that I yearned for a normal and peaceful life and to have a happy family. I wanted to write successful books "rich in ideas, of a high moral quality," loved classical music, wished that I had money enough to buy records and a record player and a radio, and had a strong desire to travel around the world!

Sometime during that memorable spring of 1947 I was visited by the widow of Léon Pfeffer, the martyred hero of the Resistance and friend of my father, whom I remember as the man with a hollow cheek. I don't know what occasion brought Madame Pfeffer up from Lyon, but one of the objects of her journey was to unburden herself of a painful secret: the truth about the fate of my father, the real reason why nearly three years after supposedly joining the Free French Forces he had still not returned. What my aunt and uncle had told me in Lyon no longer seemed believable to me in any case, but I could not contemplate emotionally the possibility that I had lost both of my parents; I continued to live with the dream that Papa and I might yet be reunited. Madame Pfeffer's visit forced me to grasp the dreadful reality. I thus learned from her that Papa had been arrested one month before the liberation of Lyon on September 3, 1944. Over the decades I learned all the terrible details of what had happened to him.

In the summer of 1965, I met in Lyon a man named Wolf Klein, who had been Papa's companion in misfortune and in whose arms he died at the end of the death march from Auschwitz when they reached the camp of Landsberg in Bavaria early in 1945. In 1994, I had a reunion with my childhood friend Pierre Meyer in Sydney, Australia. Pierre's mother, then eighty-eight years old, gave me her account of how she had been arrested together with my father after he had lunch with her at her apartment. They were arrested by plainclothes French policemen who handed Papa over to the Gestapo, while she was unaccountably released the same evening. Papa left Lyon on the last train from that city bound for Auschwitz. The detailed story of that harrowing nine-day trip is narrated in Ted Morgan's *An Uncertain Hour*, a book about Lyon under German occupation. There were more than 600 prisoners of the sinister fort of Montluc aboard that train, many of whom were Jewish. In the heat of summer the poor victims of Klaus Barbie travelled four days without food or drink until they reached the spa city of Vittel in the hills of the Vosges. There the courageous president of the local Red Cross, Madame Bouloumy, rallied townspeople to prevent the train from going any further, until the prisoners had all been let out on the platform, where they were hosed down by firemen and served mineral water, soup and sandwiches, while those in urgent need were given medical treatment. I found out as much as was possible about the fate of my father, but I never came across any witness to my mother's death.

~

In the final quarter of 1947, the pedagogical direction of our home was assumed by my former *moniteurs* in Andrésy, Heini and Hanka, who had become his second wife. We were now taken firmly in hand;

there was no more freewheeling permissiveness. Our life became more structured, but it was also enriched culturally. The home of Le Raincy-Côteaux was closed in January 1948 and we were all moved to a newly opened, much larger home in Livry-Gargan, a contiguous suburban city to the west of Le Raincy. The move did not impact our schooling, except that I had to walk a much greater distance (over two kilometres) four times a day to classes at the École Thiers, likewise the following year to the École Jean Macé in Les Pavillons-sous-Bois and, two years later, to the Lycée Charlemagne annex of Le Raincy.

Within days of our arrival in the new home a general assembly was called, at which we unanimously voted in favour of establishing a children's republic, that inspired creation of Dr. Janusz Korczak. Central to Korczak's teaching was the conviction that the child is a person and deserves to be heard and respected, that children should be consulted in decisions affecting them. The other great pedagogue whose teaching the CCE followed was Anton Makarenko, who successfully raised young delinquents orphaned by the Russian civil war that followed the seizure of power by the Bolsheviks in November 1917. While Korczak's pedagogy centred on the personal development of the child, Makarenko stressed the primacy of nurturing loyalty to the collective.

In our "republic" of Livry-Gargan every one of the forty-odd children, who ranged in age from twelve to eighteen, belonged to one of eight commissions: hygiene and cleanliness (which assigned the housecleaning chores on Thursday mornings); sports and leisure; culture; press; workshops; etc. The chairpersons of the eight commissions were elected by the general assembly, which met about once a month. Together with Heini, Hanka and the occasional third counsellor, these eight chairpersons formed the governing body of our republic — the *Direction*, directorate, which met weekly to decide on current matters. Matters ruled important were referred to the general assembly and decisions were made on the basis of majority vote. One significant element of Dr. Korczak's model, however, was missing: that of the children's court. When a serious breach of discipline occurred, Heini and Hanka resorted to the prerogative of their adult authority, although they did on occasion consult members of the directorate in a rather non-binding fashion. One such case caused me real pain. My friend Henri Moreno had been caught stealing and was promptly expelled from the home and handed over to the care of his uncle. I felt that Henri should have been given the chance to redeem himself; he was very intelligent and promising and not at all a bad person, unlike a certain Claude R., who took pleasure in bullying and blackmailing.

Our "republic" even had an anthem, for which, as the home's "established" poet, I wrote the lyrics and the composer Ilya Holodenko, a friend of our home who often visited us, wrote the music. Another visitor friend of our home was Oscar Fessler, former director of a Yiddish theatre in Buenos Aires, who led us in staging theatricals. Ours was a richly varied life. Installed in a large cabin behind the house were photographic frames, embroidery, bookbinding, printing and other workshops, in which we spent hours on days off from school. We attended different schools, academic and vocational. Every Saturday night after dinner the tables of the dining room were set aside and the stools arranged in a circle for an evening of games, singing, storytelling or reading, individual or group performances, just as we used to do in Andrésy. In addition, Heini formed us into a choir, which performed at various venues, notably on Jewish occasions, in Paris. We even participated in programs alongside the outstanding Chorale populaire juive de Paris. Once or twice we went on air in radio station studios and even won prizes competing against adult choirs. Then, every June we held a well-attended open house fair at which we displayed and sold the products of our workshops, sang as a choir and put on performances of gymnastics, dancing, stage and puppet theatre skits under the direction of Fessler.

Besides the modest revenue generated by the fairs, the CCE collected donations from Jewish merchants and businessmen in Paris, but that did not suffice. Although it seems that no delegations were visiting our home any longer, American financial support for the CCE continued to be channelled through the Joint. At the same time a number of American Jews personally contacted some of us. I thus corresponded with a very kind young "auntie" named Shirley Schwartz, who lived in Chicago; besides letters, she occasionally sent me parcels containing American delights and clothes. Reading her letters and answering them was good English practice for me.

Unfortunately, the communist orientation of the CCE caused friction with the Joint. In the fall of 1948 it was explained to us that the Joint had decided to suspend its aid to the CCE, in consequence of which children who were orphaned of "only" one parent were to be turned over to the care of the surviving parent. As a further consequence, we were told, the CCE would seek aid from a different source: the affluent Jewish communities of South America. Toward that end Szmulek Farber travelled to that distant part of the world. I remember that whenever any of us needed clothing, Madame Hélène took us to the *vestiaire*, the clothing distribution store of the CCE at 14 rue de Paradis, where we were fitted with suits and sundry woollens made in Argentina. My childhood classmate and roommate Émile J., who conducted research in the archives of the CCE, discovered that, to put it mildly, we were not told the entire truth. Apparently, not only did the Joint never suspend its aid earmarked for the children's homes of the CCE, but the CCE hid a "dark secret": it made financial contributions to the French Communist Party. Mindful of the fact that Heini had us secretly produce in our printing workshop (in which I worked) leaflets and other propaganda material for the local organization of the Communist Party, this revelation perhaps should not have shocked me as much as it did.

A revelation even more disturbing to me was the case of at least one "full orphan" who was transferred to the care of relatives. Annette Zaidman, a long-time collaborator of Nazi hunters Serge and Beate Klarsfeld, recalls with bitterness in her autobiographical work

Mémoire d'une enfance volée (*Memoir of a Stolen Childhood*) how the CCE treated her. She spent only one year at Andrésy, where she belonged to the same group as I, and one year at the home in Sainte-Maxime in Provence. She suffered from emotional handicaps that kept her from being happy yet was removed to the care of an uncle. Had such been my fate, I would certainly not have fancied being placed under the care of my uncle and aunt in Lyon, for instead of pursuing my schooling, I would likely have been forced to help Uncle Paul at daily street markets, like my cousin Freddy.

I was a member of the directorate through the entire period of nearly three years that I lived in Livry-Gargan. At first I was the librarian and in that capacity a member of the culture commission headed by Madame Hélène's son Jojo. The library was the room in which many of us did our homework and read novels after supper until bedtime, which was ten-thirty for the older children. I next headed the press commission, which was responsible for three "publications": the first was the *journal mural* for which, as in Andrésy, we sought contributions every month in the form of articles that had to be edited and illustrated, and drawings or paintings. In addition, we issued a small weekly bulletin that was pinned on a board, and an occasional printed brochure that contained articles selected from the *journal mural*. Émile J. and I wrote a novel in weekly instalments that were posted on the bulletin board. It was about the adventures of a boy who leaves Lyon after the terrible air raid of May 26, 1944. The novel was never completed, due perhaps as much to our running out of imagination as to lack of time.

The Livry-Gargan period of my life happened to be a time when the attention of Jewish people everywhere was focused on the painful birth of the State of Israel and its heroic fight for survival. Since the Soviet Union at the time backed Israel, and Golda Meir became Israel's first ambassador to Moscow, the communists momentarily let go of their animus against Zionism and joined other Jewish organizations in their support of the fledgling state, which contended with overwhelming numbers of Arabs in opposition, backed by Britain. Until 1948 the only Jewish content in our education had been learning some Yiddish songs and the occasional lesson in Yiddish, but now our choir sang a couple of Israeli songs and there was even talk of learning Hebrew. The paucity of Jewish content in our lives did not go unnoticed. Even my Uncle Paul in Lyon, who was a communist sympathizer, expressed indignation at us not being taught Yiddish.

Alas, support for Israel turned out to be a passing fad, which served the Soviet purpose of driving British influence out of the Middle East. Stalin's accommodation of Zionism or, for that matter, any measure of Jewish life in the USSR, did not last. Already in 1948 Jewish writers and theatre directors in the Soviet Union were being assassinated on the orders of the ogre of the Kremlin, a crime of which we in France were not aware. Worse was to come.

Rich and varied though our life in the home was, I found it nevertheless confining. At one of our general meetings I expressed the view that at least some of us among the older children (I was fifteen) should get to know non-Jewish working-class youth by joining the local branch of the Union de la jeunesse républicaine de France (UJRF; Union of Republican Youth of France), the youth organization of the Communist Party. Heini enthusiastically approved my proposition and, a few days later, I became one of several adolescents of our home to be welcomed into membership at a meeting of the local UJRF circle. The members of that circle were by and large older than us and were very friendly and supportive. The activities in which we participated included the hawking of the UJRF weekly newspaper L'Avant-Garde, the Vanguard, at the Sunday market, putting up posters, distributing flyers and collecting signatures under the Stockholm Appeal for the abolition of nuclear weapons adopted by the World Peace Council, a Soviet front organization chaired by the French nuclear physicist Frédéric Joliot-Curie. The first time that I sold the Avant-Garde at the market, an activity prohibited under municipal regulations, a policeman ran out of a café and chased after me, but I was a faster sprinter than he. I was so proud of myself when I rejoined my comrades and told them how I had outrun the *flic* (cop)! Some time later I was elected as one of the delegates of our circle to the regional congress of the UJRF held in Argenteuil.

But I was no mere political animal. In the three years that I lived in Livry-Gargan I wrote a great deal of poetry; there were times when I wrote one or even several poems a day. At the same time, at the age of fourteen, I took up the study of the Russian language on my own using Nina Potapova's text book for speakers of French. When in doubt about pronunciation or any problem I turned to Ilya Holodenko or Rose Averbuch, who was also of Russian origin and for a time replaced Madame Hélène as director. On one of my rare visits to his palatial apartment, my cousin Simon Domb remarked on my gift for learning languages and urged me to take up Asian studies after I graduated from secondary school. I took that advice all the more to heart since I already nourished a genuine interest in China, where at the time the civil war between the communists led by Mao Zedong and Chiang Kai-shek's Kuomintang was entering its conclusive stage. I often studied maps of China to follow the progress of the People's Liberation Army on its southward march. When more than a decade later, after my return to Paris, I found myself at loose ends, not knowing what the future held for me, Simon denied ever having given the advice that launched me on my career as a sinologist. He pretended not to comprehend why I did not choose a more "normal" field of studies.

Meanwhile, the organization France-URSS, which published a glossy magazine vaunting the Soviet paradise, put me in correspondence with a high school student in Moscow named Tania Korzhikhina. Madame Averbuch helped me with translating her letters and I wrote to Tania in a mixture of Russian and French. Unfortunately, I never met Tania in person. When in 1955 I visited Moscow for the first time, I spent an evening with her parents in their apartment, but Tania had by then left for Sakhalin Island.

Not all of the children living at Livry-Gargan and other CCE homes became as enraptured as I did with communism. But, regardless of how much or how little impact the communist indoctrination had on them, the children of the CCE homes still marched as a group in the demonstrations or parades organized by the French Communist Party, notably on May Day and July 14, the national day. As mentioned previously, shortly before the end of the parade we marched past a reviewing stand on which sat or stood the triumvirate of the top leaders: Secretary-General Maurice Thorez, rotund former pastry chef Jacques Duclos, and tall, lanky André Marty. None of us at the time knew (and few know to this day) that, as Stalin's anointed political commissar of the International Brigades during the Spanish Civil War, Marty had ordered the execution of anti-fascist fighters such as Trotskyists, anarchists and, at Albacete, even volunteers who belonged to neither "deviant" current. After falling out with Thorez and Duclos and being repudiated by them in true Stalinist fashion, Marty was expelled from the Communist Party in December 1952.

In the fall of 1947 and in 1948, France was repeatedly shaken by politically motivated strikes. One afternoon, as we emerged from a metro station with the intent of joining a solidarity demonstration, truncheon-wielding policemen suddenly charged the crowd and Heini promptly pressed us back into the underground station. During the long and bitter coal miner strike of 1948, each table group of five or six was made to "adopt" one miner family to correspond with.

Whether to any degree "politically conscious" or not, many of my companions, as they grew into adulthood, became resentful and alienated from the CCE and its successor organizations. Tragically enough, they also grew up estranged from Judaism, having never been effectively introduced to the immense spiritual and cultural legacy of our people, except for a few Yiddish songs and some eviscerated observance of Passover and Chanukah. One reporter describes us children of the CCE as "those who did not believe in Santa Claus yet honoured him at Chanukah."

Only a very few of us later on willed to be Jews in an active, positive manner, by seeking to possess that invaluable heritage accumulated by our people over the millennia, a heritage of which we were deprived by the misguided policy of "full insertion into French society" of our educators. Ignorance of what Judaism is all about was aggravated by indoctrination in communism — that pernicious ideology that derides what Judaism stands for and is the greatest lie ever inflicted on suffering humankind. We were led to believe in the Soviet Union as a paradise, in Stalin as a god and in communism as the ideal for the realization of which we were to devote our lives when we grew up. What tragedy!

I still grieved, sometimes angrily, at the loss of my parents. I have, all my life, keenly felt the deprivation of a carefree childhood. Wanting to be a revolutionary, I felt obligated to adopt the outlook of an adult before my time and to suppress a deep-down urge to be the child that I actually was. I often felt depressed and fled into escapist dreams, fantasizing about living in an earlier, seemingly more romantic time, and in a different country. Then, in my mid-teens, as adulthood seemed to beckon, I yearned to be and look younger, becoming what some called "a serious child."

In December of 1948 I received a letter that filled me with excitement when, on the back of the envelope, I read the name "Goldman" with a return address in Toulouse! To my indescribable surprise and delight the writer of the letter introduced himself as Léon, a brother of my father; he had survived the Nazi camps and immigrated to France as a displaced person the year before. Uncle Léon's first wife and their infant son, Heniek (Henry), had been murdered by the Nazis and he now was remarried to a young woman named Genia, who was likewise a displaced person from Poland. The first of the three children of Uncle Léon's new family, a girl named Paulette, was born in Toulouse. It so happened that Uncle Léon's letter arrived just as I was about to travel to Lyon for my annual or semi-annual visit with my maternal family there. It was therefore agreed with my newly found paternal family that I would meet them in Toulouse during the following Easter vacation.

Uncle Léon had spent nearly two years searching for me and I was astonished and pained to learn from him that in 1947 he happened upon my uncle David Domb in Toulouse, an encounter during which my uncle pretended not to know my whereabouts. I was further saddened to discover not many years ago, in the archives of the CCE, that the organization knew about the existence of Uncle Léon several months before I received his letter, since it was informed in August 1948 by a Mr. Ankelewicz visiting from Toulouse that a brother of my father had recently arrived there.

In April 1949 I travelled to Toulouse. Though he had only seen me briefly when I was four years old in 1938, Uncle Léon recognized me as soon as I walked out of the railway station and held me in a warm embrace, as did Aunt Genia. I instantly loved this stocky little thirty-nine-year-old man (one year older than my father) and his ebullient, affectionate young wife. Like Papa, Uncle Léon was a tailor; he worked at home in the cramped little apartment of Place Saint-Georges where he lived with Genia and their three-year-old daughter, Paulette. She amused me greatly when, on the morning after my arrival, she woke up to find me sleeping on the other side of her father and asked insistently in a sing-song Toulouse accent who that "little boy" was. She was so endearingly playful and affectionate! In the two weeks that my first visit in Toulouse lasted, Léon and Genia made me feel, more than my other two uncles and aunts, that I had a family indeed. Aunt Genia had a brother in Toulouse, whose son Marcel would become a good friend to me years later. I was introduced to a friendly boy also named René and a girl — a native of Luxembourg — who lived upstairs, and these two showed me around the beautiful "pink city," so called on account of its brick houses.

I visited Toulouse again during the Easter vacation of the following year, 1950, and in the intervening time Uncle Léon and Aunt Genia visited me in Livry-Gargan, when they came to Paris to make visa arrangements in preparation for immigrating to Canada. They offered to adopt me and take me along. Unfortunately I had other plans. In 1950, what should have been a tantalizing prospect, had I been in my right mind, did not appeal to me at all. Canada was such a peaceful country, a country where life was good, but at the time I looked upon it as not essentially different from the United States, which inspired hostility. Less than a decade later, living in Canada would become a dream seemingly impossible for me to realize.

Yet, supposing that I had accepted my family's offer, I am not sure that I would have been happy living through the last of my teen years in Toronto, a city that, in the 1950s, was not culturally stimulating. I would likely have felt indescribably bored and found Canadian high school and teenagers and their ways not at all congenial. Besides, as I was to discover when I finally did come to live in Canada, the material condition of my family was not prosperous. Uncle and Aunt worked hard and lived in very modest conditions. But in 1950 my aunt and uncle were looking forward to a new life in Canada, where Aunt Genia's two sisters were already established, having been brought there after the war by an uncle who lived in Edmonton. The happiness Uncle Léon and Aunt Genia felt when they left Europe for the New World must, alas, have been overshadowed by worries about what I was up to.

In the years that followed, when I lived in Poland and in China, my contact with them was suspended. Fortunately, a letter that I wrote to them from Beijing reached them, in spite of several address changes, in December 1958, just as Aunt Genia was giving birth to Susie, my youngest cousin. Two years later we were happily reunited in Canada.

Vacation in Poland

In the summer of 1949, the course of my life led once again to a cross-road. This time, however, the path that I was about to tread was not laid out by circumstances independent of my will, but by a premature decision that I was allowed to make at the young age of fifteen.

That summer the CCE again chose to include me in a group of children to be sent on a summer vacation abroad, this time to Poland. At the time, the communist government of that country annually invited a thousand or more children of Polish immigrants in Western Europe to vacation for one month at luxurious summer colonies situated in scenic parts of the country, such as the Baltic coast, the mountainous regions of the south or the Masurian Lakes. Our group was invited by the official Jewish organization of Poland and attached to the convoy formed to transport mainly children of Polish coal miners in the north of France.

On the day of our departure Heini accompanied our small group to the office of the CCE on 14 rue de Paradis, where we lunched at the canteen and were placed in the charge of the principal pedagogue of the CCE, Luba Pludermacher, who walked us to the special train awaiting us at the Gare du Nord. Luba had been a counsellor at the OSE's château du Masgelier during my brief sojourn there. She was a motherly woman, vibrant and effusive, yet a strict disciplinarian at the same time. Her voice was known to rise from caressing suasion to thunderous yells when angered and to just as quickly settle back into a gentle tone that soothed fear and ruffled feelings. When thus carried away by a fit of anger, she was prone to make such mistakes of grammar that we strained to suppress our giggling. Her sixteen-year-old son was a member of our group. Also travelling with us were Sophie and another director of the CCE, a bald, jovial little man named Leizer.

The train on which we travelled to Poland was not a regular one — it was a very long convoy of boxcars divided into compartments, which was shunted hither and thither across Belgium and Germany for several days. Sometimes we were immobilized for hours on side-tracks, but there were entertaining and even exciting moments on that journey. As soon as the train came to its first major stop across the border in Belgium, we rushed to exchange some money and huddled around vending machines to buy tablets of the most delicious chocolate in the world. The most challenging moment for the adults accompanying us came when our train crossed from Belgium into Germany. They had to restrain us and even force the windows shut, so irresistible for us was the temptation to lean out and shout insults at the Germans who stood on station platforms and either did not react or smiled blandly.

Then came the long-awaited, suspense-filled moment when we crossed the line into the Soviet Occupation Zone of Germany. The train rolled to a stop in front of a long wooden hut which, curiously enough, had two doors, both at one end and side by side: one marked *vkhod*, entrance; the other *vykhod*, exit. At the sight of the Soviet soldiers wearing rubashka-style jackets and red-star-marked caps, we cheered wildly, only to be taken aback by their lack of response and the blank expressions on their faces. We filed out of the train into the hut, where our passports were stamped. One child-faced beardless young soldier walked us back to our car, and I undertook to practise on him the skimpy bits of Russian that I had so far learned. For a moment his face lit up and, caressing my hirsute chin, he asked how old

I was. "Fifteen," I answered, upon which he exclaimed in disbelief, "And you already have a beard?"

When our train finally entered Poland and stopped at the first station, we stepped out on the platform and received a rousing welcome. Officials spoke and a band struck up the national anthem followed by the "Internationale." Sophie, who stood next to me, was moved to tears and reminisced how, back in the 1920s in her hometown of Lodz, she had seen police beat with truncheons demonstrators who sang the "Internationale," that stirring hymn composed soon after the crushing of the Paris Commune of 1871 by a poet and a composer who fought in its defence. After the ceremony Sophie took leave of us and boarded a train bound for Warsaw, where she planned to make arrangements for a permanent return to her native country.

We continued our journey in the boxcar train until we reached the port of Szczecin (Stettin), where our CCE group spent an afternoon in some reception hall. The next day we were conveyed to our intended destination in the south of Poland, a home for Jewish orphans of the Shoah situated in a Silesian village called Pieszyce (the former German Peterswaldau). Pieszyce was our home base for the duration of our stay in Poland; from there we travelled to various places around the country. In Pieszyce we were joined by a small group of Belgian boys, who became our friends and travel companions and whom we, the French, good-humouredly teased for their accents and curious expressions.

Pieszyce was set in the scenic hilly country of Lower Silesia, a few kilometres outside Dzierżoniów, a town that in the immediate postwar years housed so many Jews looking to emigrate from there to Israel or to the West that some nicknamed it "Żydoniów" (the word Żyd meaning "Jew" in Polish). Of the three million Jews who lived in Poland before the war not more than about 50,000 remained: most of them had survived in remote areas of the Soviet Union, notably Uzbekistan. Some had fought as partisans in the forests of Belarus or Ukraine, others in the ranks of the Soviet army or the "reborn Polish army," which marched alongside it into Poland. By and large, these survivors had little desire to settle permanently in the country of their birth and left as soon as opportunity beckoned and travel documents were procured. The pogrom of Kielce in 1946 and other outrages swelled the flight out of Poland. Yet, there were idealists, who were determined that the 1,000-year Jewish presence in the country must not be extinguished and laboured to recreate community organizations, children's homes, schools and cooperatives.

Paradoxically enough, there were Jews who had emigrated to France or Belgium before the war and now sought repatriation to Poland, a land that had become a cemetery of our people and of the vibrant civilization it had created there. These were mostly communists motivated by the idealistic desire to contribute to the building of a new socialist Poland. Many had distinguished themselves as fighters in the ranks of the International Brigades of the Spanish Civil War and the multi-ethnic MOI underground created by the French Communist Party in 1940.

At the time of the liberation of France, MOI leaders were summoned by that party's leaders to a secret meeting, at which they were praised for their heroic struggle and told that by their sacrifice they had earned the right to call themselves French men and women. Then, in the next breath, they were urged to return to their countries of origin "liberated" by the Soviet Army, there to serve as experienced "cadres." It seemed as if the French communist leaders were anxious to see as many of these immigrant combatants leave the country as soon as possible in order to appropriate to themselves credit for the sacrifice made by the Jewish and other immigrant heroes, so many of whom had perished because of the refusal of the Party leaders to allow them to flee from Paris in 1943, at a time when the special brigades of the police and the Gestapo were closing the trap they had set for them. Having recognized the foreign communist combatants as "French," the French Communist Party now boasted of its 75,000 martyrs and called itself "le Parti des fusillés" (the party of those who were shot).

Jewish communists who, like Sophie, returned to Poland after the war, were indeed recognized as valuable "cadres" and given positions of responsibility in the party apparatus and government administration. Adam Rayski, who had commanded the Jewish section of the MOI underground in Paris, was put in charge of all press and book publishing houses, except for those belonging to the Catholic Church. As I recall, Sophie, as Rayski's subordinate, became the national director of the International Book and Press Club, an amazing cultural organization that operated branches in all cities of importance. Others were given diplomatic postings. For two decades the veterans of the MOI invested their dedication and talents into what they believed would be a new society free of injustice and "exploitation of man by man." However, when an antisemitic, semi-fascist clique assumed the leadership of the ruling party in 1968, these veterans were thanklessly driven out of Poland with a passport valid for a one-way trip to Tel Aviv. Rayski had already defected to France in 1956; Sophie followed in his footsteps in 1969, after she was dismissed from her job as a "Zionist," an epithet pinned on all Jews by the communist bosses of Poland after the Six-Day War in Israel in 1967.

Nonetheless, all this was in the future. In that summer of 1949, our CCE group vacationed in Poland. I remember us going out as a group to a cinema in Dzierżoniów and, on one occasion, to an evening reception by the local communist youth organization ZMP, where at the behest of our hosts we had to rise, clap and chant in unison the names of the communist leaders of Poland, the Soviet Union and France: "Bierut-Stalin-Thorez"!

My most pleasurable memory is of the several days that we spent in Poland's lovely ancient capital, Krakow, which, luckily, had not been destroyed by the Nazis. I delighted in its fabled historical sites: the royal palace on Wawel Hill, Saint Mary's cathedral with its stunning gigantic sculptured altar by Wit Stwosz, the central square fronting it on which stands the ornate Sukiennice market, the Barbikan gate and other remnants of medieval enclosures. Not far from Krakow is the town of Wieliczka, where we descended into Europe's largest salt mine, in the depths of which one wanders through a maze of halls filled with sculptures and even a chapel, all carved in the salt. Such an awe-inspiring place!

From Krakow we were taken to Auschwitz, which had not yet been turned into the museum that it is today. Words cannot express the distress that engulfed my heart as we trod through expanses still strewn with human ashes and even fragments of bones. I stared in shock at the ground beneath my feet, wondering whether my mother's remains were right there mingled with those of other victims. Symbolic of the mind-numbing scale of destruction of human life that took place in the killing fields of Auschwitz and Birkenau is the railway platform at the foot of that grim tower with its arched gate. Here the daily convoys of tortured human cargo arrived from all over Europe. Here the heavy iron-barred doors of the cattle cars were slid open, disgorging the starved, thirsty and shivering survivors of several days of agony on rails: men, women, and children in a state of shock, stunned by the light of the day or the violently bright spotlights used at night, hurtled amid whip-wielding SS, who barked even more ferociously than their vicious dogs, into line-ups past those who selected them — now to the left, now to the right, now to immediate death in the gas chambers, now to a life of a few months, or perhaps one year, of starvation and indescribable suffering and humiliation.

Remembering how very close I came to being murdered there with my mother sends shivers up my spine. Would my mother, petite and frail as she was, and I, a child of eight, have survived the several-day-long journey of horror from the "antechamber of death" in the Parisian suburb of Drancy? If we had, we would no doubt have been transported on arrival to one of those fictitious shower chambers, in which naked men, women and children uttered pathetic screams at an indifferent heaven as the poison gas was being released. Often did these unspeakably horrible visions of the gas chambers and crematoria of Auschwitz, Treblinka, Majdanek, Sobibór, and other death camps torment my imagination as I was growing up....

That my father did not perish in that manner, but of exhaustion at the end of a death march, is hardly comforting. And what of all my uncles, aunts and cousins who saw me when Mama took me on a visit to Poland in 1938 but whom I could not remember because I was only four years old? I shall never know how they perished: whether by starvation or disease in a ghetto, or in the gas chambers of Treblinka or Auschwitz. I have now lived almost my entire life without closure, if in reality there is such a thing.

Fifty-four years later, I revisited Auschwitz in the company of my wife. From the red brick barracks of Auschwitz proper we wandered to the remaining rows of wooden barracks at Birkenau and other vestiges of the satanic Nazi murder machine that ground pitilessly day and night. We approached the ruins of a crematorium just as a group of Japanese was filing past it: they were visibly shaken and I could not help wondering how aware they were of similar atrocities perpetrated by special units of the Japanese army against innocent Chinese peasants and Allied prisoners of war in secret camps in Manchuria.

Our CCE group's excursions of that memorable summer of 1949 included visits to Warsaw and Wrocław (Breslau). Both cities still lay largely in ruins, but we were assured that their reconstruction proceeded apace. The most memorable moment of our stay in the capital was the heart-rending agony of a walk in the ruins of the Warsaw ghetto and the sight of the monument erected in memory of the young heroes of the uprising, who knew that they were doomed and isolated in the very middle of Nazi-occupied Europe yet fought to the last to resist.

In every place that we visited we were hosted in Jewish children's homes, which was an edifying experience, for even more than was the case with us, the survival of orphans of the Shoah in Poland was miraculous, considering how dramatically more cruel the German occupation had been in Poland than in France. Those orphans had endured more searing terror and suffering than we had; some had even seen their parents and siblings murdered before their very eyes.

The traumas endured by the child survivors of the Shoah in Poland made us feel, almost uncomfortably, as if we had been lucky. Indeed, we sometimes felt awkward in the presence of our Polish peers, awkwardness made worse by the difficulty of communication, since none of us knew Polish or even spoke Yiddish to any effective extent. I muddled through a weird combination of equally meagre Yiddish and Russian.

During our Warsaw visit we stayed in the children's home of Sródborów, a village scattered over a vast extent of pine forest and sand dunes near the town of Otwock. There, a girl of my age who had survived in the Soviet Union congratulated me on my very limited Russian and, after my return to France, we struck up a correspondence in Russian. Alas, in the fall of 1950 when Sródborów became for a while my home as well, that friendship petered out. Curiously enough, from our visit in the summer of 1949, I had gleaned the superficial impression that the children's homes in which we stayed in Poland were luxurious compared to ours in France. When I passed that observation on to Heini in the wake of our return, he agreed that such was indeed the case and that he had criticized "our Polish comrades" for raising the children in Sródborów and other homes in unnecessary luxury. Furthermore, it seemed to me that the boys and girls of the Polish homes were allowed to live like carefree children. They seemed so innocent and genuine compared to us: I almost envied them for that. At the age of fifteen, the communist ideology rubbed into my consciousness with such effectiveness by our educators, particularly Heini and Hanka, demanded of me that I act like a young adult and suppress the secret yet understandable inclination of actually preferring to be a child.

These conflicting emotions no doubt contributed to the ill-considered choice of a future that I made upon my return to Livry-Gargan. What our group saw and was made to believe during that vacation convinced me that a new Poland was in the making, in which Poles and Jews would live in brotherhood, where socialism would eradicate poverty and guarantee everyone a decent existence. And since, furthermore, my father had been a communist, I persuaded myself that my parents had left pre-war Poland because of antisemitism and unemployment, and that, had they survived, they would have returned to live in their "homeland." I thus resolved to return to Poland in order to live there, complete my education, and participate in the building of a socialist society. Genuine as this motivation was, it was also underpinned by a belief that I dared not recognize: that, away from Livry-Gargan and all who knew me as a budding "politico," I could, without losing face, be free to be a child for at least a few more years.

Our return to France was followed by a brief sojourn in Andrésy and we settled back in the home in Livry-Gargan before the beginning of the school year in October. I was admitted in the *classe de troisième*, equivalent to Grade 9, of the prestigious Lycée Charlemagne of Le Raincy, along with one other boy and one girl from our home. On the first day, we entered the classroom several minutes late but armed with valid excuse papers. In answer to the questions of the professor of French, told him that we had spent our summer vacations in Poland, to which he exclaimed, "And you returned alive from there?!" Such were the ridiculous notions that some people in the West held about countries behind the "Iron Curtain."

Farewell to France

The *lycée* offered students a choice of two curricular sections: Classic and Modern. The Modern section placed more emphasis on mathematics and the sciences. Students enrolled in it studied two modern languages, the first one being English, which was compulsory beginning in the sixth form. For a second foreign language the Lycée Charlemagne offered the choice of German or Spanish, beginning in the fourth form. Students in the Classical section studied, in addition to two modern languages, Latin and Greek. Foolish as I was in my young years, I allowed myself to be persuaded by Heini and my two classmates from the home to register in the Modern section. While I excelled in the humanities, I was mediocre in mathematics and poor in the sciences. To make matters worse I chose German as a second language, notwithstanding an emotional handicap I suffered about that language in these postwar years. To this day I bitterly regret that I did not study Latin and Greek, for I grew to delight in classicism after I studied Classical Chinese, Biblical Hebrew and even a touch of Aramaic. I would have blossomed in the Classic section.

Although by nature I was not wilfully undisciplined, I almost inadvertently ran afoul of two professors and received two *consignes*, detentions, in as many weeks: one from the professor of mathematics, who inflicted four problems on me, the other from the professor of fine arts. He was a mean and despicable individual who sported a moustache à la Dali. He seemed to derive inordinate pleasure from uttering remarks replete with sexual innuendo and watching the girls blush. The arts class occupied the entire Saturday morning and was held in a pavilion isolated at one end of the park. One balmy spring morning we students all strolled lazily toward the pavilion and arrived three minutes late at the door of the classroom. This caused the arts professor, Monsieur Lambert, to fly into an entirely uncalled-for outburst of rage. He slammed the door shut in the face of the students and ordered us all to wait in the stairwell until it pleased him to summon us in. A typically French scene then ensued: a loud explosion of general indignation, followed by the group deciding to walk out of the pavilion and move to Permanence, a hall in which students were expected to spend any free period they had between classes, to quietly read and study under the supervision of a teacher.

That we should have a morning of free time was clearly not the intent of the arts professor. As we all descended the steps, one student after another had a sudden change of heart and precipitously ran back up the two flights of stairs. Once outside I discovered that there were only nine of us left willing to defy Lambert: eight girls and I, the only boy. Looking laughingly at me, the girls expressed no end of derision at the cowardice of the boys. We had not been sitting in Permanence more than fifteen minutes, when a boy entered the hall and informed the teacher that Monsieur Lambert had asked for his students. As we filed into the arts room, Lambert's moustache seemed to bristle with fury at the sight of me holding up my head, which was my usual way of walking, not a pose of defiance. With a contrived expression of surprise he remarked sarcastically, "Oh, there is a young gentleman chaperoning these damsels and he is so proud!" He then ordered me out of the classroom, shouting that I was the most insolent student he'd ever met. Taken aback by this unexpected and unjustified verbal assault I returned to Permanence, only to be almost immediately summoned back by Lambert's messenger boy.

The outcome of this unwanted confrontation was that I was

served a *consigne* and had to write a French composition on the subject of "politeness." Fired by irrepressible anger, I penned an essay
that was sarcastic in tone: I began by arguing that politeness was the
foundation of civilized society and proceeded to castigate, without
naming him, Lambert as a capricious professor, who vents his anger
at students over trifling matters. I concluded that such a teacher is not
worthy of his calling and deserved no respect. I still wonder whether
Heini read my discourse before apposing his parental signature to it.

A few weeks passed. One morning when our class sat down to a
written geography test made up of two questions — one I could answer to perfection, the other I had no idea at all how to answer — the
janitor walked in and handed a note to the professor of geography. It
was a summons for me to appear forthwith before the *conseil de discipline*, disciplinary council, assembled to sit in judgment over me in
the principal's office. I marched across the park like one condemned
to the scaffold. Seated around the principal's desk were two professors
who had cause to hate me (one of them being Lambert) and two on
whose support I could count: the motherly professor of physics and
her husband. I stood as the principal read aloud my essay and was
then ordered to move to the next room while my fate was being de-
bated. Before long I was called back in and informed by the principal
that, in consideration of a number of facts in my favour, the committee had decided that I would not be expelled from the *lycée* but that,
instead, a formal reprimand would be inscribed in my records. Sigh-
ing with relief, I ran back across the park to the classroom. Since half
the time for the test had already passed, the professor of geography
decided I needed to answer only one of the two questions — and left
the choice to me. Suppressing my glee I chose the question I knew I
could answer so well and, in the bargain, received a very high mark!

During the rapid succession of weeks and months in the last year
of my childhood in France, I increasingly lived in two worlds. One
was that of current reality, in which I acted as if my future lay in
France and, harbouring no thought of emigrating, looked forward to

being recognized as a *pupille de la nation*, "ward of the nation," and a naturalized citizen of France. Had I stayed in this class of orphans "adopted" by the state, I would have enjoyed certain benefits in pursuing my education and undergone a less rigorous military service when I reached the draft age of twenty.

But would my intellectual ambitions have been gratified? Nothing is less certain, for in 1951, the year that followed my departure from France, CCE policy in the children's homes was reframed by tunnel-vision-afflicted leftists, who ruled that we should not be so privileged as to all pursue secondary schooling, when most working-class French children had to work and make a living from as early an age as fourteen. Some of my companions were forced out of *lycées* into vocational schools. This absurd policy wrecked the dreams of adolescents who, as they grew into adulthood, harboured grudges against the CCE, which previously, notwithstanding its "proletarian" ideology, had been so enlightened in matters of education and culture.

The other world was that of speculations about my future life in Poland and, beyond it, the beckoning communist world. For my dreams reached even further east to vague career ambitions in the Soviet Union and the emerging new China. Czechoslovakia also held a certain fascination for me; I knew that Prague was a magnificent city and I sometimes fantasized about living there. Looking back at the fantasies that populated my musings at the time, I can only regret having looked elsewhere for the happiness that might have been within reach had I exerted my imagination in a different manner and not concerned myself with what others might have said or done. I was heavily influenced by communist teachings and wanted to be a good communist.

Although my relatives forever after accused the CCE of having in effect sent me to Poland, the decision to immigrate there was truly mine. As a matter of fact, the CCE pressed me to reconsider. Heini used his characteristically doctrinaire approach and suggested that if I were a true communist, I would face whatever risks and fight for socialism in France, instead of running away to a country in which socialism was already being realized. Mathilde used gentle persuasion to urge me to change my mind.

Sophie invited me for at least two talks in her office at 14 rue de Paradis. Her approach was not intimidating like that of Heini or the brutally dogmatic Szmulek Farber; it was essentially sensible, pragmatic. She urged me not to idealize Poland but to be aware that I would face great difficulties of adjustment there, that it would not be like returning to Pieszyce and that, if I failed to adjust, there would be no running back to France for me, at least not under the protective mantle of the CCE, which would pay for my move to Poland. She further explained that to leave the "camp of socialism and peace" in disenchantment and return to capitalist France would cause me to be regarded as something of a traitor by "the comrades." By way of illustration of the possible predicament that might await me, she cited the example of Naftali (Tolly) Skrobek, son of her close friend Sarah Kutner. As a teenager Tolly had fought in 1944 in the Resistance. His father, a truly heroic figure, had perished in Struthof, a Nazi concentration camp located on French soil, in Alsace. Soon after the war Tolly immigrated to Poland, filled with idealism, only to return defeated to France. As a result, he and his mother were ostracized by "the comrades," with the single exception of Sophie.

I wonder, in retrospect, how unshakeable my resolve to emigrate from France to Poland was. As I probe deep into memories of what my daily reflections were at the time, I instinctively feel that, had I known a politically well-informed person who was not a communist, but whose views I could respect, one whom I trusted and in whom I could confide, I might have seen the light. Or was I so hopelessly indoctrinated that only a brutal confrontation with the reality of communism could bring me to my senses?

As the school year progressed and the time to pull up roots grew nearer, I vividly remember that doubts tugged at my musings, particularly on the long walks home from school when I was alone with my thoughts. I sometimes happened upon negative views of the Soviet Union coming from Jews who had found refuge there during the war. I caught myself wondering how it was possible for old Bolshevik leaders — Lenin's companions Grigory Zinoviev, Lev Kamenev and Nikolai Bukharin, those tragic victims of Stalin's purges of the late 1930s; or veteran communist leaders like Nikola Petkov and Traicho Kostov Djunev in Bulgaria; or László Rajk in Hungary — to turn traitors? During my 1948 stay in London, Sonia had sought to open my eyes by indignantly asking how these men were made to confess unlikely crimes at their trials. And then, how believable could it be that Josip Tito and the entire Yugoslav leadership became secret "agents of American Imperialism"? The witch-hunt for "Titoists" or "Trotskyists" in the ranks of the French Communist Party and even the UJRF circle in Livry-Gargan, to which I belonged, troubled me. I was, as yet, not aware of the persecution and murder of the Jewish writers and theatre directors in the Soviet Union at the time, and the Slánský trial in Prague was still a few years ahead.

I can now in all candidness recognize that I even caught myself anxiously wondering whether communism was not the greatest lie of the century, if not of all time. Why was it so difficult to travel to the Soviet Union, and why did no one return from there? Was it because they had something to hide? Yet, as soon as such doubts skirted my mind I brushed them aside, because it was simply inadmissible to conclude that my father and all the communist heroes and martyrs of the Resistance had devoted their lives to a lie. Also, so many persons I admired and loved were communists. Last but not least, I recognized that without the gigantic contribution and sacrifices of the Soviet Union, Hitler would not have been crushed. These thoughts, more than any other reason, helped to silence my doubts.

I also misguidedly persuaded myself that had my parents survived, they would, for the same reason, have wished to return to the country of their birth. In truth that would have been unlikely. I have grounds to believe that my father would have outgrown his communist convictions in the face of mounting evidence of the evil nature of the system that the Soviet Union imposed on the countries its armies traversed as they crushed Nazi Germany. As a hardworking and skilled tailor Papa would have prospered in France in the postwar years, as so many in his profession did. A distant cousin told me that in 1944 he confided to her his ambition to become his own boss after the war and vacation on the French Riviera, wearing a white suit!

And there were further reasons to suppress doubts. I could not afford to lose face before my companions who viewed me as an exemplar of political consciousness. Some of them were hostile to me and would have mocked me if I had become a renegade. At the home of Le Raincy-Côteaux, Sergent had nicknamed me "Reporter Renégo," and that nickname stuck and would have lent itself to my being ridiculed as a *renégat*, renegade. To cease believing in communism could also have placed me in an awkward situation as a "child of the CCE."

And so time hurtled me relentlessly toward that fateful day when I would leave the secure life that I enjoyed in the home of Livry-Gargan and say farewell to France. There were actually two of us preparing to immigrate to Poland. The other one was my roommate Georges Borenstein, a red-haired boy two years my senior, who was not the least "politically conscious." Like me, he was a member of the group sent to Poland during the previous summer. While there he was reunited with two uncles who had survived the Shoah, and they urged him to return and live with their family in Płock, a city situated about one hundred kilometres northwest of Warsaw.

On that historical date of Sunday, June 25, 1950, our home held its annual *kermesse*, an exceptionally successful day of celebration of our accomplishments, attended by many guests who came from Paris for the occasion, among them the Polish ambassador, the writer Jerzy Putrament. We displayed and sold the products of our workshops and held performances by our choir, our gymnastic team and the puppet theatre directed by Fessler. The following morning, being perhaps the first to rise, I went to the mailbox to pick up the daily newspaper, which was, of course, *L'Humanité*, central organ of the French Communist Party. The front page featured a map of Korea with a headline that reported the outbreak of war in that country. It is no exaggeration to say that until that day, almost no one in France knew of a country called Korea. Even I, enthusiastic geographer that I was, had only learned about its existence quite recently, from reading in the publication of the Cominform (the information bureau of the leading communist parties of Europe) an article authored by Kim Il-sung (misspelled Kim Ir-sen). Turning facts upside down, the communist press mendaciously accused South Korea of having attacked the so-called Democratic People's Republic of Korea in the north.

Two or three days later the North Korean communist forces "liberated" Seoul and relentlessly drove the South Korean forces and the Americans who were rushing to their assistance ever further south, until they held no more than the narrow southeast corner of the peninsula around the port of Pusan. This stunning course of events, which foreboded the victory of the North, made me wonder how it was possible for the South and the Americans to be the aggressors, when they seemed so utterly unprepared. It was not until the fall, by which time I was already in Poland, that the fortunes of war were reversed, thanks to the brilliant strategy of General Douglas MacArthur.

During that eventful summer the CCE sent me for one last time to its summer colony at Lacroix-Saint-Ouen near Compiègne. There was much excitement in the air due to preparations that were being made for a major communist youth rally, which was to begin with a torch relay across France. A beautiful song had been composed for the occasion, beginning with the words, "Sur les routes d'été, sur les routes de France, nous allons par milliers au rendez-vous de l'espérance" (Along the roads of summer, along the roads of France, we march by the thousands to the meeting with hope). The lyrics then evoked the forests, the fields, across which, from the north to the Savoy, the youth of France would bring joy to all. The awareness that I would no longer be in the country when that rally took place fed the hesitation that on and off hovered over my resolve. Besides, I was having such a good time at the colony, taking part in walks in the Forest of Compiègne, in that historic city, and to such sites as Pierrefonds, the gigantic medieval castle reconstructed in mid-nineteenth century by the architect Eugène Viollet-le-Duc.

It is said that good times never last, and it saddened me to part with friends old and new and to return to Livry-Gargan. Now that the date set for my departure was near I was no longer sanguine, just when many of my companions and adults connected with the CCE were warmly bidding me adieu. I was nervous and suppressed my anxiety, but I was convinced at this stage that I could not afford to withdraw and therefore had no choice left but to hope for the best.

That fateful day, August 19, finally arrived. Lugging our suitcases and accompanied by a couple of well-wishers, Georges Borenstein and I walked along our street, the Avenue du Colonel-Fabien, on our way to the bus stop, casting last glances at our home. We were met on the platform at the Gare de l'Est by a lady from the office of the CCE, who entrusted us with the care of Marcel Schachet, a simple boy nearly twenty years old, but mentally still a child. We were to hand him over to his father in Międzylesie, a border town in Poland that was the site of the repatriation camp where most people aboard our train were to disembark. I was also given a letter of introduction to the official Jewish organization in Warsaw.

The train would take us through Stuttgart and Prague. Our excitement mounted as, on a glorious sunny day, we approached the border of Czechoslovakia. The crossing at Cheb, our gateway into the "Camp of Socialism and Peace," was nothing like the musical welcome our train of vacationing children had received the summer before in Poland. Rather, it seemed to confirm Churchill's bemoaning of the "Iron Curtain" that had descended across the heart of Europe. A tall and glum moustached guard with an icy manner handed out long and detailed questionnaires in several languages, which he collected once completed. After a long delay the train moved again and I sat for a while in an empty car, calmly admiring the stunningly beautiful scenery of Bohemia, when a Czech man sat down across from me and, upon learning that I was travelling from France to Poland, whispered to me, "Communism no good. Hard work, no pay!"

After a couple of hours the train entered the Czech capital, one of the most beautiful cities in the world, whose incomparable panoramas, fleetingly embraced from the train's window, filled me with enthusiasm, and I anticipated my meeting with my Czech correspondent Jiří Davidek. There he stood on the platform at Wilson Station. We spotted each other instantly. He welcomed me with great warmth, introduced me to his fiancée and handed me a bag of plums. As the stop was long enough, he led me outside the station for a walk to the nearby world-famous Wenceslas Square, which is the heart of Prague. Along the way I noticed a huge billboard with a map of Korea that bore the inscription "Korea Vojuje!" (Korea fights). Even more surprising, I caught sight of passing North Korean soldiers. Oh, how I would have loved to see more of Prague but, all too soon, the time came for Jiří to walk me back to the train and bid me adieu. Thereafter we still exchanged a few letters, but our correspondence lapsed before long.

We arrived in the Polish border town of Międzylesie at night. We were met on the platform by Marcel Schachet's father, come from nearby Wrocław, where he lived. He looked not at all happy when we handed him his son. Georges and I then parted; he travelled north to Płock to be reunited with his uncles and I remained in Międzylesie. Here I posted the letter of introduction from the CCE to the Jewish organization in Warsaw, instead of simply continuing my journey to Warsaw, where I should have arrived the next morning and gone to the office of the Jewish organization to hand the letter to its director in person. But the CCE lady who saw us off at the Gare de l'Est in Paris had not explained matters clearly to me, so instead, I followed the crowd of Polish coal miners returning from the north of France and went with them to the repatriation camp, where in the next several days they all were processed and left as soon as work and resettlement places were found for them. In consequence of my confusion I wasted, it seems, at least two precious weeks in Międzylesie and Wrocław while the CCE and the Jewish organization in Warsaw worried, wondering where I had disappeared to.

Within days of my settling in the repatriation camp, a young official came to process the immigrants. He gave me a round-trip railway ticket to Wrocław, some money, and a form to hand in at a place called *urząd zatrudnienia*, a name I was told how to pronounce without being informed exactly what it meant, which is "employment office"! The official did not seem to realize that, beyond a few rudimentary expressions, my knowledge of Polish was almost nil. And so I wandered into a wild adventure in Wrocław.

When I arrived, carrying a carton with a few belongings, in that sprawling city that still lay largely in ruins, it was near sunset. Wandering through fields of rubble and streets where only a few buildings stood, I asked passersby the way to the "employment office"; in response I met with vaguely pointed directions and explanations hardly intelligible, or simply stares and shrugs. As I crossed a bridge a woman approached me and rubbed against me. Annoyed and embarrassed I abruptly interrupted her chatter with a rude "ja nie rozumiem"(I don't understand). Undeterred, she asked, "Sprechen Sie Deutsch?" (Do you speak German?) Having shaken off the dame I approached a very young policeman, or rather "militiaman," since under the communist regime the police was called *Milicja Obywatelska*, Citizens' Militia. The friendly militiaman invited me to follow him and left me in what must have been a hostel for transient men. The hostel's manager led me to a bed in a room where several men were sleeping. To my dismay, he woke me and the others at five in the morning and threw us all out into the street. Hungry, tired and in near despair I wandered along unknown streets again until, I no longer remember how, I found myself in some office, where two women recorded my particulars and called in a gentleman, who bore the title of "curator."

Before the morning was over I was taken by streetcar to a *pogotowie*, shelter for children, set in a small building with a large garden in a beautiful undestroyed suburb. In it lived a small number of boys and girls of all ages. I stayed there for a week or perhaps longer. I was free to move around and almost daily rode a streetcar to the centre of the city to visit the father of Marcel Schachet, whom I knew from France. Mr. Schachet had placed his son as boarder in a vocational institution and lived alone in his apartment. He always received me warmly and once, upon saying goodbye, expressed with a sigh the wish that I were his son. Then one afternoon, as he joyfully greeted me, he produced a telegram from the Jewish organization in Warsaw asking him to find me and send me immediately to Warsaw! After retrieving my belongings with his help, I took an overnight train to Warsaw, where I rushed to the office of the Jewish organization. The director mildly reproached me for causing everybody anxiety about my disappearance. He telephoned Hanka, who happened to be vacationing in Poland, in the resort town of Otwock not far from the capital, and sent me on my way to her.

As she met me at the railway station in Otwock, Hanka effusively embraced me and affectionately scolded me for having caused her so much anxiety. She had in the meantime arranged for my admission in the children's home of Śródborów, where our group had enjoyed such a pleasant visit the summer before.

Challenges and Friendships

My return to the children's home of Sródborów, this time as a ward instead of a visitor, was no homecoming. The children's home, *dom dziecka*, had in the intervening time been nominally transferred to the authority of the Polish government, although the non-Jewish children in it were few. The natural surroundings were attractive enough: the three houses of the colony were separated by wooded spaces and sandy trails. Indeed, the entire village of Sródborów was scattered across a seemingly endless expanse of pine forest and sand dunes. The air was bracing and fragrant and Sródborów counted several sanatoriums. But seeing nothing but pines and sand whichever direction I ventured and as far as the eye reached, never beholding a vista nor seeing a horizon, soon caused me to feel claustrophobic.

Having experienced the richness of life in a "children's republic," it surprised me that in a children's home situated so near Warsaw, where before the war Janusz Korczak had directed two orphanages, the educational methods taught by the great pedagogue did not seem to be much practised. The Weisbrot couple who directed the home were addressed formally as "Pan Dyrektor" and "Pani Kierowniczka" (Mr. Director and Mme. Director); the counsellors, and even the gardener and the washerwoman, were addressed by prefixing their names with *pan* and *pani*, titles once reserved for the nobility. *Wy*, the Polish equivalent of the French *vous*, is conventionally used in the Polish language only as the plural of *ty* (French *tu*), except among communists who used it as a semi-formal second person of the singular. Furthermore, the use of the third person *pan* and *pani* instead of the second person singular as the polite form of address makes Polish speech rather cumbersome.

Mr. Weisbrot was a soft-spoken, kind gentleman. His wife, however, was rather peremptory: a cold, authoritarian woman, she exuded even less warmth than Hélène Hercman, the only adult to whom we said *vous* in Livry-Gargan. But Madame Hélène had been only an administrative director: her calling was not education. Beyond this, Willa, the girl with whom I had corresponded since the summer of the previous year, now became indifferent to me. I very much missed the intimate egalitarian relationship we had enjoyed with the adults in the homes of the CCE, and also the spirit of spontaneous cooperation that had been bred into us in these homes. There was a "children's council" in Śródborów, but its activity seemed to be limited to occasional formal meetings preceded by standing at attention. At Livry-Gargan we'd had permanent seats around small tables in the dining room and each one of us performed in turn the duty of *chef de table*, someone designated to fetch the food from the kitchen and serve everyone around that table. If, because of some outside activity, several children happened to return home past the set meal time, one of them would spontaneously volunteer to assume the functions of a *chef de table*. In a similar situation in Śródborów, it was each child for himself.

The cultural life of the home could at best be described as mediocre; there was none of the vibrancy, intensity and diversity of cultural and creative activity that had enfolded us in Livry-Gargan. All things considered, or perhaps reconsidered, it seemed as though when I returned to the children's home of Śródborów to live in it, nothing conformed to the appearances that had so impressed me the year before.

Within days of my arrival I was faced with the challenge of attendance at school. The secondary school was situated a few kilometres away from the home and out of the forest in the city of Otwock in what was, I believe, a former aristocratic mansion. My knowledge of Polish being less than rudimentary, I was admitted to the school as a "free auditor," rather than a regular student in Grade 10, from where I was moved a few days later to Grade 9. To say that I felt *dépaysé*, lost, when my secondary schooling had to be resumed in a new country and in a new language would be something of an understatement. I felt positively frightened! Everything looked strange, beginning with the classroom, in which the portrait of communist president Bolesław Bierut hung on one wall and a cross on the opposite one. When in the third period of the morning a Catholic priest in cassock walked into the classroom and the students rose to cross themselves and recite a prayer, my fellow "Weisbrot children," as some called us, motioned to me to follow them out of the classroom. Fortunately, attendance in the religion class was optional.

My progress in the Polish language seemed to me frustratingly slow, in spite of the private tutoring dispensed to me by a retired lady teacher who spoke fluent French. My limited knowledge of Russian was of some help, since both languages are Slavic. Still, to this day I hold Polish to be the most difficult language that I ever tasked myself to master. Neither Hebrew nor even Chinese strained my faculties of linguistic absorption as did Polish, with its tortured phonetics and devilishly complicated grammar, which features nouns and adjectives that undergo seven cases of declensions that differ not only with each of the three genders and three numbers (singular, dual, plural), but also include many exceptions; verbs that change their form, depending on whether the action is one-time or repetitive, and even their meaning depending on the prefix attached to them. Russian, by comparison, seemed significantly simpler. I further reckon that no matter how fluently a non-native learns to speak Polish, he is not likely to acquire a native accent. For my part, I retained a slight French accent that to Polish ears sounded charming.

By the time winter came around, I could communicate at a very basic level and to a small extent understand textbooks and lectures. In January 1951, I successfully pleaded with Mr. Weisbrot to let me leave the children's home and move to the *Bursa*, the adult Jewish student hostel situated in Praga, the half of the metropolis of Warsaw situated on the east bank of the Vistula River. I was one of a small number of secondary school students admitted into the hostel and permitted to live in it on a small stipend granted by the Jewish organization. This I supplemented by giving private lessons in French. Although I now became independent, I nevertheless felt far from happy. Living in the city enabled me to call frequently on Larissa Wuzek, my childhood friend from the CCE home of Andrésy. She was usually alone in her family apartment after school. Before he took her to Poland in 1948, her father had married a woman with two daughters who were older than Larissa. Larissa was not happy; her two half-sisters treated her like a Cinderella and her father, a veteran of the Spanish Civil War, was a hard man who worked with the UB secret police. Larissa and I reminisced about our happy times in Andrésy and consoled each other. One evening her father came home early and surprised us in conversation. He made it clear that I was not to visit Larissa again and informed Sophie that he did not wish his daughter to continue meeting her friends from France.

Throughout the month of January, I continued to attend the school in Otwock. This required that I rise every weekday morning at an ungodly hour in bitter winter weather to catch an early streetcar that would bring me to Warsaw East Station in time to catch the first train to Otwock, where I still needed to walk at least one kilometre before arriving at the school in time for the morning gathering at eight o'clock. Unfortunately at the time, but fortunately in retrospect, I was expelled from the school on the pretext that I had been disrespectful to the geography teacher, a mean woman who deserved no respect and whose ignorance I challenged when she "taught" that the capital of China was Nanjing and I rose to firmly insist that since the founding of the People's Republic it was Beijing.

In the *Bursa* I shared a bedroom with four university students, one of whom was not Jewish. The young men and women who lived in the hostel were a complex lot, emotionally impacted by the dreadful experiences they had survived in the ghettos or remote places of refuge in the Soviet Union. Few of them were congenial, but I did make some friends nonetheless. One of them was Felix Lewin, a gifted twenty-year-old painter who had recently arrived in Poland with his parents from Belgium. The other two were immigrants from France: Rachel Mayerfeld and Jean (Janek) Rosenbaum. Rachel was an exuberantly cheerful and friendly young woman, whom I had the pleasure of meeting again some thirty years later in Tel Aviv, where she was established as a creator of splendid paintings and exceedingly fine ink drawings of scenery. She was married to a man named Chaim Beilis and was the mother of two wonderful children, a boy and a girl who, when I visited in 1980, were doing their military service.

Janek Rosenbaum, a twenty-six-year-old man (to whom Felix and I referred as *le vieux*, the old man), was a student of sinology at Warsaw University. I credit him with having so stimulated my latent curiosity about China that I elected sinology as my future field of study. I often dropped in on Janek in his room and looked on with envy as he read Chinese texts printed the old-fashioned way, coursing down the columns of intricate characters with scissors in his hand. One afternoon that curiosity led me to visit him at the university, where he introduced me to Professor Witold Jabłoński, Poland's premier sinologist. Jabłoński was an amiable, ruddy-faced, modern-day Taoist sage. I saw him again in 1957 when I was a student in Beijing. At that time I conversed with him briefly before he set out, on a hot summer afternoon, to roam around the Buddhist temples of the Western Hills for several hours. He then returned to his hotel to rest before a reception organized in his honour and died in his sleep of a heart attack.

After my transfer from Otwock to the *Bursa* I was accepted as a "free auditor" at an exclusive high school for boys situated on the same street. That school, named after King Ladislaus IV (Władysław

Czwarty) was reputed to be one of the very best in Warsaw, thanks to the presence on its faculty of some outstanding professors, such as the dreaded elderly count who taught mathematics and liberally insulted students, calling some of them "caveman," "swineherd" and other such epithets. For the second time since my arrival in Poland I underwent the intimidating experience of entering a classroom in a strange school, when I hardly knew the language. But the anxiety was soon dispelled by the warm welcome the boys gave me, even though I caused some raised eyebrows by walking out of the classroom upon the entrance of the Catholic priest, nicknamed Ksiądz Pomidor (Father Tomato) on account of his plumpness and rosy cheeks.

When the mid-morning break came, the boys all burst into buzzing after one of them spied the approach at the end of the corridor of the chemistry professor, an elderly man whom they nicknamed "Pszczółka," "Bee," on account of his frequent retelling of his adventures with the bees that he raised. The boy with whom I shared a desk asked me whether I knew what *pszczółka* meant. Not noticing that the professor had at that very moment entered the class, I answered that, yes, it was an insect that goes "buzz, buzz." Silence fell as the professor cast a severe glance upon me and, ordering me to stand up, asked whether that was all my *mądrość*. Not knowing that the word meant "wisdom," I innocently asked, "What is 'mądrość'?" sounding like a Jewish boy engaging in a Talmudic dispute. The boys burst into peals of laughter but promptly jumped to my rescue by explaining that I was a new boy from France, who did not yet fully understand Polish.

Considering Poland's sad reputation as a land of virulent anti-semitism, I must say that neither at Ladislaus IV, nor at the school which I attended afterwards, nor in the summer colonies, did I ever meet with overt manifestations of antisemitism, even though my surname was evidence enough of my Jewish origin. I made friends among the Polish boys, some of whom invited me to their homes to do our homework together after school or with whom I went together to cinemas.

At Ladislaus IV my best friend was Jurek Wróblewski. His father had been killed fighting the Germans in 1939 and he lived with his mother a few buildings away from the *Bursa*. I often walked after school to Jurek's flat and, together with a younger boy named Jacek, we went hand in hand on long walks around Warsaw. Jurek's mother always welcomed me warmly and sometimes reminisced about Jewish neighbours she had before the war, whom she obliged on Shabbat by switching their lights on or off. Amazingly enough, Jurek, who after graduating from high school studied to become a theatre director, learned to speak Yiddish in order to perform in Warsaw's world-famous Jewish theatre, directed at the time by the great Ida Kamińska.

Notwithstanding occasional bright moments, the year 1951, or at least the first half of it, was one of the unhappiest years of my childhood. I was unhappy living in the *Bursa* and unhappy at school, even though my classmates were good to me. I whiled away hours sitting in class unable to understand much of what the teachers were saying, almost despairing of ever mastering the impossibly difficult Polish language. To complicate that endeavour even further, the curriculum of Grade 9 comprised Polish literature from the time of the Renaissance to the eighteenth century, written in a language that differed significantly from modern Polish writing. That was a period when Polish authors let go of the grip of Latin and learned to express themselves in their native language. As the Renaissance poet Nicholas Rey famously put it, "Let people everywhere know that the Poles are not geese, that they have their own language!"

I rose every morning with a burning urge to return to France, which I well realized was an unrealistic dream. In my more despairing moments I fantasized about secretly riding on the roof of a train. Fortunately, the evening hours brought consoling thoughts and the hope that once I mastered the language I would adjust to life in Poland and be happy. Early in the spring of 1951, I contracted a severe case of what I believe was pneumonia and I spat blood. Without adequate medical attention and, more importantly, the caring human attention that I yearned for, the illness lingered and, in a fit of despair, I wrote a letter to Marcel A., a Parisian boy who had befriended me in the CCE summer colony of Compiègne the summer before and with whom I corresponded. In that letter I gave vent to my disillusionment. Little could I have anticipated that Marcel's parents would publicize my letter and use it to attack the CCE and accuse it of having sent me to Poland.

I was beside myself with surprise when one afternoon Sophie unexpectedly entered my room. My delight at seeing her was brief, as she looked visibly upset. The cause of her understandable anger was the publicity given my letter to Marcel A. and the dismay it had generated among the leaders of the CCE. They called on Sophie to investigate. Sophie scolded me copiously but soon regained her true countenance, that of the tender and loving person that she genuinely was. She took out of the bag that she was carrying a package of freshly baked delicious bread rolls and pastry and comforted me by saying that when I mastered the language, I would see Poland differently and learn to love the country.

Sophie was exceedingly attached to the country of her birth and rejoiced at the sight of Warsaw being rebuilt, particularly the new schools, the new apartment buildings and all the social benefits that the government was conferring on working people in spite of the poverty of the country. She was an honest communist who believed with all her heart in the promised bright future, in which there would be "bread and roses" for all, as the poem by James Oppenheim says. Her kind of communists, whose hearts vibrated with sympathy for the exploited and oppressed and in whose commitment there was not one ounce of expediency or cynicism, were doomed to become disillusioned years later and to be cruelly betrayed.

With the arrival of summer my mood became more upbeat. Not far from the *Bursa*, the main avenue of Praga coursed by the side of a vast park through which I walked almost every afternoon, either by myself or in the company of Jurek or one of the other adolescent boys who lived in the *Bursa*. We swam and sunbathed on a beach on the Vistula, right across from the Old City, Stare Miasto, which was being lovingly rebuilt to look just as it had in the eighteenth century. In July, Ryszard Krzyżanowski, a tall, handsome and cheerful university student who befriended me, invited me to vacation with him at his sister's cottage in the scenic Karkonosze (Riesengebirge) mountain region of Silesia. One day when I hiked alone to the peak of that range, the Śnieżka, I inadvertently crossed the ill-marked border and found myself among a Czech-speaking crowd. A Czech guard turned up and brusquely ordered me to return to the Polish side. This insignificant moment heightened my awareness that, at the time, communist countries were not only separated from the West by an "Iron Curtain" but also from each other by lesser "iron curtains." One even needed a special pass to travel to the border regions of Poland.

As September neared, the question of my further schooling became a pressing matter. Sophie went with me to plead with Mr. Kubiak, the gruff professor of Polish who had the power to authorize or refuse my admission into Grade 10, but there was no coaxing him; he categorically refused to let me move up to the next grade. Luckily, a solution to my dilemma soon materialized.

One evening I was invited with Sophie to dinner at the home of Lola Zajączkowska, an austere-looking but inordinately kind lady who worked in the history section of the Central Committee of the United Polish Workers' Party, the official name of the governing communist party. Lola had two sons, Włodek (a diminutive for Włodzimierz) who was my age, and Geniek (Eugeniusz), who was two years older. Both attended an eleven-grade school, which belonged to a network run by the TPD (Society of the Friends of Children), a secular educational society. The TPD schools differed from the general run of Polish public schools in that their curriculum excluded the teaching of religion. This made them more congenial to minorities such as Lutherans, Jews or agnostics. Lola arranged for me to be admitted into Grade 10 at the TPD No. 3 School attended by her sons in nearby Mokotów. The two boys became my friends and over the years that I lived in Poland I was a frequent Sunday guest at the Zajączkowskis.

No longer a "free auditor" and now seemingly in possession of the language, I felt at ease in the new school. Unlike musty old Ladislaus IV, TPD No. 3 was a modern building surrounded by greenery in a suburb of low-rise new apartment buildings widely spaced apart by lawns, gardens and playgrounds. The ambiance was decidedly more congenial than in the two schools in which I had spent the previous year. The teachers were less formal: one addressed them as *pan* and *pani*, but without the addition of the title "professor." I was particularly taken with Pani Knothe, the professor of Polish, a radiant lady, always smiling, always elegantly dressed, with discreet makeup. On winter days she was seen in the streets wearing a fox stole around her neck, in the style of Warsaw's elegant ladies of pre-war years. Under a regime whose activists regarded such display of refinement as a manifestation of bourgeois decadence, she was bound to run into trouble. When my class moved up to Grade 11 in September 1952, Pani Knothe was dismissed by decision of a numbskull Party boss. Fortunately, the irrepressible anger of students and their parents compelled the authorities to reinstate her.

Pani Knothe was a captivating, witty lecturer who held me spellbound. Inspired by her teaching, I made ever more rapid progress in mastering the language. She led me to discover the greatness of Poland's literature, particularly of its Romantic period, which was the subject taught in Grade 10. I discovered a rich literature confined in a parochial language with few of its authors translated into other languages as yet. Among the translated authors, Henryk Sienkiewicz stood out for having been awarded the Nobel Prize for his *Quo Vadis*, even though that was not his best novel. Poland's great romantic poets, particularly Adam Mickiewicz and Juliusz Słowacki, belong in a league with Pushkin, Goethe, Heine, Schiller, Hugo, Byron and Keats.

Besides Sophie, who still lived with friends, there were now two other women who kindly looked after my well-being: Lola Zajączkowska and her friend and fellow worker in the Party history institute, Pola Barska, who was childless and lived alone. Pola even gave me the key to her apartment, so that after school on certain days I could let myself in and do my homework there, until she returned home from her office and prepared supper, after which I returned to the *Bursa* for the night. Pola and Lola had both lived in the Soviet Union during the 1930s and through the war years. Lola's husband had perished in Stalin's purges, yet she remained entirely devoted to the cause of communism. To these two women their Jewish origins seemed inconsequential. Lola advised me to cease corresponding with family and friends in the West; she pointed out to me that her much beloved brother lived in Paris, yet she did not correspond with him, this being the politically wise thing to do.

In November 1951 I fell ill with a serious case of jaundice, which necessitated my hospitalization for nearly six weeks. The unpleasantness of the experience was somewhat relieved by the presence in the bed next to mine of a very friendly Albanian student named Skender Koja, who spoke French and introduced me to fellow Albanian students who visited him. I received frequent visits from classmates and my "aunties." On the day of my release from the hospital, Lola and Pola arrived by taxi to take me back to the *Bursa*. At least so I presumed, but to my utter astonishment, they explained that the *Bursa* was not a proper place for one so young to live, that I needed a family life and that, consequently, they had arranged for my adoption by a childless couple who were "good comrades"! This unilateral decision concerning my future, made without consulting me first or even consulting Sophie, left me speechless, dumbfounded all the way to my new "home."

My would-be "adoptive parents" were Colonel Alexander Zatorski and his wife, Ala, who bore the rank of major and was the director of the Polish army's publishing house. "Olek," the colonel, was a man of few words: reserved, pensive, wise in the counsel he dispensed when sometimes I accompanied him on his walks with the couple's two small dogs. He inspired respect. His wife, by contrast, was outspoken and assertive. She took to chiding me for my lack of political enthusiasm and for not associating with the boys to whom she introduced me, who were sons of high-ranking Party members. These boys attended meetings after classes, sometimes until late into the evening, and were otherwise active in the ZMP (Union of Polish Youth), the Party's youth organization. Like many high school students, I held a membership in the ZMP but was not motivated to become an "activist." In Poland, unlike in France, there was no long lunch break; classes went from eight in the morning until one or two in the afternoon. In order to avoid Ala's sermonizing about my coming home right after classes, I took to spending afternoons in the school library, at the homes of classmates, doing homework together, or going to a cinema. I also resented Ala's remarks that I no longer needed to be looked after by all those "aunties," by which she meant Sophie, Sophie's friend Rózka, who lived around the corner, Lola, and Pola.

The Zatorskis lived in an apartment behind the great department store in the centre of Warsaw. They had a maid, a country woman in poor health who liked me and confided to me facts that she would not dare to mention in the presence of her employers — facts about the painful living conditions of the "toiling masses" whom the regime pretended to serve. Some of that reality was evident to anyone who cared to look, particularly the sight of immense queues of housewives who spent entire nights even in the bitter cold of winter in front of meat stores waiting for them to open in the morning, only to then walk away empty-handed or with little more than a piece of sausage. Whatever one sought to buy in those years, the most frequent answer one received to queries in the stores was *nie ma* (there isn't any). One met with rudeness at every step.

But at least in Poland people did not seem afraid of badmouthing communism and loudly chiming how good things had been before the war. Some of my classmates did just that, particularly a sixteen-year-old one-eyed boy who had spent six months in jail for his bad-mouthing of the regime yet had not "learned his lesson." By contrast, members of the "red bourgeoisie" — I first heard that term uttered cynically by Ala Zatorska — only had to send their servants, driven in office cars, to special "stores behind yellow curtains," where food and goods of all kinds, including imported ones, could be obtained without the need to queue up. It did not seem to me, however, that the Zatorskis abused the privileges allowed the *nomenklatura*, as members of the Party hierarchy and government officials came to be known in later times.

When the school year ended in late June, I judged the time opportune to have a frank talk with the Zatorskis. I told them that at eighteen I was too old to be adopted, that living with them would never work out, and that therefore with the onset of the summer vacations the time had come for me to leave them. I thanked them for their kindness and all they had done for me and I believe that we parted amicably, although I never communicated with them afterwards.

In July I was admitted to a four-week summer vacation colony for boys operated by my school at the small resort town of Rewal, on the Baltic Sea near Szczecin. Upon my return to Warsaw I moved with Sophie into a two-bedroom apartment that had temporarily been allocated to her, its regular tenants having been appointed to a long-term diplomatic posting abroad. The apartment was in a house on a quiet street in a pleasantly green district near Narutowicz Square. From there I often walked to school through fields past parcelled gardens. Bordering on that square was the largest student residence in Warsaw. I often called there on the Albanians whose acquaintance I had made while in hospital, as well as on some North Korean students. During the Korean War, Poland sheltered thousands of orphaned children and students from that unfortunate country once called "the Poland of the Far East," on account of it being torn between China, Russia and Japan. The North Korean students I encountered were a surprisingly freewheeling lot: they went out with Polish girls, made friends and learned Polish much faster than the Chinese students. The latter were far fewer in numbers and remained rather aloof. I fear that many of those Koreans, particularly the orphaned children raised in the fairly open society of Poland, must have met a sad destiny when their totalitarian government demanded their return several years later.

Sophie became like a mother to me, but I am afraid that as a teenager I must have caused her some worries, particularly since I did not share her enthusiasm for life in the "People's Poland." I was able to make modest contributions to our living expenses by working part-time after school at Polskie Radio, the national radio station, in the building from where broadcasts were made in foreign languages. I was hired by the French-language department; for a time I read news and commentaries and then was assigned to the translation bureau, where news and sundry materials were being readied for broadcast to France and Belgium. I worked in that bureau for several hours after school two or three times a week, in addition to a full day on Saturday or Sunday, and earned more per month than factory workers who toiled full time. I was assigned a desk in a large common room where my fellow employees were two men and several women, all native speakers of French. French was the working language in the department.

The atmosphere in the room was livened up by congenial exchanges of light and often funny remarks. The women fussed over me as the kid whom they could call on to run down the three flights of stairs to the snack bar and bring back trays with refreshments. This pleasant ambiance was occasionally disturbed by the momentary entrance of the director or the Party secretary. A heavy silence of intense concentration over the work at hand then descended. Both chiefs were intimidating: the director, a Pole from France who always had a cigarette dangling from his lips, would inquire about some matter or other and cast suspicious looks around the room to assure himself that no one touched files marked "confidential." A man dreaded even more than him was the Party secretary, curiously enough a dark-skinned Corsican who likely did not speak any Polish. How and why he had been brought to Poland was a mystery. No one heard him speak except when called to his office, which would occur when he appeared in the door of the common room and motioned at a person with his finger. I remember once being thus summoned and asked inquisitively why I had translated a certain verb the way I had, whether there was some dark political motivation behind my admitted error. One Sunday I ran into him on a streetcar. Not wishing to acknowledge me, he pulled his Borsalino hat, which made him look like a mafioso, down over his eyes.

My work at Polskie Radio and regular reading of French newspapers at the international book and press club made me wonder why no mention was made in the Polish media of the trial of Julius and Ethel Rosenberg in the United States, now in its third year. The Rosenbergs were charged with having divulged the secret of the atomic bomb to the Soviet Union. Before I had left France, the communist and allied media vociferously denounced the trial as a fabrication and angry demonstrations were held in front of the American embassy in Paris, but in Poland no one seemed to have even heard of the Rosenberg trial.

One evening when I briefly dropped in on Jeanne Pakin, a veteran of the Jewish resistance in France and a friend of Sophie's, I joined a conversation she was having with a neighbour, in the course of which I expressed my puzzlement over the silence of Poland's media. The neighbour, as could be expected, was not aware of the Rosenberg affair and looked surprised. After she left, Jeanne vibrated with anger as she scolded me, asking whether I had not lived in Poland long enough to understand that when the Party kept silent over a particular matter, there was a reason for that. When the Rosenbergs were sentenced, the affair at last became news in Poland and their execution was met with suitably organized indignation.

At age eighteen I had not yet shaken off the communist ideology

214 A CHILDHOOD ADRIFT

in which I had been raised, even though I felt deeply troubled by much of what I saw and heard. The year 1952 was marked by particularly disturbing events, notably the frightful Prague trials at the end of which Rudolf Slánský, former secretary-general of the Czechoslovak Communist Party, and seventeen other members of its central committee, most of them Jews, were convicted of being agents of American imperialism and Zionism plotting to overthrow the "people's democracy" system. Twelve of these veteran communists were sentenced to death and hanged. Similar judicial murders following investigation under the supervision of Soviet specialists in mental and physical tortures took place between 1947 and 1953 in all satellite countries, except Poland.

Troubling thoughts coursed through my mind as I wondered once again how it was possible that dedicated communists who had suffered imprisonment under right-wing regimes before the war or fought in the Spanish Civil War and the anti-Nazi resistance could have turned traitors, just like Lenin's Bolshevik companions sentenced to death in the Moscow trials of the late 1930s. Worse yet, the Prague trials witnessed the introduction of Zionism as the object of vilification.

Then, in the winter of 1952, a similarly sinister judicial farce known as the Doctors' Plot took place in Moscow — a trial of Jewish doctors accused of murdering Soviet leaders and plotting to assassinate Stalin. Sophie now became visibly concerned. Thankfully, most of the doctors were saved by the timely death of Stalin, who was mourned with varying degrees of sincerity, or insincerity, by everybody around me. I admit to having felt sadness on March 5, 1953, not being as yet conscious of the criminal character of Stalin and his regime. Every page of the Party's daily newspaper *Trybuna Ludu* lauded Stalin, while stashed in a corner of the back page, barely noticeable, a short paragraph reported the death of the great Russian composer Sergei Prokofiev. To top the official adulation of Stalin, the government renamed the great industrial city of Katowice Stalinogród but reversed that decision in 1956.

The fall of 1952 was marked by national elections in Poland following the promulgation of a new constitution, which changed the official name of the country from Republic of Poland to People's Republic of Poland. Sophie and I both voted for the first time in our lives, Sophie at age forty-eight and I at age eighteen. But while Sophie exuded what seemed to me a naive enthusiasm over the matter, I was not the least excited about having no choice other than voting for the PZPR or not voting at all. Even though I still believed in the merits of the "people's democracy" system, this looked to me like a parody of an election.

Earlier that year the government had decreed that all Polish citizens must apply for a newly minted identification card. High schools students were mobilized for the campaign. Following a brief training, we fanned out with lists of addresses at which we were to hand out applications, instruct the residents in how to answer the questions and what documents to provide in support of their applications, and then return to collect these papers after they had been suitably prepared. Some people required repeated visits before they did what was expected of them, which was exasperating. My route included an Ursuline convent, where my work was made easy by the efficiency of the cooperative and amiable nuns. The mother superior even invited me to dinner, but I politely refused.

In the fall of 1952 I entered Grade 11, the final year of high school in those days, the year at the end of which one had to pass very demanding written and oral examinations in all subjects taught since Grade 8 in order to graduate with the Certificate of Maturity, the *Matura*. The Polish language no longer presented a challenge to me, except perhaps for a desire to strive for excellence in my writing style. The foreign language courses presented no difficulty whatsoever. Being a native speaker of French and fairly good at English, I was free to take either of these language classes. I settled for English, which my friend Jan Pogruszewski was also taking; I was envious of his proficiency in the language. The second foreign language on the curriculum, Russian, was compulsory for all. There I had no problems either. While in hospital the year before I had spent hours every day studying all kinds of Russian texts, from articles in *Pravda* to poems of Pushkin and Lermontov, so that by the time I returned to school I had mastered Russian to the point of receiving top marks in the subject. Perhaps there was not much merit in that achievement since, apart from Włodek Zajączkowski and a few others who were native speakers, my classmates by and large were not earnest about learning Russian, such was their deep-seated animosity toward Russia.

One morning the lady who taught English entered the class and announced with a sad countenance the passing of King George VI. All in the class became silent, except for the Soviet-born little Bolshevik who was the ZMP group leader; he made crude, sneering remarks. Voices of indignation rose from the class; I could not contain my fury and lashed out at him, upon which he mocked me as a "Western liberal"; I took what he meant as an insult to be a compliment!

At about that time, Jan and I and a bright fifteen-year-old Grade 9 friend met like three conspirators after school to learn the international language Esperanto, created by the genius of the Polish Jewish doctor Ludwig Zamenhof. We even joined the Polish Association of Esperantists and met with adult members at its office. Though not illegal, the Association was frowned upon, since 1952 was the year in which Stalin revealed yet another side of his incomparable genius by publishing a series of articles on linguistics (!) in which he reviled Esperanto as a "cosmopolitan" (code word for Jewish) product.

Much of the spring term was devoted to intense preparation for the *Matura*. I crammed mathematics and the sciences, all subjects in which I felt weak. I spent nights studying with my friends Józef Wasilewski and Andrzej Stankiewicz at the latter's home; we would test each other while Andrzej's kind mother sustained us with sandwiches and tea. The examination assignments were drawn up by the Ministry of Education, and the teachers prepared us academically as well as practically for what everyone anticipated to be an ordeal, down to such practical details as how to be properly dressed for the occasion. One teacher even insisted on making sure that all buttons were sewn on firmly!

The tensely anticipated week began with the Polish composition assignment: we had to write an essay on one of the four historical figures chosen by the World Peace Congress as cultural figures of the year. One of these figures was Victor Hugo and I chose to write my essay about France's most honoured poet and novelist, his literary and political legacy. When the results of the *Matura* were announced, I was delighted to discover that I had earned the grade of five, which was the highest and signified excellence, in all the humanities, the grade of four (good) in mathematics, and three (pass) in the sciences. The principal of our school, a usually stern lady, effusively congratulated me; she thought that my mastery of the Polish language after only three years in the country was such an achievement that I deserved a special recompense. She therefore recommended that I be sent to one of the special summer colonies that the regime reserved for children of Polish ancestry living in Western Europe.

Now no longer a schoolboy, I contemplated an uncertain future. At the beginning of 1953 a commission from the ministry of higher education visited our school and invited interested students to submit applications for studies abroad, which in those years generally meant studying in the Soviet Union. Having been told that a student exchange agreement had been signed with China I applied to be included in it, but by the time summer came around, applicants wishing to study at Soviet universities had already been selected while I had received no communication from the ministry. Larissa's application to study in the Soviet Union had been rejected on the grounds that, having lived in Poland only five years, she was not sufficiently "assimilated" to qualify as a Polish student abroad. I had lived in Poland for not quite three years and was not even active in the ZMP as Larissa was, therefore it was obvious to me that I stood even less chance of being selected. Having concluded that my application would be rejected, all that remained for me was to make up my mind as to which department of Warsaw University I should apply to. Besides, I still cherished dreams of returning to France.

China Beckons

At the beginning of July 1953, I was one of several native speakers of French included in a group of high school students that was sent to a summer colony in Bardo, a castle in a hilly region of Silesia. Bardo was one of the special colonies intended for children of the "Polonia," the Polish diaspora of Western Europe, whom the government sought to impress. These colonies were of a higher standard than the ordinary summer colonies to which schoolchildren were sent, such as the one in Rewal, where I had vacationed the year before. The boys who were to join us two weeks later were mostly sons of coal miners of the north of France with the odd Parisian among them. The stated purpose for which we Warsaw kids had been sent down to Bardo was to "prepare" the place for the boys from France, most of whom would be younger than us. I and the few other French speakers, one of whom was Benoît, the son of Adam Rayski, the great leader and future historian of the MOI Jewish resistance in France, looked forward with intense excitement to the day of their arrival.

In the course of the evening preceding their arrival, between dinner and bedtime, the director signified what he meant by "preparation," when he gathered us French speakers in his office for a highly confidential meeting. With a grave face and in solemn terms he invested us with what he explained to be a weighty mission. We held our breath as he went on to ask that we not reveal to the boys from France that we knew their language and were in any way different from the other Warsaw boys, so that at the end of every day, when all were in bed, he could open the mailbox at the entrance to the colony and bring into his office the letters that the boys wrote to their parents. We were then to read these letters and translate for him whatever they wrote about Poland. The supposed purpose of this indiscretion was to help the government improve its work with the "Polonia." Having been raised in the conviction that personal correspondence was confidential, I could not believe what I was hearing. Moreover, I had for two weeks excitedly anticipated the arrival of our guests, so that I could indulge in the pleasure of speaking French every day.

Unable to contain my indignation, I informed the director that I would not let him keep me from speaking my native language and that he had no right to violate the confidentiality of personal correspondence and force us to become spies. Stunned by my heated expression of insubordination, the director screamed at me that his was not a personal request but a mission entrusted to us by "the Party." I countered that "the Party" would never demand that we act so deceitfully. (I now know better, of course!) The other boys, who up to that moment had stood in stunned silence, now echoed my objections. This unsettled the director to such a degree that, with a sweeping movement of his hand, he shouted, "Get out, all of you!"

On the following morning, as the train was not expected until the afternoon, we strove to keep a low profile; we moved about the castle and its grounds so as not to cross paths with the director, lest he summon us back for additional pressure. Since the entire colony was to walk down the hill to meet the train, we ran down ahead of the others to the station. We positioned ourselves on the outdoor platform in a manner calculated to introduce ourselves to the guests as they came off the train. And so, by the end of the day I had already become friends with two of the boys from France: Gabriel Meretik, future journalist for the Parisian daily *Le Monde*, probably the only Jew in the group, and Stanislas Kocik, who was the son of a coal miner and an amazingly accomplished fifteen-year-old poet. Stanis, as I called him, was a genius cast in the pattern of the young French impressionist poets of the late nineteenth century; stupendously prolific, he composed verse in both French and Polish. After our brief time together at Bardo, he and I entered into an almost decade-long correspondence. When I saw Stanis again in Paris in 1960, he had, alas, fallen on sad days of physical and mental illness. I lost contact with him after I moved to America and a letter I wrote to him was returned as undeliverable.

Happy days now followed the arrival of the boys from France, marked by long walks, outings to places of interest and excellent meals. But there were not to be many of these days for me. The colony had been in full swing, so to speak, for not even two weeks when I unexpectedly received a telegram from the ministry of higher education, summoning me to present myself immediately at the summer school for candidates accepted for studies abroad. The school was being held near Plac Narutowicza. That was the area in which I lived with Sophie, but unfortunately, I would not be allowed to stay at home. The night train from Bardo brought me to Warsaw early in the morning. After collecting my registration papers from the ministry, I presented myself at the office of the school. Instead of simply asking the reason for my arriving at the course one month after it had begun, the director bellowed at me. I promptly produced the telegram, which I had received only the day before, along with the forms from the ministry. Thereupon he informed me about the classes and assigned me a place in a dormitory room of the student hostel.

The course was intended primarily for high school graduates accepted for studies in the Soviet Union. The few of us who were chosen to study in China under a Poland-China exchange program were somehow included in that course. The daily schedule featured hours of Russian language and political study, much of which repeated what we had already learned in Grade 11. Four other boys slept in the dormitory room to which I was assigned, in addition to a senior student on vacation from the University of Leningrad, who was a member of the Party. The purpose of his presence was obvious: it was to monitor our ideology and assess our "political maturity," a quality as important for study abroad as high academic grades. That "comrade" cleverly provoked us into political discussions, usually at bedtime when our guard was lowered.

One evening one of my roommates naively asked the "comrade" what faults exactly were attributed to Gomułka, a legitimate question when one considers the nebulous wording in which that former leader's alleged activity was wrapped by official propaganda. Władysław Gomułka had been the most important figure in the Party leadership next to President Bierut and would eventually become the leader of the country in the years 1956–1970. In 1949, however, he was accused of "nationalist deviation" because of his unhappiness over mounting Soviet encroachment on Poland's sovereignty and was imprisoned for five years. Stalin's edict to have him tried and executed was not carried out due to Bierut's clever manoeuvres, which spared Poland the Moscow-style judicial farces leading to executions of disgraced veteran communist leaders that took place in all other "people's democracy" countries of Eastern Europe.

The evening that my roommate put that question to our "comrade," instead of addressing his query to us, we all gasped. Fortunately, a few days later, the "comrade" had his afternoon off and went into town. Having discovered that he kept his notebooks on the top shelf of our room's closet, we organized ourselves to investigate what he had written about each one of us: one of the boys stood watch in the corridor while the rest of us moved the table to the closet, placed a chair atop the table and drew out the notebooks, making sure that they would be placed back precisely the way they were found. Not surprisingly, our friend's naive query had been duly recorded and he was rated as politically immature. About me, the "comrade" noted that I was politically savvy but displayed a Western European liberal mentality. We now all knew how to change course verbally in order to win more favourable political assessments.

One late afternoon when I was sitting alone in my room I heard a knock on the door and beheld an utterly unexpected visitor: Heini! About one year before, I had, to my astonishment, run into Heini when I stepped into a streetcar. At that time he had arrived in Warsaw only days before with Hanka, his wife. Hanka, who did not have French citizenship, had been expelled from France on account of her political activities. Heini, who was Alsatian and spoke no Polish, followed her to Poland with their two small sons, Guy and Claude. Surprisingly enough, he adapted amazingly well: he learned to speak the language in a remarkably short time and became a worker at the Żerań automobile factory, happy to have for the first time in his life learned a trade. I often visited the family in their Praga apartment and we spent pleasant hours together. In 1953, they had a third son, Joseph, named, alas, after Stalin. Heini never came to Sophie's apartment, perhaps because she did not think highly of him. Now it was he who, to my surprise, came to see me. But enjoying a visit was decidedly not Heini's purpose. He bore the most severe countenance that I had ever seen on him, and I instantly realized that the cause for his crossing the entire width of the city to call on me was a letter that I had written to him, in which I had poured out my unhappiness about living in Poland and my resolve to return to France, should my candidacy to study in China be rejected. But Heini said little and only asked whether I could come to his home for dinner and to discuss matters when I had a free evening.

I had not looked forward to the evening, in the course of which Heini shouted, as was his wont, mercilessly lambasting me until very late into the night for wilfully blinding myself to the objective reality of the extraordinary achievements of People's Poland in the face of so many difficulties. One of the accusations he hurled at me was that of seeing only the drunks prostrated at the foot of the rising new constructions, and not the constructions themselves in which working people were now being housed. This long, drawn-out evening gave me a foretaste of the mentally unsettling methods of "brainwashing" that I would later discover in China. In spite of parting with expressions of affection from him and Hanka, I left their home thoroughly shaken.

In the weeks that followed, I convinced myself that Heini was right and endeavoured to change my views about Poland and to marshal myself into a positive frame of mind, which, to be honest, stood me in good stead during the more than three-month-long wait until my departure for China and for long afterwards. Once the preparatory school was over, all that was left for the four of us selected to study in China, and the newly appointed eight additional students who were lucky not to have had to endure the gruelling preparatory course, was to patiently wait for the date set for our departure, a date that was deferred time and again.

In the meantime I resumed my work at Polskie Radio and even participated in volunteer labour sessions, clearing rubble on Warsaw reconstruction sites. I genuinely admired the progress made in the reconstruction of the capital, destroyed during the uprising of 1944. Regardless of my political views then or now, one must admire a country that at the time was poor and beset by so many pressing needs, not least of which was housing the people, yet found the funds, energy and know-how to rebuild the Stare Miasto (Old City) and only slightly less ancient Nowe Miasto (New City), not as they looked before the war with their modern accretions but fully restored to their eighteenth-century splendour, complete with the panoramas painted by the landscape painter Bellotto, who used the name of his uncle, Venetian master Canaletto.

I now gladly assumed my Polish citizenship, and Sophie expressed delight at the happier disposition she noticed in me. I cultivated a relationship with three different girls, one of whom had been my classmate at the TPD school and was a native of France. Since the death of Stalin and the assumption of leadership in the Soviet Union by Georgy Malenkov, the political atmosphere seemed to have noticeably relaxed. Some prisoners were released from the Gulag, among them the Jewish doctors who had been tried on the fabricated charge of attempting to assassinate Stalin. Shortly before his death, Stalin mooted the plan to emulate Hitler by deporting the Jews from European Russia to Siberia, and it has been rumoured that the opposition of his colleagues on the Politburo to that criminal plan caused him to suffer the massive stroke that killed him.

The period from 1953 to 1956 soon became known as the "Thaw," after the title of the latest novel by Soviet writer Ilya Ehrenburg. In the years when I read, willy-nilly, a great deal of Soviet Russian literature, Ehrenburg was an author I truly enjoyed. He was a great lover of France, its culture and way of life, and was decorated with the medal of the Legion of Honour in 1944. In two of his major novels, in which much of the action unfolds in France before, during and after the war, the luminousness of the passages set in France contrasts with the greyness of the passages set in the Soviet Union. It still amazes me that in spite of Ehrenburg's sympathies for France and evident Jewish consciousness, the Ogre of the Kremlin tolerated him. But years later Ehrenburg did relate in his memoirs the constant fear under which he lived in the grips of Stalin's terror.

Delay followed delay, but the day anticipated with trepidation finally arrived. On a cold, rainy December morning our group of twelve prospective students arrived at Warsaw's Okęcie airport and boarded an Ilyushin airplane bound for Moscow. We were led by Gusta, a graduate student in sinology at Warsaw University, whose husband, Stasiek Kuczera, was already doing research in Beijing. I was brimming with excitement because my long-held dream of seeing Moscow was about to be realized. Alas, at the end of a five-hour flight, the first travel aboard an airplane in my life, we were met at Vnukovo airport by the representative of the Polish embassy in the Soviet capital, who informed us that we had only a five-hour layover and were already booked on a flight to Sverdlovsk (Ekaterinburg) leaving at midnight. Our pleading was in vain. How bitter the disappointment! It was not until two years later, in the summer of 1955, that I would at last have occasion to enjoy the sights of Moscow.

It was bitterly cold and still dark at six o'clock in the morning when, after a six-hour flight from Moscow, we landed at Sverdlovsk and trudged across a snow-covered tarmac toward a wooden shack inside which incongruously hung a huge crystal chandelier. There, we were served breakfast and then rushed to a plane bound for Krasnoyarsk in the heart of Siberia. That flight was five hours long and was followed, after a two-hour break, by another flight of the same duration that ended in Irkutsk. For me each landing was an ordeal of extreme pain in my ears and sinuses, and we all felt in a state of exhaustion so extreme that we were on the verge of rebellion: we resolved that we would not endure another five- or six-hour flight without a night's rest! Luckily, we were offered dinner and a night's rest at the airport of Irkutsk. My anguish was relieved altogether when we were informed that only half of our group, namely six of the boys, would be included in the next morning's flight for the final leg of our long journey to Beijing; the five girls and I were to fly twenty-four hours later!

The following morning, notwithstanding a temperature of about thirty degrees below zero, I ventured to walk away from the airport in the expectation of exploring Irkutsk. But the city was a long distance away and I had to content myself with nothing more than a stroll through a nearby village of wooden *izbas*, log cabins. On the second evening at the airport hotel a Polish diplomatic courier who was to fly the following morning joined our group. The courier was a chubby, jolly man, who regaled us with detailed accounts of all the airplane disasters he had survived in the course of his career in different parts of the world. These disasters all happened in Dakotas, small airplanes reputed to be "flying coffins," as he amiably confirmed. One can only imagine our shock and dismay when, before dawn the next morning, standing on the open airfield shivering in a temperature of thirty-two below zero, we heard the call to board a tiny Dakota, which carried only a dozen passengers and looked as if it had been pieced together with plates of metal of different colours and pointed skyward at an angle of almost forty-five degrees. But at least all seats were window seats and we flew at low altitudes.

What with two stopovers, that final leg of our journey lasted almost the entire day. Soon after take-off from Irkutsk the scenery changed from boundless expanses of snow-covered plains to a landscape of seemingly uninhabited mountain ranges. Our first landing was a brief lunch stop at the airport of Ulan Bator, the capital of Mongolia, Genghis Khan's homeland, which in 1924 had the sad distinction of becoming the first satellite state of the Soviet Union. During the plane's descent we caught a glimpse of a city largely made up of shacks and yurts surrounding a miniature replica of Moscow's Red Square, on which one could discern the mausoleum of Sükhbaatar, the country's Lenin. Inside the tiny airport a group of smiling Mongolian men in colourful robes stood along the wall behind us as we ate our lunch; they waved goodbye when we walked back to the airplane. The next landing was in the middle of the Gobi Desert in a place called Sainshand. There was no settlement that we could discern there: only a few yurts and a herd of camels, chased away from our landing path by lasso-wielding horsemen. This was only a refuelling stop and we were soon up in the air again.

Before long we were again flying over a range of barren mountains. Suddenly, with suspended breath I beheld that wonder of the world: the Great Wall of China! Its majestic silhouette, punctuated with turrets at regular intervals, snaked up and down the barren mountains from boundless horizon to boundless horizon. During the five years of my stay in China, I would several times have occasion to walk on top of the Great Wall in the company of other foreign students at Beijing University. We travelled to and back from it on an amazing antique train across the final stretch of the North China plain, flat like a table top, up to the walled town of Nankou and then, with a second steam engine pushing from behind, abruptly up mountains, through a succession of tunnels, to Badaling station. In that station stood a statue of Zhan Tianyou, China's first railway engineer, who had built that marvel of engineering, the Imperial Peking-Kalgan Railway, in the 1890s.

Our plane now began its descent into Nanyuan airport, south of Beijing. What a sight the ancient capital was in those days, when it was girded with rings of monumental walls and gates and resplendent with thousands of tiled roofs gleaming in the bright winter sun! The sight of it was too fabulous for words, a sight beyond what the present-day traveller could even imagine as he lands in the indifferent modern megalopolis that Beijing has become.

The arrival formalities completed, we were met by a welcoming committee from Beijing University (or Beida, its familiar name) and driven to that revered institution across the historical Outer City and Inner City. The inner wall that separated these two parts of historical Beijing, like its outer ring walls, were all torn down in the late 1950s. As soon as we passed Da Qianmen, the "Great Front Gate" to the Inner City, I beheld Tiananmen, the famous and imposing "Gate of Heavenly Peace," which is the southern entrance to the Forbidden City of the emperors of the Ming and Qing (Ch'ing) dynasties. Fronting Tiananmen in those days was not the vast concrete glacis of today, the site of so many self-congratulatory parades of the regime and protest demonstrations against it. Whereas today the glacis is framed by the mausoleum of Mao Zedong, the National People's Congress and other Chinese versions of Stalinesque architecture, in 1953 it was a much smaller square framed with trees and red walls, almost reminding me of the Tuileries garden in Paris. After about another half hour we passed Xizhimen, the "West Straight Gate," and continued several kilometres beyond it to the walled campus of Beijing University. By the time we reached our dormitories, night had descended. These dormitories were attractive Chinese-style pavilions with curved roofs built not many years before, when the campus belonged to Yenching University, known as "Harvard in China."

The next morning we returned to the heart of the capital to be introduced at the Polish embassy and collect our scholarships. The embassy was located in the part of the old Legation Quarter that abutted the southern end of Tiananmen Square. Coming out of it we hired bicycle-drawn rickshaws for a short ride to the fabulous Dongan Bazaar on Wangfujing, the attractive commercial street once known to Europeans as Morrison Street. But first I stood for a while in the square silently admiring the monumental gate through which we were to pass a day or two later on a guided tour of the Forbidden City organized for foreign students. How many times had I seen pictures of Tiananmen in books and illustrated magazines and dreamt that perhaps some wonderful distant day I would behold it before my very eyes. That oft-imagined and dreamt-of moment had now, almost unexpectedly, arrived!

Thoughts of a hopeful future in this blessed moment of my first day in China mingled with a flood of images of my past life. I was nineteen years old, standing on the threshold of adulthood. But I was also a child of the Shoah — the catastrophe that had carried away my parents and imprinted on my life an entirely different direction than would have been the case had my parents lived. But for now I was happy to have come to live in a country that had no tradition of antisemitism; in Europe, even when teachers, schoolmates and others were good to me, I remained aware that "something" about me set me apart from them, and I was as a rule on my guard. For, although I did not look Jewish, I assumed that merely from knowing my surname gentiles would naturally deduce that I was Jewish and comment about it when I was out of their sight.

Classes began for us on the second day. Beida had a foreign student office, which operated a two-year intensive Chinese language course: students who elected to study in specialized schools, notably the Central Academy of Fine Arts or the International Trade College, spent only one year in the language course, but those who intended to study Chinese literature or history, the latter being my case, spent two years in the language course. In the second year we would be introduced to Wenyan, classical or literary Chinese. I graduated from the language course in 1955 and became a first-year student in the history department of our university.

Three years earlier, China had adopted the Soviet model of education in which university studies lasted five years, the first three constituting the undergraduate portion and the final two years the pre-MA graduate section. Unlike the North American system, which allows students to choose from a wide selection of subjects in order to obtain a liberal education in the humanities or the sciences, the Soviet model required that one elect a field of specialization as soon as one entered the first year of university. Also, the education dispensed at universities embraced only the humanities and the sciences; more technical fields like medicine or engineering were taught in specialized institutes similar to the French *grandes écoles*. A major urban centre had, as a rule, only one general education university and countless specialized schools of higher learning. This vast reorganization of higher education was accompanied in 1952 by the nationalization of foreign-established universities, such as American missionary universities like Yenching and Tsinghua outside Beijing; these were broken up in order to reassemble their faculties. That was how Beijing University was moved from downtown Beijing to the former campus of Yenching on its outskirts, and its Faculty of Arts absorbed those of Tsinghua and Yenching.

Not long after the arrival of our Polish contingent, one girl, who had been all smiles and sweetness to me, confided to Gusta, the graduate student who had been our leader during the journey, her annoyance that "even here," in China, a Jew should sneak among Poles. Little did she know that her confidante, who was blond like herself and whose maiden name was concealed by her marriage to a Polish gentile, was Jewish also. Gusta reported the girl's utterance to Mrs. Kiryluk, the ambassador's wife, who was Jewish as well! That lady acted like a mother to the Polish students and invited, or should

I say, summoned us, once a month for a meeting, usually followed by a delicious lunch. At the first such meeting attended by our newly arrived group, she lashed out against unnamed individuals who dared to spread antisemitic gossip, all the while staring at the culprit who burned with shame and looked as if at any moment she would slide under the table.

Most Chinese people did not even know what a Jew was, and when asked what they know about the Jews, many ventured to express curious notions gleaned from hearsay, such as that Jews were smart at business — something they admired — and that they were supremely clever, citing as proof the few Jews whose names they knew, usually Karl Marx, Albert Einstein and, alas, Henry Kissinger!

One of the earliest friends I made among Chinese students at Beida was Liang Pengfei, a native of Harbin in Northern Manchuria who, not surprisingly, spoke fluent Russian and studied French in the department of Western languages. Coming from Harbin, a major city that had once had a large and flourishing Russian Jewish community with a magnificent synagogue, he had met Jews before. One summer day he and I bussed into the centre of Beijing and rambled around Beihai (Northern Sea) Park, whose dominant feature is a white Buddhist pagoda on a rise overlooking the lake. Moments after we left the park a massive rainstorm hit the street and we ran for shelter under the porch of the Beijing public library nearby. The storm lasted long enough for us to stand there and chat at leisure. Suddenly, Pengfei looked at me with a mischievous smile and remarked, "I suspect that you are not a real Pole…." As I turned to him in surprise, he added, "I think that you belong to a certain national minority known to be the most intelligent people in the world!" I cherished the friendship offered me by Pengfei. Like many Chinese in the 1950s, he avowed that the communists had done much good for the country but could not comprehend why they had to be so oppressive, when they enjoyed the people's support. The well-meant criticisms he sometimes uttered eventually earned him several years in China's Gulag. Grateful for having survived terrible suffering, he converted late in his life to Christianity.

I readily made friends among Chinese students; when some praised me for not being "like other foreigners," for being more like them, that made me truly happy. Even though with the passing of time I suffered many a cruel disenchantment, I yearned to immerse myself in the land and its people. As I grew familiar with the Chinese and their ways, I became increasingly critical, yet at the same time some string in my heart continued to vibrate with them. Lu Xun (Hsün), who is generally regarded as the greatest Chinese writer of the twentieth century, subjected the failings of his compatriots to blistering criticism and even ridicule, yet he loved them deeply and they forever love him. Later in life I became aware of parallels and even similarities between the Chinese and the Jews and researched and wrote on that subject.

A few years after the liberation there still lingered something of the old China and the charming side of its ways; the cruel side, however, did not wane and if anything, grew worse. I loved to wander about Beijing's *hutong*, winding lanes, to watch the people go about their daily activities, even when I was myself the object of their curiosity, and to peer through open gates of the walled houses whose windows faced secretive inner courtyards. There was something sensual about these northern Chinese dwellings and lanes, which were often adorned with porticos erected in memory of chaste widows or eminent men. All of this is, sadly enough, long gone.

Even more unfortunately, in the "New China" of Chairman Mao, foreign students were restricted in their movements, pigeonholed by nationality and compelled to leave the country after completion of their studies. In the late 1950s the segregation of foreign students grew, even as the repression inflicted on educated Chinese became ever more stringent. By the time I left China in October 1958, Chinese students had become truly afraid of befriending foreigners. I envied foreign students in Taiwan, who could study and live where they wanted, even with Chinese families if they so chose.

Like the Soviet Union after 1953, China began to experience a period of "thaw," which gave rise to guarded optimism about the future. Although in 1956 the Chinese Communist Party disapproved of Soviet leader Nikita Khrushchev's revelation of the horrendous crimes perpetrated by Stalin, it also approved of the Soviet army's intervention in Hungary to crush the "counter-revolution." Nevertheless, that year Mao Zedong coined the slogan "Let a hundred flowers bloom; let a hundred schools of thought contend." The following spring he initiated a campaign of "Rectification of the Work Style" of Communist Party leaders and invited people, particularly intellectuals and students, to "boldly" express criticism, promising that no one would be punished for expressing opinions, even if these were deemed "incorrect."

Alas, millions who took the "Great Leader" at his word and criticized the misdeeds of the communists in speech or in handwritten big character posters pasted on walls, discovered that they had been lured into unmasking themselves as rightists or "counter-revolutionaries" in what turned out to be a crude trap. Accused students, professors and public figures, were subjected to "struggle meetings," at which their own colleagues and even relatives were forced to denounce them, repudiate them, even beat them up, until they thoroughly debased themselves and wrote and rewrote abject confessions that were not only self-incriminating but also incriminated others. I personally witnessed, as I peered into the window of a classroom without being detected, how some poor fellow stood on a chair in the middle of a circle, while at a signal given by a cadre official, everybody screamed at him. Many who could not endure such humiliation and loss of face committed suicide. Others suffered condemnation to long years at *laogai*, reform through labour, in the Gulag. A degree of totalitarian mind control of such intensity had not been experienced even in the Soviet Union in Stalin's time.

The tragic aftermath of the 1957 "Rectification" was for me the last straw. My initial discovery of "New China" had rekindled my enthusiasm for the cause of communism and restored my trust in its promise of a better future for mankind. Misgivings began to cause cracks in that confidence in September 1955 when I travelled on the Moscow-Beijing train back to China after spending two months in Warsaw, which that summer had been the venue of the wonderfully exciting World Festival of Youth and Students, organized every second year by the world communist movement. And that summer I was at last given the opportunity to visit Moscow and was suitably impressed with its sights and the splendour of its metro stations. One afternoon in the course of that nine-day ride our train came to an unscheduled stop at a minor station in Siberia. A few of us stepped outside to stretch our legs. On the tracks next to where our train was stopped stood a long train of sealed boxcars. That train warranted no curiosity, until what sounded like muffled groans were heard coming from inside it, and then hoarse voices loudly swearing, calling for something to drink. Lifting my eyes up to where these troubling sounds emanated from, I noticed horizontal slits under the roofs of the cars and, to my shock, saw hands hanging out from them. My companions and I looked at each other in stunned silence. Then, before we even had time to react, the all-aboard call urged us back into our train.

The discovery that there were concentration camps in the Soviet Union and that people were being transported in cattle cars was a prelude to the ultimate shock that awaited me the following spring when I read the speech that Soviet leader Nikita Khrushchev made at a supposedly secret session of the 20th Congress of the Soviet Communist Party. In that speech Khrushchev revealed the crimes of Stalin: the mass murders, the tortures, the deportations of entire ethnic groups. To learn that Stalin had been a murderous tyrant belonging in a league with Hitler caused me immense grief and an unutterable feeling of betrayal, for I thought of all the good people who had died believing in the cause of communism and in Stalin — among them my father. And I thought of Sophie and others who had endured prison and no end of sacrifices fighting for that cause. Many years later I accepted that Mao Zedong belonged in that league of champion mass murderers as well, but by then I had long lost my illusions, and I rejoiced when the Soviet Union disintegrated and its subject nations won their freedom. My only regret is that the Chinese empire did not also disintegrate, for martyred Tibet would then have regained its independence.

I expected to graduate from Beijing University in 1960. I was only a third-year student in the terrible school year 1957–1958 when the long drawn-out witch hunt for rightists and a succession of insane campaigns of the kind that George Orwell lampooned as organized mass hysteria made normal academic activity impossible. Students and professors were being sent for long periods to rural villages to undergo "thought reform" by labouring with "poor and lower middle peasants"; they had to participate in sessions of "criticism and self-criticism" and "offering their hearts to the Party." As normal academic activities were suspended, foreign students in the departments of history and Chinese literature were told to keep themselves busy writing papers. I chose to travel for three weeks in the South.

In the mid-fifties it was still possible for foreigners to socialize with their Chinese student peers and even establish bonds of friendship, in spite of varying degrees of watchfulness on the part of those who wielded political authority. Authorities did not ban such spontaneous relationships, lest such actions give the lie to their claims and propagandistic boasts about how they promoted friendships between the people of China and other countries.

When I became an undergraduate student in the history department, I even marched with my classmates in the May 1st (International Labour Day) and October 1st (National Holiday) parades past the reviewing stands on Tiananmen Square. On a few occasions I was invited to the homes of classmates whose parents lived in Beijing — a rare privilege at the time.

The year 1958 was the first of the *Dà yuè jìn*, or Great Leap Forward, which ended with the setting up of the People's Communes, the most extreme form of collectivization of agriculture ever devised.

As part of the Leap Forward people everywhere were mobilized to produce steel; city courtyards and fields bristled with millions of furnaces of every size. The peasants were urged to cast their household pots and pans into these furnaces, as the collective eating halls set up in the people's communes made these utensils unnecessary.

Mao's inane ideas hurt nature as well, when he launched a campaign to eliminate the "Four Pests": flies, mosquitoes, rats and... sparrows! The latter were guilty of eating too much grain! Travelling across Jiangsu province that May I witnessed people standing on roofs or running from tree to tree, screaming and using every imaginable noise-making implement to cause the frightened birds to fly until they dropped dead. Back in Beijing I was informed that flocks of birds had found refuge on the grounds of foreign embassies and that the Chinese authorities had asked permission to enter and cull the hapless winged refugees, which were then taken out by the truckloads.

The goal of all this frenetic activity was to turn China, within three years, into an industrial power surpassing Britain and even the United States. Instead, the year 1960 saw the onset of the greatest famine in Chinese history, all the worse for being man-made. Estimates of the number of people who died in that famine range from thirty to forty million. But I had left China two years before that catastrophe, determined to depart from the Bloc and remake my life in France or in Canada, since in any case it was no longer possible to pursue normal studies in China.

In the final months of my life in China, and with time on my hands, I was seized with a veritable wanderlust. I strolled about the streets and lanes of Beijing, visited isolated temples describe in old travel guides, and called on veteran foreign residents of the capital, among them Robert Winter, a retired elderly American professor of English who lived in an isolated part of the university campus, and Walter Zeissberger, an Austrian professor of German who in pre-communist times had taught at the Catholic University of Beijing.

These men, and others whom I was privileged to know, were gold-mines of information about what life had been like before the communist revolution.

Until the fall of 1957 I had given no thought to my future after graduation from the university, but the political circumstances compelled me to focus on the future. By 1958 my disenchantment with Mao's China and communism in general was profound and I had resolved to leave, a move that required that I first return to Poland. After 1950 my correspondence with Sonia and Monty had become sporadic and ceased altogether when I was persuaded by well-meaning persons that for the sake of my future in Poland it was not wise to correspond with people in the West. Luckily, in 1958 I succeeded in renewing contact with my family in France and in Canada. I became anxious to return to Poland as soon as possible, fearful lest the exceptionally liberal political climate of the country of which I was a citizen might deteriorate due to Soviet pressure and I could then lose all chance to depart from there to the West.

As 1958 wore on and the day of bidding farewell to China approached, I grew ever more depressed. I had grown attached to the country and had in better times considered making it my home. I worried over the fate of my Chinese friends entrapped in the regime's repression and forced into estrangement from me. My last school year in China was marked by frequent upsets and sleepless nights. I even had nightmares evocative of the anguished times of my childhood during the Shoah.

I arrived back in Poland in October 1958, embarrassed to have to keep my ultimate purpose of returning to France hidden from Lola and Pola, all the more since I had been warned by Luba Brojde, the wife of Léopold (Lejba to those with whom he was familiar) Trepper, that Pola was an informant of the UB secret police. In the summer of 1959 I deceptively assured the two women that I was going to France for only a three-month visit with my family and would return in the fall. This seemed plausible, since I was a student on scholarship at

Warsaw University. I had reconnected with Sophie once I was back in Poland and had moved with her into a two-bedroom apartment.

My intention was to remain in the West and return to Poland only if I failed to settle in France or North America. The only persons other than Sophie who knew of this plan were Lejba Trepper and his family. Sophie and Lejba were long-time friends. Both had been secretly active in Paris in the years 1940–1943: Lejba as *le grand chef* of the "Red Orchestra," the major Soviet intelligence network in occupied Europe that communicated to Moscow some of the best-kept German secrets; Sophie as one of the leaders of the Jewish section of the MOI. The two were, however, not allowed to have contact with each other. In January 1945 a Soviet airplane had landed in liberated Paris. It brought back Maurice Thorez, secretary-general of the French Communist Party who had spent the war years in the Soviet Union, and on its return flight the plane carried Trepper back to Moscow. Alas, notwithstanding his meritorious contributions to the Soviet victory, Lejba soon found himself locked up in Moscow's notorious Lubyanka prison for nine years. His wife and sons were falsely informed that he had been executed as a traitor. One year after the death of Stalin he was released to his family. In 1957 an agreement was signed between Poland and the Soviet Union, which allowed for the repatriation of residents of the Soviet Union who could claim Polish origins. Lejba and his family availed themselves of that opportunity.

Lejba, Luba and their three sons, Michael, Edward and Peter, were now settled in Warsaw, where they lived in far better conditions than they had in Moscow. While Lejba was a native of Poland, his family were Russian-born immigrants who, like others we knew in their situation, experienced much difficulty adjusting to Poland, learning the language and dispelling the curtain of hostility toward Russians. Lejba found employment with the Jewish Cultural Society as an editor of literary works translated from Yiddish and thus looked forward to a life of tranquility at last. The calm would, alas, last not even a decade.

Sophie and I grew very close to the Trepper-Brojde family. I became friends with their sons, particularly Michael, the oldest one, who was a graduate student of English literature. I had met the brothers previously during a stopover of a few days in Moscow on my way back to Beijing from a summer vacation in Poland in 1957. Back from China, I became a frequent visitor at their Warsaw apartment, and when Sophie travelled to New York in the spring of 1959 to reconnect with her two brothers and her sister, Michael stayed with me in her apartment.

Sophie did not approve of my plans to move back to the West but assured me of her discretion. Seeing the firmness of my resolve to leave Poland, Sophie asked me to seek the benefit of Lejba's wise counsel, which I did. Lejba simply advised me not to say or do anything (such as applying for political asylum) that could possibly harm Sophie.

One August morning at dawn, as the train on which I had left Poland neared Paris, the castle of Lacroix-Saint-Ouen on the River Oise, site of the CCE summer colony in which I had stayed three times, came into view. The city of my dreams looked the same as when I had left it, except that now its arteries were clogged with automobile traffic and the smell of gasoline filled the air.

After a few weeks of visiting with my family in Lyon and Nancy, I returned to Paris, where I eventually found employment and settled in a rented room in the suburb of Antony. I was hired by UNESCO to compile a volume of Chinese popular short stories of the Sung period, which I translated into French. I also attended courses at the Sorbonne, as well as seminars at the contemporary China research centre of the École pratique des hautes études, whose director, General Jacques Guillermaz, honoured me with his friendship. Having lived nine years under communism I was aghast at the hold that its ideology held over the minds of so many people in France. Many of the students and intellectuals whom I met seemed to me unbelievably gullible. Students spoiled by the French welfare state, which provided them with tuition-free education, besides cheap meals and cheap accommodation, deluded themselves with the astonishing beliefs that their peers in communist countries were paid salaries to study, that the Soviet Union was technologically ahead of the United States, and that the people's communes had brought the Chinese peasantry prosperity! I tried, without much success, to counter these myths. If I mentioned Stalin's crimes, some retorted that one could not make omelettes without breaking eggs, an inhuman but sadly typical reflection of French intellectuals fluttering above the world of reality.

I renewed contact with a few of my companions from the children's homes but, except for the former Andrésy *monitrice*, motherly Mathilde, I kept my distance from the CCE and its successor organizations, which exist to this day. The fourteen months that I lived in France in 1959–1960 were a happy time and, notwithstanding the exciting prospect of sailing to America to study on scholarship at Columbia University, I felt sad when the time came to leave. I sailed from Le Havre to Montreal, where I rejoiced in the three-day-long reunion with Uncle Léon and Aunt Genia, who had travelled from Toronto to meet me at the arrival of the SS *Homeric*.

I embraced my new surroundings in New York almost from the moment that I detrained at Grand Central Station in that most stunning metropolis in the world, in the glorious East Coast autumn days of October 1960. I pursued graduate studies in the department of history and the East Asian Institute at Columbia University for the next three years, then accepted a position on the faculty of the University of British Columbia, where I completed my post-graduate studies alongside my teaching. The wonderful port city of Vancouver became the end destination of a life of wandering from country to country.

Afterword

In March 2005 I revisited the château du Masgelier, accompanied by my childhood friend Bernard Ebenstein, who had also survived the war in hiding. Bernard, who once was a professor of French literature and rhetoric at the University of Limoges, has now for many years achieved recognition as deputy mayor in charge of the finances of that large city. His office was in the *hôtel-de-ville*, the city hall. It was the anticipation of a reunion with him that brought me for a few days to Limoges after sixty-three years. Bernard and I had not only been companions in the Jewish children's home of Andrésy in 1945–1946, but also classmates in the elementary school for boys in that village. Indeed, one particularly exciting event of my return visit to Limoges was a drive with Bernard down to the city of Brive-la-Gaillarde for a reunion with Lucien Fraysse, who had been our teacher in Andrésy during that first year after the war. He was now ninety-five years old and remembered me well and, I believe, fondly. How fortunate I was to see him again, for the following year he died.

On that morning when Bernard drove me to the Masgelier, we strolled about the grounds and peered into the windows of the locked-up castle. The place looked abandoned and sorely neglected. Furniture was piled up helter-skelter in the darkened dusty halls and the only living presence we could detect was that of a few ponies grazing in a small enclosure. Coming to the detached annex below the castle, we were surprised to find the door unlocked. We climbed the steps to the loft, where I discovered that the dormitory in which I'd slept had been divided into several rooms. Just as we walked out of the annex a car drove onto the grounds and a lady, who happened to be the caretaker, inquired what we were looking for. I explained to her my past connection with the place. She confirmed my guess that, indeed, the loft had until recently been one single large dormitory and informed us that the castle was now a summer vacation colony.

On the wall below the steps that led to the main entrance of the castle we came upon a historical plaque bearing the inscription that hundreds of Jewish children had been sheltered on the premises between September 1939 and February 1944. Why February, I wondered: were the remaining children all arrested in that month by the police or the Gestapo? Or had it been possible to evacuate and hide the last of the children precisely that month? Looking down at the surrounding countryside and the narrow road leading up to the castle, it seemed to me that any of the sinister black Citroën cars favoured by the Germans and the police seen driving along it would have been noticed in time to enable at least the older children to flee. My questions were answered in part by what I read in the records of a symposium held in 1996 in Guéret, the chief city of Creuse — namely, that whenever feasible, the children of the Masgelier were released in groups under the care of the brave young women of the Garel Circuit, and also that because the château du Masgelier had suffered the greatest number of arrests, the ose decided to close its gates in February 1944.

In a documentary film on French Resistance heroine Thérèse Monot, who survived the hell of Ravensbrück, there is a sequence dating probably to 1940, which shows Marshal Pétain ascending the steps of the *hôtel-de-ville* of Limoges, welcomed by a delirious crowd. Viewing that scene I mischievously imagined Pétain brought back to life half a century later for not more than a moment and for no purpose other than that of ascending these steps again so that, as soon as he walks into the lobby of the *hôtel-de-ville*, he catches sight of a plaque marked with an arrow that points to the right and the inscription "Bureau de Monsieur Ebenstein"!

Poems

I became drawn to poetry at the age of eleven, but of the childhood poems in which I poured out my emotions few survive. I have appended to my memoirs four poems, roughly translated into English, which reflect the pain and longing that tormented me for years after the loss of my parents. I wrote three of them in the years 1948–1950, between the ages of fourteen and sixteen. As could be expected considering my age at the time, they are naive and childish, for which I beg the reader's indulgence. I have also included in this selection one poem from my adult years, "Lons-le-Saunier 1942–1992," inspired by the fiftieth anniversary of that day when my mother and I were violently separated.

Mama

Mama!
   That is the first word to burst forth
   from the lips of a child in his cradle.
   Mama!
   Your name reflects the purity of the angel
   the harmony of a summer sky
   the whiteness of the blanket in which you wrapped me…

   Sometimes, when I half raise my eyelids
   after a long sleep
   and a warm ray of light
   projects on the wall the shadow of a curtain
   your face appears before me as in days of yore
   tenderly smiling at my awakening.
   Your large blue eyes are moist
   and a minute tear rolls down your cheek
   and sparkles like a pearl of dew…

Thinking of My Father

Day after day, month after month, years follow up on years,
Time passes and the images just perceived
Fade away already and appear little more than waning silhouettes.
But there is one image among all others,
a face which for me will never fade
a face which to me is painfully dear:
the face of my father.
Oh Father, where are you now?
Of your friends of yore, those who survived
say to me that you are no more,
that your corpse lies among millions of corpses,
formless remains of bone and flesh in a Bavarian mass grave.
No, that is not possible!
Father, tell me that you are not dead
that you live still in my heart heaving with bitterness and regret
and that as long as I exist you will not die…

Anthem of the Children's Home of Livry-Gargan

By our work, with joy and cheerfulness, we live in a republic,
Youth brimming with strength and health toward a good life we
  move.

(Refrain) Friends, onward to life, onward on the highway of
  friendship!
We are young, brimming with strength and health.

Our parents fought for their ideal: like them we shall struggle,
And by our work reach the goal, following the road which they laid
  out.

As we behold spring and life, joy and work as our guides,
Youth our banner, life for us will be splendid.

And when for us in turn the day comes to be artisans of freedom,
We will with pride remember that in friendship we were formed.

Lons-le-Saunier: 1942–1992

English adaptation of my poem by Netta Zukerman, freelance journalist and poet

I am eight years old…

A nondescript High Street
Runs down from the railway station
At Lons-le-Saunier.

Is there anyone today,
Anyone at all,
Aimlessly strolling along it
Who might just remember
That it had been transformed
Into a corridor of death,
Sweeping in its wake
A misery-stricken procession?

1992: arriving from another continent,
a train glides into obscure Lons-le-Saunier
Ghostly reminder from another era…
I glance through the window
And recognize
In spite of automobiles
And other signs of modernity
This, so very commonplace High Street.

My heart contracts
As it recalls
The void of that obscure morning,
This same shabby little High Street,

Devoid of clatter and mundane conversation,
In which we walked, my mother and I,
Marshalled by black-uniformed *flics*,
Captained by a bullying watchdog, mustachioed and menacing
Harrying us with coarse words and blows.

That railway station so nondescript, so grey,
Where today travellers lug their suitcases,
Reverberates for me a different hubbub.
For this is where cries resounded,
Tears flowed like rivers
From the unfortunates who were earmarked for Rivesaltes,
Of my mother dragged along the ground, struggling,
And of the children torn from their parents
Thrown into the train
Bound for the station before the final solution…

The train stops for only one minute.
It warms up, starts and slowly speeds along
Toward Lyon, toward Avignon and the luminous South.
Those low-lying hills gently caressed by a pallid sun.

Was that the scenery traversed by that other train
From the distant past,
Which she must have seen through her tear-dimmed eyes?
Oh, Mother, what were your last thoughts?
Alas, no one will ever know.

I was eight years old…

Glossary

aliyah (Hebrew; pl. *aliyot*, literally, ascent) A term used by Jews and modern Israelis to refer to Jewish immigration to Israel; the term is also used to refer to "going up" to the altar in a synagogue to read from the Torah.

Allies The coalition of countries that fought against Germany, Italy and Japan (the Axis nations). At the beginning of World War II in September 1939, the coalition included France, Poland and Britain. Once Germany invaded the USSR in June 1941 and the United States entered the war following the bombing of Pearl Harbor by Japan on December 7, 1941, the main leaders of the Allied powers became Britain, the USSR and the United States. Other Allies included Canada, Australia, Czechoslovakia, Greece, Mexico, Brazil, South Africa and China.

American Jewish Joint Distribution Committee (JDC) Also known colloquially as the "Joint." A charitable organization founded in 1914 to provide humanitarian assistance and relief to Jews all over the world in times of crisis. It provided material support for persecuted Jews in Germany and other Nazi-occupied territories and facilitated their immigration to neutral countries such as Portugal, Turkey and China. Between 1939 and 1944, JDC officials helped close to 81,000 European Jews find asylum in various parts of the world.

Amitié Chrétienne (French; Christian Friendship/Fellowship) An organization founded by Alexandre Glasberg in 1940, it established shelters for hundreds of Jews released from French internment camps, enabling them to hide from the Nazis. Also active in the organization was Pierre Chaillet (1900–1972), a Jesuit priest who helped hide Jewish children of Lyon during World War II. Chaillet was recognized as Righteous Among the Nations in 1981. *See also* Glasberg, Alexandre; Righteous Among the Nations.

Association des Juifs de Belgique (French; Association of Jews in Belgium, AJB) The association established by the Nazis in November 1941 to consolidate all the Jews in Belgium under one administrative umbrella. Ostensibly created to organize Jewish schools, oversee the welfare of the Jewish population in Belgium and facilitate Jewish "emigration," the AJB's main tasks were in fact to implement the Germans' anti-Jewish measures and facilitate the transport of Jews in Belgium to compulsory labour and death camps. Like the *Judenräte* in occupied Eastern Europe, officials of the AJB were in a difficult position. Some members of the AJB were affiliated with the Belgian Resistance and worked to rescue Jewish children through their orphanages and underground networks. *See also* Judenrat.

Attlee, Clement (1883–1967) The British Labour Party leader from 1935 to 1955 and prime minister of the United Kingdom between 1945 and 1951. Attlee followed the pro-Arab policy of foreign secretary Ernest Bevin regarding British Mandate Palestine. Although he publicly declared the Mandate unworkable in February 1947, his government continued to preside over British Mandate Palestine until Britain's official withdrawal on May 14, 1948. *See also* Bevin, Ernest; Palestine (British Mandate).

Bevin, Ernest (1881–1951) British Labour Party politician who was foreign secretary of the United Kingdom from 1945 to 1951. With regard to Britain's mandate in Palestine, Bevin adopted a pro-Arab stance, not yielding to postwar pressure to change Britain's restrictive immigration policies against Jews, regardless of the plight of the hundreds of thousands of Jewish displaced persons after the war. The British mandate was withdrawn on May 14, 1948, when the State of Israel was declared. *See also* Palestine (British Mandate).

Bierut, Bolesław (1892–1956) General-secretary of the Polish United Workers' Party. Bierut served as president of Poland from 1947 to 1952 and prime minister of Poland from 1952 to 1954.

boches (French) A derogatory term for Germans used in both world wars.

Bolesław the Pious (circa 1224–1279) Duke who governed all of Greater Poland from 1257 to 1273. In August 1264, he enacted the Statute of Kalisz, also known as the General Charter of Jewish Liberties, which allowed Jews various privileges in Poland, including settlement and trading rights, as well as freedom of religious practice.

Bolshevik (from the Russian word *bol'shinstvo*, majority) A political party in Russia that originated in 1903 after separating from the Russian Social Democratic Labour Party and came to power during the second half of the 1917 Russian Revolution. The Bolsheviks, founded by Vladimir Lenin and Alexander Bogdanov, were hailed as a proletariat-focused party and eventually became the Communist Party of the Soviet Union.

Bund (Yiddish, short for Algemeyner Yidisher Arbeter Bund in Lite, Polyn un Rusland, meaning the Jewish Workers' Alliance in Lithuania, Poland and Russia) A Jewish social-democratic revolutionary movement founded in Vilnius, Lithuania, in 1897 to fight for the rights of Yiddish-speaking Jewish workers in Eastern Europe, advocate Jewish cultural autonomy in the Diaspora and champion Yiddish language and secular culture.

catechism A reference text and guide to the Catholic religion in a question-and-answer format to help teach the doctrine of the faith.

Chagall, Marc (1887–1985) Artist of Russian-Jewish descent who was famous for his paintings and stained glass windows.

cheder (Hebrew; literally, room) An Orthodox Jewish elementary school that teaches the fundamentals of Jewish religious observance and textual study, as well as the Hebrew language.

Chiang Kai-shek (1887–1975) Leader of the Republic of China from 1928 to 1975, he opposed the communism of Mao Zedong. *See also* Mao Zedong.

Commission centrale de l'enfance (French; Central Commission for Children, CCE) A communist committee that grew out of the wartime efforts of the Union des juifs pour la résistance et l'entraide (UJRE) to protect Jewish children. Founded after the liberation of France and operating under the leadership of Sophie Schwartz Micnik in Lyon, the CCE ran group homes for Jewish children. *See also* Micnik, Sophie; Union des juifs pour la résistance et l'entraide.

Compiègne A municipality in northern France about seventy kilometres from Paris that was the site of the Royallieu internment and transit camp after the German occupation of France in 1940. Between 1941 and 1944, between 40,000 and 45,000 prisoners passed through the camp, before being deported to Auschwitz and other Nazi camps.

Dannecker, Theodor (1913–1945) An SS-*Hauptsturmführer*, or captain, who worked under Adolf Eichmann in the Reich Security Main Office. As head of the Nazi Jewish affairs department in Paris, he supervised the roundups of Jews by French police, resulting in more than 13,000 being deported to Auschwitz. *See also* Eichmann, Adolf.

Darquier de Pellepoix, Louis (1897–1980; born Louis Darquier) Head of the Commissariat général aux questions juives, General Commissariat for Jewish Affairs, from May 1942 to February 1944, succeeding Xavier Vallat. *See also* Vallat, Xavier.

D-Day The well-known military term used to describe the Allied invasion of Normandy, France, on June 6, 1944, that marked the onset of the liberation of Western Europe during World War II.

de Gaulle, Charles André Joseph Marie (1890–1970) French general and statesman who opposed both the Nazi regime and French collaborationist Vichy government. De Gaulle, a World War I veteran and Brigadier General in World War II, escaped to London after the fall of France in 1940. In London, de Gaulle organized the Free French Forces, a partisan and resistance group comprising French officers in exile. After the war, de Gaulle served as head of the French provisional government from 1944 to 1946, and as president of France from 1958 to 1969.

Degrelle, Léon (1906–1994) The founder of the Belgian conservative nationalist Rexist Party in November 1935, which called for increased influence for the Catholic Church in Belgian society and the abolition of liberal democracy. The party was dissolved in 1945.

Demarcation Line The boundary between the northern part of France occupied by the Germans (Occupied Zone) and the southern Unoccupied Zone that was under the control of the Vichy government. *See also* Vichy.

displaced persons People who find themselves homeless and stateless at the end of a war. Following World War II, millions of people, especially European Jews, found that they had no homes to return to or that it was unsafe to do so. To resolve the staggering refugee crisis that resulted, Allied authorities and the United Nations Relief and Rehabilitation Administration (UNRRA) established Displaced Persons (DP) camps to provide temporary shelter and assistance to refugees, and help them transition toward resettlement.

Doctors' Plot An alleged conspiracy by a group of doctors — most of them Jewish — to eliminate the top leadership of the Soviet Union by poisoning them. The accusations in 1953 against the "assassins in white coats" were an escalation of Stalin's campaign against Soviet Jews that began in 1948 and were accompanied by press coverage that produced antisemitic hysteria throughout the country. Stalin planned to use the Doctors' Plot to instigate a major purge directed against Jews in the Soviet Union. Fortunately for the accused, Stalin died only days before their trial was about to begin. A month after his death in March 1953, the newspaper *Pravda* declared that the case had been fabricated and that the doctors had been released.

Drancy A northeastern suburb of Paris that was the site of an internment and transit camp from which about 65,000 people, almost all Jews, were deported to concentration and death camps. Established in August 1941, the camp was run by the French police until it was taken over in July 1943 by the Nazi SS, who ran it until its liberation in August 1944.

Duclos, Jacques (1896–1975) A member of the French Communist Party who was elected to the French National Assembly in 1926 and filled a variety of roles, including vice-president of the National Assembly, deputy to Maurice Thorez and acting secretary general of the Communist Party from 1950 to 1953. *See also* French Communist Party; Thorez, Maurice.

Eichmann, Adolf (1906–1962) The head of the Gestapo department responsible for the implementation of the Nazis' policy of mass murder of Jews (the so-called Final Solution), Eichmann was in charge of transporting Jews to death camps in Poland. In 1942, Eichmann coordinated deportations of Jewish populations from Slovakia, the Netherlands, France and Belgium; in 1944, he was directly involved in the deportations of Jews from Hungary. After the war, Eichmann escaped from US custody and fled to Argentina, where he was captured in 1960 by Israeli intelligence operatives; his ensuing 1961 trial in Israel was widely and internationally televised. Eichmann was sentenced to death and hanged in May 1962. *See also* Gestapo.

Einstein, Albert (1879–1955) A German Jew who became an influential physicist. He was famous for his theory of relativity and theory of gravitation, which involved ideas about space-time, mass-energy and movement of light, and published more than 300 scientific papers and more than 150 non-scientific papers.

Engels, Friedrich (1820–1895) A German philosopher and writer who is best known for co-authoring, with Karl Marx, *The Communist Manifesto. See also* Marx, Karl.

Esperanto An international language created by Dr. Ludwig Zamenhof in the 1870s in Bialystok. Zamenhof's intention was to create a language that would foster communication between people of different ethnicities. Esperanto is currently spoken in 115 countries and estimates of Esperanto speakers range from 10,000 to two million.

Fabien, Colonel (1919–1944; born Pierre Georges) A member of the French Communist Party and a leader in the French Resistance. Colonel Fabien was involved in assassinations of German soldiers and the formation of a Free French fighting battalion.

Feldman, Valentin (1909–1942) French communist and philosopher who joined the French army in 1939 and the Resistance by 1941. Feldman wrote newspaper articles against the Germans; after his arrest in February 1942, he was tortured and subsequently executed by a German firing squad in July 1942.

Franco, Francisco (1892–1975) Spanish general, dictator and head of state of Spain from 1939 to 1975. Franco, who led the Nationalists in victory against the Republicans in the Spanish Civil War, at first remained officially neutral and then "non-belligerent" during World War II but lent military support to the Axis powers. Paradoxically, his authoritarian, fascist regime did not follow an antisemitic policy of interning Jews unless they were stateless, instead allowing approximately 30,000 Jewish refugees who had documentation into Spain, often on their way through to neutral Portugal. *See also* Spanish Civil War.

Frankl, Viktor Emil (1905–1997) Austrian psychiatrist and survivor of Theresienstadt, Auschwitz and Dachau, who created logotherapy, a form of psychotherapy based on finding meaning in life. Frankl is best known for writing *Man's Search for Meaning.*

Free Zone (in French, *Zone libre*) The southern region of France that was under French sovereignty between June 1940 and November 1942, after which it was occupied by Germany. *See also* Vichy.

French Communist Party (in French, *Parti communiste français*; PCF) A political party founded on communist principles in 1920. The party was led by Maurice Thorez in 1930 and supported the Popular Front government of 1936. The Jeunesses Communistes (Young Communists), a previously independent organization, became an auxiliary of the PCF by 1931 and was an essential element in the party, recruiting youth. *See also* Thorez, Maurice.

French Forces of the Interior (FFI) The formal name given to the French rural and urban resistance fighters after the Normandy landings on June 6, 1944. In June 1944, the forces comprised approximately 100,000; by October of that year the numbers had grown to 400,000. *See also* Maquis; Resistance.

Friedländer, Saul (1932–) A Czech-born Israeli and American historian. During World War II, Friedländer was a hidden child in a Catholic boarding school in Vichy France. He immigrated to Israel in 1948 and has taught at universities in Geneva and Israel. Since 1988, he has been teaching history at the University of California in Los Angeles.

Garel, Georges (1909–1979) A Lithuanian-born French engineer who was active in the French Resistance and joined the OSE (Œuvre de secours aux enfants) in 1942, becoming its director in 1943. He created the Circuit Garel (Garel circuit) in 1942 to organize the rescue of Jewish children during World War II by hiding them, often in Catholic and secular institutions or with families in the countryside. *See also* Garel circuit, OSE.

Garel circuit The underground network in southern France named after one of its organizers, Georges Garel, who helped rescue Jewish children from transit camps and orphanages, and provided them with false identification papers and refuge with Christian families. The Garel circuit, which was organized in 1942 and began operating in early 1943, was part of the OSE (Œuvre de secours aux enfants) and saved more than one thousand children. *See also* OSE.

Gerlier, Pierre-Marie (1880–1965) Archbishop of Lyon and Primate of Gaul from 1937 to 1965. Though a supporter of Maréchal Pétain, Gerlier aided Amitié Chrétienne and helped to save a group of 108 Jewish children. He was named Righteous Among the Nations in July 1981. *See also* Amitié Chrétienne; Pétain, Philippe; Righteous Among the Nations.

Gestapo (German; abbreviation of Geheime Staatspolizei, the Secret State Police of Nazi Germany) The Gestapo were the brutal force that dealt with the perceived enemies of the Nazi regime and were responsible for rounding up European Jews for deportation to the death camps. They operated with very few legal constraints and were also responsible for issuing exit visas to the residents of German-occupied areas. A number of Gestapo members also joined the Einsatzgruppen, the mobile killing squads responsible for the roundup and murder of Jews in eastern Poland and the USSR through mass shooting operations.

Gomułka, Władysław (1905–1982) First Secretary of the Polish Worker's Party (1956–1970). At first, he promised economic reforms and liberalization under Communist rule. However, his reforms (known as Gomułka's thaws, Polish October or October 1956) were temporary, and soon came under Soviet criticism.

Glasberg, Alexandre (1902–1981) A Ukrainian-born Jew who converted to Catholicism and, in 1940, founded Amitié Chrétienne in France to assist Jews hiding from the Nazis. Glasberg was also involved postwar in Jewish emigration from Europe and from Arab countries to Israel. He was recognized as Righteous Among the Nations in January 2004. *See also* Amitié Chrétienne; Righteous Among the Nations.

Gulag (Russian) Acronym for *Glavnoe Upravlenie ispravitel'no-trudovykh Lagerei*, meaning Main Administration of Corrective La-

bour Camps. The term refers both to the bureaucracy that operated the Soviet system of forced labour camps in the Stalin era
and to the camps themselves. Gulag camps existed throughout
the Soviet Union, but the largest camps lay in the most extreme
geographical and climatic regions of the country (such as in the
Arctic north, the Siberian east and the Central Asian south). Prisoners endured hard labour, violence, extreme climate, meagre
food rations and unsanitary conditions, all of which resulted in
high death rates. Historians estimate that from 1934 to 1953 more
than a million prisoners died in Gulag camps.

Hauptsturmführer (German; head storm leader) A Nazi paramilitary rank equivalent to that of a captain.

Iron Curtain A term coined by Sir Winston Churchill in 1946 to describe the metaphorical boundary that physically and ideologi-
cally divided Europe into two separate spheres of influence at the
end of World War II: one in Eastern Europe, controlled politically,
militarily and economically by the Soviet Union; the second in
Western Europe, allied with Western liberal democracies, economically predisposed to market economics and under the military protection of the United States.

Judenrat (German; pl. *Judenräte*) Jewish Council. A group of Jewish leaders appointed by the Germans to administer and provide
services to the local Jewish population under occupation and
carry out Nazi orders. The *Judenräte*, which appeared to be self-
governing entities but were actually under complete Nazi control,
faced difficult and complex moral decisions under brutal conditions and remain a contentious subject. The chairmen had to decide whether to comply or refuse to comply with Nazi demands.
Some were killed by the Nazis for refusing, while others committed suicide. Jewish officials who advocated compliance thought
that cooperation might save at least some of the population. Some
who denounced resistance efforts did so because they believed
that armed resistance would bring death to the entire community.

Khrushchev, Nikita Sergeyevich (1894–1971) First Secretary of the Communist Party of the Soviet Union from 1953 to 1964. Nikita Khrushchev stunned Party members when he denounced the excesses of the Stalin era and Stalin's cult of personality in 1956. Khrushchev's regime was characterized not only by de-Stalinization of the USSR but also by a foreign policy that espoused peaceful co-existence with the West. Bitter power struggles within the leadership of the Communist Party, a political split with Communist leadership in China, and Soviet humiliation over the 1962 Cuban Missile Crisis led to Khrushchev's ouster in October 1964.

Kielce pogrom The July 1946 riots in a city in Poland where about 250 Jews lived after the war (the pre-war Jewish population had been more than 20,000). After the false report of a young Polish boy being kidnapped by Jews, police arrested and beat Jewish residents in the city, inciting a mob of hundreds of Polish civilians to violently attack and kill forty Jews while police stood by. Combined with other postwar antisemitic incidents throughout Poland — other pogroms occurred in Rzeszów, Krakow, Tarnów and Sosnowiec, and robberies and blackmail were common — this event was the catalyst for a mass exodus; between July and September 1946, more than 80,000 Jews left Poland.

Kissinger, Henry (1923–) A German-born Jewish-American who came to the United States in 1938 and served as Secretary of State from 1973 to 1977 under Republican presidents Richard Nixon and Gerald Ford. He is considered a controversial figure for his role in ending the Vietnam War and in US policy toward Chile and Pakistan.

Klarsfeld, Serge (1935–) A French lawyer who, with his wife, Beate (b. 1939, née Künzel), has sought to bring Nazi war criminals to justice. He also serves on the board of trustees of the Fondation pour la mémoire de la shoah (Foundation for the Memory of the Shoah).

Korczak, Janusz (1878–1942) Pseudonym for Henryk Goldszmit.

A Polish-Jewish educator, doctor and writer who advocated for respecting children's rights and independence, focusing on understanding their emotions. In 1912, Korczak established a Jewish orphanage in Warsaw called Dom Sierot and also created a children's newspaper. In 1940, when his orphanage was moved into the Warsaw ghetto, Korczak was given many opportunities to escape but always refused, instead choosing to stay with the children. On August 5, 1942, Korczak steadfastly accompanied "his" children on a deportation to the Treblinka death camp, where he perished. Korczak's works include more than ten fiction and four non-fiction books, including *How to Love a Child* and *The Child's Right to Respect*.

Koshevoy, Oleg Vasilyevich (1926–1943) A leader in the Young Guard, an anti-Nazi Soviet youth organization founded in summer 1942. Koshevoy was arrested, tortured and executed by the Nazis in February 1943 at the age of sixteen.

Kosmodemyanskaya, Zoya Anatolyevna (1923–1941) Member of a partisan force while still a high school student. Assigned to burn a village where a German regiment was stationed, she was caught, tortured and hung by the Nazis in November 1941 at the age of eighteen.

Laval, Pierre (1883–1945) A French politician who served as prime minister of France from January 1931 to February 1932 and again from June 1935 to January 1936. Laval also headed the Vichy government between April 1942 and August 1944. A right-wing collaborator, Laval went beyond compliance with German requests to actively seek out foreign-born Jewish children for deportation from France. He was tried for treason after the war ended and was executed by firing squad.

Leguay, Jean (1909–1989) Leguay served as second in command of the French National Police and helped to organize the Vél d'Hiv roundup. *See also* Vélodrome d'Hiver.

Lenin, Vladimir (1870–1924) The founder of the Russian Communist Party and leader of the Bolsheviks throughout the October Revolution in 1917 and Russian Civil War (1917–1923). Lenin is considered the architect of the USSR (Union of Soviet Socialist Republics).

Loinger, Georges (1910–) A specialist in physical education and member of the French Resistance who worked with the OSE (Œuvre de secours aux enfants) to teach and save Jewish children. Loinger and his team smuggled 1,500 children from southern France to Switzerland, and also worked at and provided training to staff at OSE children's homes. *See also* Œuvre de secours aux enfants.

Lustiger, Jean-Marie (1926–2007) Archbishop of Paris from 1981 to 2005. Born to Jewish parents, Lustiger was attracted to Christianity in the late 1930s and was baptized, against his parents' wishes, in August 1940. His mother was killed in Auschwitz-Birkenau in 1943.

Mackenzie King, William Lyon (1874–1950) Prime minister of Canada from 1921 to 1930 and again from 1935 to 1948. Until 1947, his government followed an extremely restrictive immigration policy, and Frederick Charles Blair, director of immigration from 1936 to 1943, was also openly antisemitic. Between 1933 and 1939, Canada admitted 5,000 Jewish refugees, the lowest number out of any country during that time.

Main-d'œuvre immigrée (French; Immigrant Workers' Union, MOI) A trade union created in the 1920s that was affiliated with the French Communist Party and had a membership consisting mainly of immigrant workers. The MOI became active in the French Resistance after the Vél d'Hiv roundup of July 1942. *See also* Vélodrome d'Hiver.

Makarenko, Anton (1888–1939) An influential Soviet teacher and writer who became known for creating an effective pedagogical approach to dealing with delinquent children based, in part, on meaningful work and participation in decision-making.

Malenkov, Georgy Maximilianovich (1902–1988) A Soviet communist party member who, after Stalin's death, served as premier of the Soviet Union from 1953 to 1955.

Malinovsky, Rodion Yakovlevich (1898–1967) A Soviet military leader who was appointed Marshal of the Soviet Union in 1944 and served as defense minister from 1957 until his death. During World War II, he fought in the Ukraine, Romania, Hungary and Manchuria, a region between China and Russia.

manoir de Denouval A mansion in Andrésy, France, about twenty-five kilometres from Paris that was bought by the UJRE (Union des juifs pour la résistance et l'entraide) in December 1945 to house and support Jewish war orphans. Between 1945 and 1949, approximately 200 children lived in the mansion. *See also* Union des juifs pour la résistance et l'entraide.

Mao Zedong (1893–1976) A Chinese military leader who became head of the Chinese Communist Party in 1935 and chairman of the People's Republic of China in 1949, serving in those roles until his death.

Maquis (French; abbreviation of *maquisards*; literally, thicket) The term for French Resistance fighters in rural areas during World War II. The *Maquis* originated from a group of men, mostly communist and socialist, who fled to mountainous terrain (hence their name, which loosely translates as "bush") to avoid being arrested by the Gestapo in occupied France due to their political orientation. By early 1943, the *Maquis* had grown in strength and organization due to the thousands of new members who were avoiding the new law of conscription in France, the *Service du Travail Obligatoire*, which led to forced labour in Germany. The *Maquis* at first focused on sabotaging German communication and transport lines, as well as providing protection to Jews and refugees, and later were able to organize armed resistance due to British and American support. After the Normandy landings on June 6, 1944, the *Maquis* became formalized into the French Forces of the Interior. *See also* French Forces of the Interior; Resistance.

Marty, André (1886–1956) A member of the French Communist Party and, from 1924 to 1955, of the French National Assembly.

Marx, Karl Heinrich (1818–1883) The German philosopher, historian, sociologist and theorist who inspired the revolutionary communist ideology known as Marxism. According to Marx's vision, a communist society would be classless and stateless, based on a common ownership of the means of production, free access to the material goods that people need for wellbeing, and an end to wage labour and private property. Two of his most famous works are *The Communist Manifesto* (1848) and *Capital* (1867–1894).

Milice (short form of *Milice française*; French militia) A paramilitary force, created by the Vichy regime, that operated in France between 1943 and 1944 to counter the French Resistance. Members of the *Milice* were sympathetic to Nazi ideology and helped the Gestapo to round Jews up for deportation. *See also* Gestapo.

Minc, Joseph (1908–2011; born Joseph Minkowski) A Russian-born Jew, living in Paris, who was involved in several anti-Nazi organizations, including the French Resistance, Main-d'œuvre immigrée, Union des juifs pour la résistance et l'entraide and Commission centrale de l'enfance, through which he helped to organize the rescue of Jewish children. *See also* Resistance; Main-d'œuvre immigrée; Union des juifs pour la résistance et l'entraide; Commission centrale de l'enfance.

Minkowski, Eugène (1885–1972) A Polish-born French psychiatrist who was involved in the French Resistance and was a director of the Œuvre de secours aux enfants, protecting Jewish children during the Holocaust. *See also* Resistance; Œuvre de secours aux enfants.

Obersturmführer (German; senior storm leader) A Nazi military rank. Within the SS, the role of the *Obersturmführer* could vary from Gestapo officer to concentration camp supervisor.

Œuvre de protection des enfants juifs (French; Association to Protect Jewish Children, OPEJ) The successor, in 1944, of the Service d'évacuation et de regroupement d'enfants (Children's Evacuation and Reunification Service), which had been formed in 1942 by French Resistance groups to shelter Jewish children whose parents had been deported in safe homes or with Catholic families and institutions. It continues to provide child protection services and rehabilitation programs under the name OPEJ Foundation–Baron Edmond de Rothschild.

Œuvre de secours aux enfants (French; Children's Relief Agency, OSE) A French-Jewish organization that helped rescue thousands of Jewish refugee children during World War II. The OSE was founded in Russia in 1912 and its offices were relocated to France in 1933, where it set up more than a dozen orphanages and homes; hid children from the Nazis; and, among other operations, arranged for the immigration of about two hundred children to the US and the clandestine transfer of many others to Switzerland. Félix Chevrier (1884–1962) figured prominently in the OSE movement. By March 1942, the OSE, in order to continue its work, was forced under Vichy law to incorporate into the General Union of the Jews of France (UGIF), an organization that was itself forced to cooperate with the Nazis. Eventually, with the German occupation of the south of France in November 1942, and the increasing danger of arrests and deportation, much of OSE's work to rescue children went underground and it increased its efforts both to move children to safer homes in the Italian-occupied zone of southeastern France and to smuggle children across the Swiss border. *See also* Union générale des israélites de France.

Palestine (British Mandate) The area of the Middle East under British rule from 1923 to 1948, as established by the League of Nations after World War I. During that time, the United Kingdom severely restricted Jewish immigration. The Mandate area encompassed present-day Israel, Jordan, the West Bank and the Gaza Strip.

passeur (French) A ferryman or smuggler. During World War II the term was used for a person who guided people illegally across a border.

Péri, Gabriel (1902–1941) A French journalist and politician who was a member of the French Resistance and executed by Nazis for his activities.

Pétain, Philippe (1856–1951) French general and Maréchal (Marshal) of France who was the chief of state of the French government in Vichy from 1940 to 1944. After the war, Pétain was tried for treason for his collaboration with the Nazis and sentenced to death, which was commuted to life imprisonment. *See also* Vichy.

Pfeffer, Léon (1922–1944) A member of the Union des juifs pour la résistance et l'entraide (Union of Jews for Resistance and Self-Help, UJRE) and the Main-d'œuvre immigrée (Immigrant Workers' Union, MOI). He was tortured and executed by Germans in July 1944. *See also* Main-d'œuvre immigrée; Union des juifs pour la résistance et l'entraide.

pogrom (Russian; to wreak havoc, to demolish) A violent attack on a distinct ethnic group. The term most commonly refers to nineteenth- and twentieth-century attacks on Jews in the Russian Empire.

Poirier, Pierrette (1909–?) A Catholic resistance worker who looked after one hundred Jewish children while working for the Œuvre de secours aux enfants (OSE) in Châteauroux. She placed the children with non-Jewish institutions and families, visiting each monthly and paying for their upkeep. She was recognized as Righteous Among the Nations in March 1979. *See also* Œuvre de secours aux enfants.

Pushkin, Alexander (1797–1837; born Alexander Alexandrovich Bestuzhev) A Russian poet and novelist, most famous for his works *Eugene Onegin* and *Boris Godunov*.

Rayman, Marcel (1923–1944; also Marcel Rajman) A Polish-born Jew living in France who, as a member of the Main-d'œuvre immigrée (MOI), was involved in the killing of Julius Ritter, the German official in charge of rounding up forced labourers for work in Germany, in September 1943. Rayman was arrested in November 1943 and executed by a German firing squad in February 1944. *See also* Ritter, Julius.

Rayski, Adam (1913–2008; born Abraham Rajgrodski) A Russian-born Jew who immigrated to Paris in 1932, joined the Resistance and the Main-d'œuvre immigrée (MOI) and worked as a journalist for Yiddish and French newspapers. After the war, he became Undersecretary of State for the Press in Poland and was active in Zionist organizations. He helped found the CRIF (Conseil représentatif des institutions juives de France, Representative Council of French Jewish Institutions) and authored a history of Jewish life under Vichy in 2005. *See also* Main-d'œuvre immigrée.

Resistance The collective term for the French Resistance movement during World War II. In rural areas, the group was known as the *Maquis*. The Resistance published underground newspapers, helped Allied prisoners-of-war escape, sabotaged German war equipment and created intelligence networks that gathered military information in order to gain armament support from Britain. Some Resistance groups were dedicated to saving Jews. *See also* Maquis.

Righteous Among the Nations A title bestowed by Yad Vashem, the Holocaust Martyrs' and Heroes' Remembrance Authority in Jerusalem, to honour non-Jews who risked their lives to help save Jews during the Holocaust. A commission was established in 1963 to award the title. If a person fits certain criteria and the story is carefully corroborated, the honouree is awarded with a medal and certificate and commemorated on the Wall of Honour at the Garden of the Righteous in Jerusalem.

Ritter, Julius (1893–1943) An SS colonel who oversaw the conscription of French workers for forced labour in Germany. Ritter was killed by members of the Main-d'œuvre immigrée (MOI) in September 1943. *See also* Main-d'œuvre immigrée; Rayman, Marcel.

Roosevelt, Franklin Delano (1882–1945) President of the United States between 1933 and 1945. Roosevelt approved military support to Britain in 1940, but the US only officially entered into the war on the side of the Allies after Japan attacked Pearl Harbor in December 1941. Although Roosevelt publically opposed Nazi Germany's treatment of German Jews, his government did not actively pursue an immigration policy that would welcome Jewish refugees — the US even went so far as to turn away the *St. Louis*, a ship that carried almost one thousand German Jews seeking asylum in 1939. Roosevelt was aware of the Nazis' murderous policies against Jews as early as 1942, but the US did not help rescue European Jews until January 1944, through the establishment of the War Refugee Board. In June 1944, after the Swiss press published excerpts of a report that detailed the Nazi atrocities against the Jews, Roosevelt joined the escalating international pressure on Hungary to stop the deportations of its Jewish citizens.

Rosenberg trial Julius Rosenberg (1918–1953) and Ethel Rosenberg (1915–1953) were a married couple accused of selling US plans for development of an atomic bomb to the Soviet Union. Their trial was held in March 1951 amid concerns regarding legal improprieties and paranoia about the spread of communism. Despite global protests and requests for clemency following their conviction for espionage, the Rosenbergs were executed in June 1953.

Röthke, Heinz (1912–1966) An SS-*Obersturmführer*, Nazi military officer, who was jointly responsible with Theodor Dannecker for the deportation of French Jews in 1940–1944. *See also* Dannecker, Theodor; *Obersturmführer*.

Saliège, Jules-Gérard (1870–1956) A French cardinal who served as Archbishop of Toulouse from 1928 until his death. He was involved in the French Resistance and wrote a pastoral letter condemning the deportations of Jews and supporting efforts to protect Jews that was widely distributed, helping to influence public opinion against the Vichy regime. Saliège was recognized as Righteous Among the Nations in July 1969. *See also* Resistance; Righteous Among the Nations.

Sampaix, Lucien (1899–1941) A French communist, journalist and member of the Resistance who was executed by the Germans in December 1941. *See also* Resistance.

Schwartz Micnik, Sophie (1905–1999) A Polish-born Jew who moved with her husband, Leizer Micnik, to France, where he was arrested, handed over to Germans in 1942, and never heard from again. Schwartz was active in the French Resistance, running a print shop that produced false identification cards and establishing homes for Jewish children who had lost their families. Eventually she became head of the Commission centrale de l'enfance (Central Commission for Children). *See also* Commission centrale de l'enfance.

Serebrenik, Robert (1904–1965) The chief rabbi of Luxembourg. After fleeing the Nazis, he arrived in the United States in 1941, where he founded and headed Congregation Ramath Orah in New York. Serebrenik also testified at the trial of Adolf Eichmann in 1961.

Slánský, Rudolf (1901–1952) General Secretary of the Czech Communist Party from 1946 to 1951. Slánský, a Jew, had been active in the Czech Communist organization before the war, was involved in organizing the Slovak National Uprising of 1944 and, in 1946, took over the leadership of the Party. In 1951, he was suddenly ejected from the Party, accused of organizing a conspiracy to overthrow the government along with thirteen other Party members, ten of whom were also Jewish. Eleven of the accused were executed and three were given life sentences. All fourteen were officially exonerated in 1968.

SS (abbreviation of Schutzstaffel; Defence Corps). The SS was established in 1925 as Adolf Hitler's elite corps of personal bodyguards. Under the direction of Heinrich Himmler, its membership grew from 280 in 1929 to 50,000 when the Nazis came to power in 1933, and to nearly a quarter of a million on the eve of World War II. The SS comprised the Allgemeine-SS (General SS) and the Waffen-SS (Armed, or Combat SS). The General SS dealt with policing and the enforcement of Nazi racial policies in Germany and the Nazi-occupied countries. An important unit within the SS was the Reichssicherheitshauptamt (RSHA, the Central Office of Reich Security), whose responsibility included the Gestapo (Geheime

Staatspolizei). The SS ran the concentration and death camps, and also fielded its own Waffen-SS military divisions, including some recruited from the occupied countries. *See also* Gestapo.

Stalin, Joseph (1878–1953) Leader of the Soviet Union from 1924 until his death in 1953. Born Joseph Vissarionovich Dzhugashvili, he changed his name to Stalin (literally: man of steel) in 1903. He was a staunch supporter of Lenin, taking control of the Communist Party upon Lenin's death. Very soon after acquiring leadership of the Communist Party, Stalin ousted rivals, killed opponents in purges and effectively established himself as a dictator. During the late 1930s, Stalin commenced "The Great Purge," during which he targeted and disposed of elements within the Communist Party that he deemed to be a threat to the stability of the Soviet Union. These purges extended to both military and civilian society, and millions of people were incarcerated or exiled to harsh labour camps. During the war and in the immediate postwar period, many Jews in Poland viewed Stalin as the leader of the country that liberated them and saved them from death at the hands of the Nazis. At the time, many people were unaware of the extent of Stalin's own murderous policies. After World War II, Stalin set up Communist governments controlled by Moscow in many Eastern European states bordering and close to the USSR, and instituted antisemitic campaigns and purges.

Statutes on Jews The antisemitic legislations enacted by the Vichy regime in 1940 and 1941. The first Statute of October 3, 1940, defined the criteria for being Jewish, excluded Jews from professions such as public and military service and interned foreign Jews in camps. The second Statute expanded the ban on Jewish employment to include all commercial and industrial sectors and confiscated Jewish property. *See also* Vichy.

Thorez, Maurice (1900–1964) Leader of the French Communist Party (PCF) from 1930 to 1964 and vice premier of France from 1946 to 1947.

Touvier, Paul (1915–1996) Regional head of the *Milice* in Lyon, who was in charge of intelligence and operations. After having been hidden in monasteries for many years, Touvier was convicted of war crimes in 1994.

Trujillo Molina, Rafael Léonidas (1891–1961) The dictator president of the Dominican Republic from 1930 to 1938 and from 1942 until his assassination in 1961. Trujillo was open to immigration to increase the country's tax base and offered at the Evian Conference of 1938 to accept 100,000 Jewish refugees. Ultimately, only 645 Jews arrived.

UB secret police (Polish; Urząd Bezpieczeństwa, Security Office) A security service that operated under the Polish ministry of public security between 1945 and 1954 to counter anti-communist activities and engage in espionage.

UNESCO (Abbreviation for United Nations Educational, Scientific and Cultural Organization) A Paris-based United Nations agency formed in November 1945 to promote international collaboration, access to education, rule of law, human rights and freedoms, and the benefits of scientific advances.

Union des juifs pour la résistance et l'entraide (French; Union of Jews for Resistance and Self-Help, UJRE) A Paris-based and communist-led organization that was created in 1943. Originally called Solidarité and established in August 1940 to resist the Nazi occupation, the group first focused on sabotaging German industry and establishing partisan groups; by 1943, it had changed tactics and focused on hiding and protecting Jewish children from deportation.

Union de la jeunesse juive (French; Union of Jewish Youth, UJJ) A youth organization established in 1943 and led by communists from the Jewish section of the Main-d'œuvre immigrée. It was active mainly in Lyon and Grenoble. The UJJ merged in 1945 with the Union de la jeunesse républicaine de France. *See also* Main-d'œuvre immigrée, Union de la jeunesse républicaine de France.

Union de la jeunesse républicaine de France (French; Union of Republican Youth of France, UJRF) A youth organization that grew out of the Union de la jeunesse juive in 1945. Its focus was on education and on cultural and sports activities. The UJRF also sought to lower the age for voting and equal pay for equal work for young people. *See also* Union de la jeunesse juive.

Union générale des israélites de France (French; General Union of the Jews of France, UGIF) An organization created in November 1941 by Xavier Vallat, Vichy commissioner for Jewish affairs, at the request of the Nazis. UGIF was established to represent all Jewish communal and charitable groups to the Vichy regime and the Germans. It also provided social services to needy Jews and collected funds for payment of Nazi fines. The UGIF ceased functioning when France was liberated in 1944. *See also* Vallat, Xavier.

Vallat, Xavier (1891–1972) An independent member of the French National Assembly from 1919 to 1924 and from 1928 to 1940 who also served as head of the Vichy regime's Commissariat général aux questions juives, General Commissariat for Jewish Affairs, between March 1941 and May 1942. After the war, Vallat served ten years in prison for his role in implementing anti-Jewish laws.

Vélodrome d'Hiver A sports stadium, known by the short form Vél d'Hiv, in Paris that was the site of a major roundup of Jews in France on July 16 and 17, 1942. Approximately 13,000 were arrested and interned in the stadium, where they were kept for days without food, water, or sufficient medical care. They were eventually deported to transit camps and Nazi death camps.

Vichy A resort town in south-central France that was the seat of the government of Maréchal Philippe Pétain in unoccupied France. The Franco-German armistice of June 22, 1940, divided France into two zones, both of which were administered by the Vichy regime; however, in the northern zone, Vichy was subordinate to the German occupiers, while the southern region, also referred to as the zone libre ("free zone"), remained under French sovereignty. In October 1940 the administration in Vichy enacted antisemitic legislation, independently of Germany, and later collaborated with Nazi Germany by participating in roundups of Jews,

interning them in transit camps, and deporting them to concentration and death camps. *See also* Drancy; Pétain, Philippe.

von Falkenhausen, Alexander (1878–1966) The German military
governor in Belgium from 1940 to 1944 who ordered deportations
of Belgian Jews.

Weill, Joseph (1902–1988) A French physician who became medical
director of the Œuvre de secours aux enfants and helped to create
a network to save Jewish children by placing them in the countryside with families and helping them cross into Switzerland. *See
also* Œuvre de secours aux enfants.

Wiesel, Elie (1928–2016) A Romanian-born Jewish writer and professor at Boston University. Wiesel was a survivor of Auschwitz
and Buchenwald who became a human rights activist and a Nobel Laureate for his writing. His most well-known work, *Night*,
recounts his experience in these Nazi camps and is widely considered one of the most important works of Holocaust literature.

Zionism A movement promoted by the Viennese Jewish journalist
Theodor Herzl, who argued in his 1896 book *Der Judenstaat* (The
Jewish State) that the best way to resolve the problem of antisemitism and persecution of Jews in Europe was to create an independent Jewish state in the historic Jewish homeland of Biblical
Israel. Zionists also promoted the revival of Hebrew as a Jewish
national language. There are various factions within the Zionist
movement, from Labour Zionism on the left to Revisionist Zionism on the right.

ZMP (Polish; abbreviation for Związek Młodzieży Polskiej, Union
of Polish Youth) A youth organization created in 1948 out of the
amalgamation of four youth groups. The ZMP was part of the
Polish Workers' Party, later known as the Polish United Workers' Party, and served to indoctrinate youth into communism. Local branches of the ZMP determined admission to schools and
eligibility for scholarships. In 1957, the ZMP was dissolved and
replaced by the Union of Socialist Youth and the Union of Rural
Youth.

Photographs

1 René's mother, Mira Shaindl Arenstein, and father, Wolf Goldman, on their wedding day. Luxembourg City, 1931.

2 René's parents and their friends. René's mother, Mira Shaindl Arenstein, is seated in front on the far left. René's father, Wolf Goldman, is kneeling behind her. Gantenbeinsmühle, early 1930s.

3 René in the arms of his cousin Ginette. Gantenbeinsmühle, circa 1938.

4 René, centre, and his mother, Mira Shaindl Arenstein, and father, Wolf Goldman, in a public park. Luxembourg, 1939.

1 René, age 6, and his mother. Luxembourg, 1940.

2 René's cousin Simon Domb, wearing the traditional Napoleonic uniform of the École polytechnique. Paris, circa 1940.

3 René and his parents at the wedding of Joseph Lewin, eldest son of their friend Max Lewin. René is seated on the floor on the far left. René's mother is standing behind the woman holding flowers. René's father is standing in the top row, far right. Brussels, 1941.

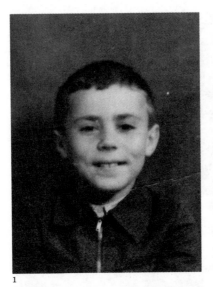

1 René, age 11. Andrésy, France, 1945.
2 René, age 12. Andrésy, France, 1946.
3 A postcard showing manoir de Denouval, which was operated by the Commission centrale de l'enfance. Andrésy, France.

1

2

1 Breakfast at Andrésy. René is holding his bowl out for more food. The children peering through the windows are from another dining room, who had likely finished their meal but had not yet been given permission to leave. Circa 1945.

2 René and students of manoir de Denouval. René is standing alone in the window frame on the top left. Adam Rayski and Marc Chagall are standing together in the centre of the second row from the back. Andrésy, 1946.

1

2

1 René is standing on the far left, leaning forward to form the letter V with his fingers over the head of his friend Evelyne, the second girl from the left in the middle row. Other friends include Elsa Zilberbogen, the third girl from the left, and Eliane Gourevitch, the fourth girl from the left. Le Raincy-Côteaux, 1947.

2 The children's choir in Livry-Gargan. René is in the back row, standing second from the left. 1948.

Sophie Micnik. Nice, circa 1990.

René. Summerland, British Columbia, 2003.

1 René standing beside a signpost marking the entrance to Kalisz. Poland, 2003.
2 René and his wife, Terry, at Morskie Oko in the Tatra Mountains. Poland, 2003.

1　René and Terry. Galapagos Islands, Ecuador, 2008.
2　René in his home study. Summerland, British Columbia, circa 2010.

1 René and his wife, Terry. Whistler, British Columbia, 2013.
2 René, his wife, Terry, and their granddaughters, Katrina and Kirsten, celebrating René's eightieth birthday. Summerland, British Columbia, 2014.

Index

The Azrieli Foundation was established in 1989 to realize and extend the philanthropic vision of David J. Azrieli, C.M., C.Q., M.Arch. The Foundation's mission is to support a wide spectrum of initiatives in education and research. The Azrieli Foundation is an active supporter of programs in the fields of education, the education of architects, scientific and medical research, and the arts. The Azrieli Foundation's many initiatives include: the Holocaust Survivor Memoirs Program, which collects, preserves, publishes and distributes the written memoirs of survivors in Canada; the Azrieli Institute for Educational Empowerment, an innovative program successfully working to keep at-risk youth in school; the Azrieli Fellows Program, which promotes academic excellence and leadership on the graduate level at Israeli universities; the Azrieli Music Project, which celebrates and fosters the creation of high-quality new Jewish orchestral music; and the Azrieli Neurodevelopmental Research Program, which supports advanced research on neurodevelopmental disorders, particularly Fragile X and Autism Spectrum Disorders.